Peg
Rankin

✱ greenhill

(✳) **green**hill

https://greenhillpublishing.com.au/

Rankin, Peter (author)
Peg Rankin: A Journey of Faith and Resilience
ISBN 978-1-923523-00-5 (paperback)
BIOGRAPHY

Typeset Calluna Regular 11/16pt
Cover photos provided by the author's family
Cover and book design by Green Hill

Peg Rankin

A Journey of Faith and Resilience

Peter Rankin SDB

"You gave her to us to be our joy and our hearts were full of happiness. And then you took her away. We gave her back without a word and our hearts were full of gratitude."

ST EPHREM 306-373

PEG RANKIN FAMILY TREE

Agnes and Bill Hughes (Parents)

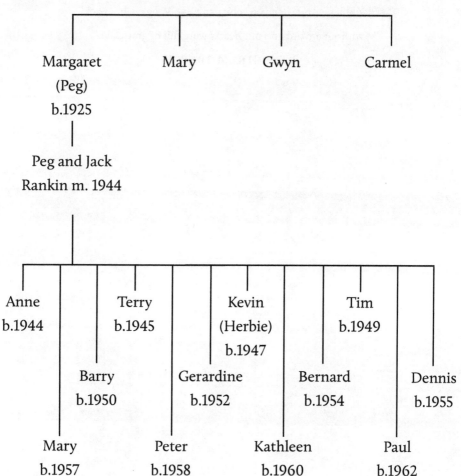

Margaret (Peg) b.1925   Mary   Gwyn   Carmel

Peg and Jack Rankin m. 1944

Anne b.1944

Barry b.1950

Terry b.1945

Gerardine b.1952

Kevin (Herbie) b.1947

Bernard b.1954

Tim b.1949

Dennis b.1955

Mary b.1957

Peter b.1958

Kathleen b.1960

Paul b.1962

ACKNOWLEDGEMENTS

THIS BOOK HAS been a labour of love. Although written in the last two years, it is the fruit of many years of listening to and observing my mother Peg in word and in deed. In one sense it has not been difficult to write as the subject matter is quite extraordinary. As a son who writes a book about his mother, I could be seen as biased, but that sits pretty comfortably with me. Peg has occasionally said I see her through rose-tinted glasses and maybe there is a little bit of truth in that.

The primary purpose of writing this book is to share Peg's rich story, the tapestry of her life. Some may have got to know Peg in her later years, and some may know snippets of her story. Others may have known her through her fifteen years of cooking at the West Gippsland Hospital, or they may remember her from the Fumina period of her life. I want to inform any reader of her entire life, her struggles, her endurance, and her capacity to make the most of any situation.

This biography is written particularly for her grandchildren, great-grandchildren and future descendants. I want them to know a little more of the faith, resilience, resourcefulness, and the extended love of this quite extraordinary woman. I want her life to impact upon theirs, so that in their time and place they in turn can strive to live life to the full, as she did.

I am indebted to my mother, who has been so helpful and encouraging in putting her life story together. Her memories of the main storylines of her life are vivid, even though the details were rather sketchy now and again. She has supported this project since the beginning. In January 2014 and again in January 2015, I spent weeks recording her oral account of significant and not so significant moments in her life. Over these last two years, countless phone calls to her unit in Leith Park, Greensborough North, to clarify and verify details of her story were met with: 'So what is on your mind today, Peter?'

My ten siblings have been highly supportive and each and every one has contributed to the book. To Anne, Terry, Herb, Tim, Gerardine, Bernard, Dennis, Mary, Kathleen and Paul, my heartfelt thanks.

I would particularly like to thank my sister Mary for her encouragement, assistance, and not least her friendship. She was the one who really got me started. Peg had expressed her disappointment to Mary that Peter had not visited her as he promised, to record her life journey. The result of that encounter jolted me into action, and Mary was present for a lot of the early interviews with Mum. Mary has written beautifully about the death of Dad and is quoted at some length.

Anne, the eldest child, has contributed significantly about

Dad and has thoughtfully unpacked the relationship between Mum and Dad.

Herb, child number three, was a mine of information for this book. His memory of family events is both acute and accurate. Without his contribution, this biography would have been much lighter on detail. I am truly indebted to both Herb and his wife Jackie for their willingness to help. Jackie went to the Lilydale Library and the State Library in Melbourne on a mission which proved very successful. I am grateful to her for her generosity and interest in this project. She was often the conduit between Herb and me in our correspondence.

Peg's three sisters, Mary, Gwyn and Carmel, were all interviewed as well. A quick trip to the Gold Coast in August 2014 to interview Carmel and Gwyn was invaluable and helped greatly with the writing of the first chapter.

Thanks to the in-laws, John Schmid, Debbie Rankin, Jackie Rankin, Marg Rankin, David Dahlenburg, Caroline West, Jo Rankin, Chris Chapple, Peter Cantwell and Brigette Rankin, for their interest assistance and comments. They have all contributed one way or another.

Thanks also to Peg's grandchildren, Isaac, Olive, Dominic, Adrian, Douglas, John, Louisa, Michael, Nicola, Jackson, Lisa, Jaryd, Sarah, Luke, Katie, Lachlan, Felicity, Markus, Thomas, Hayley and Samantha.

I am grateful to Lara and Sam West, two step-grandchildren of Peg who have also contributed. They have all helped fill in the pages of the last chapter with their special memories of 'Granny'.

Joy, Lindsay and Ian Rankin have contributed many memories and photos from the Fumina years. Joy gave me a whole day of her time, and her love of Fumina and its past is infectious. I am enormously indebted to her.

Mary and Barry Horan were also helpful regarding the Fumina period.

I would like to thank the clergy for their cooperation. Fr Herman Hengel PP has written the Foreword. Most Reverend Michael McKenna (currently Bishop of Bathurst) and Fr John Readman PE have also provided input.

Joan Robertson from the parish of St Joseph's, Warragul, had many insights into Peg's character, and her contribution to the life of St Joseph's parish greatly helped with the chapter on the Warragul years.

I have deliberately sub-titled Peg's story *A Woman of Faith and Resilience*. I wrote this book through the lens of faith, and I make no apologies for that. To understand Peg, you cannot ignore the influence of the Catholic heritage running through the very fibre of her being. For me, this is not merely a human story, but a journey in faith. Throughout history many of the outstanding men and women who have contributed so much to humanity have been saints of our Church.

Since January 2014, I have worked as Assistant Priest in the parish of St John Bosco, Engadine, New South Wales. I am indebted to my parish priest and friend, Fr Michael Court, who has encouraged me to work on this biography.

I would also like to thank Barry Chapman who assisted with

photographs, and John Casey, who assisted with the layout and general presentation. I am indebted to these two parishioners for their time and expertise.

Also, John Ryan, Maria Millward and Joan Moylan looked through the manuscript and have all made helpful suggestions which have been incorporated into the final form of the text.

Peg celebrated her 90th birthday on 19 November 2015. This date was my deadline for finishing this work. I am so pleased I have been able to meet it. I hope you enjoy reading this biography as much as I have enjoyed writing it.

Peter Rankin SDB
19 November 2015
Engadine, NSW

FOREWORD

PEG RANKIN WELCOMED me with graciousness, humour and wisdom when I arrived as Parish Priest of Warragul and Drouin at the beginning of 2003. Over the next ten years until she retired from ministry, she became my friend, mentor and inspiration on how to live my faith.

She is a most extraordinary woman, gifted with wisdom, the ability to work hard and to make the best of any situation, with an unshakeable belief in God and the message of Jesus.

She married at eighteen years of age in 1944 and with her husband ran a farm in Fumina. I like the story that after the marriage celebrations were over, they caught a bus or buses from Lilydale to Noojee and then walked seven kilometres to the farm in Fumina. They had no car and no electricity until the last of their brood of twelve was five years old. If you lived in small communities in those days, you learned to friend and to be friends with neighbours. You learned to ask for advice and help, and to give advice and help.

Another story Mary told at Peg's 80th birthday was how Peg could be cooking a gourmet meal, giving counselling on the phone, while controlling twelve children.

When Jack retired and they sold the farm, they shifted to Warragul and Peg acquired a job working in the kitchen at the Warragul Hospital. She became a special diet cook, but had no qualification whatsoever, except that she was a very good cook. Of course, eventually, rules and regulations caught up with her. Suddenly and somehow, she did get the right qualification. When she reached retiring age after her 15 years' service at the hospital, she became the Sacristan at St Joseph's Church in Warragul for the next twenty years. She set up for every Mass, funeral and liturgical celebration, ran the Legion of Mary, visited everybody in the parish, and knew everybody. She always shared her knowledge of the parish and the parishioners with wisdom and respect. She was always positive and constructive with her knowledge and advice. Her story is a story worth telling, remembering and reading.

Father Herman Hengel PP
Warragul

Contents

CHAPTER 1

Parents, Childhood
and Growing Up

MARGARET (PEG) HUGHES was born on 19 November 1925, the first of five children. Her parents, William (Bill) Hughes and Agnes Crowley, had married in 1924. Peg's arrival was followed by three sisters, Mary, Gwyn and Carmel, all born in quick succession. The youngest, a boy named John Joseph, was born in 1930, but he only lived a few months. Agnes had another child from a previous relationship. Her name was Veronica, and the Hughes sisters never knew about her until after their mother had died.

John Joseph was a sickly infant who suffered from projectile vomiting, which was a common enough ailment in those times. Bill had longed for a son after four daughters, but when he was given this blessing he possibly did not do the best by him as he was reluctant to allow an operation on his son's stomach. According to Peg, he had something against surgery. Sadly, John Joseph died when he was only five months old. Infant mortality was still reasonably high in the 1930s in Australia. Mary, the second eldest, recalls the death of John:

> *The night before the funeral Mum took us into the dining room and John Joseph was in a little coffin with lighted candles next to it. I remember Mum and Dad going off in the car and I wanted to go with them. I remember being comforted by a nurse who said, 'Come here and I will tell you a story.' None of the children went to the funeral. It is quite amazing, this definite memory I have of my brother dying.*

Psychologists tell us that even as very young children we have the capacity to remember significant events. Here is a case in point.

Bill Hughes was a small-time financier. He went into business with Agnes' brother, George Crowley, and they had their names engraved on a brass plate in a rented office in Melbourne. Before the October 1929 Wall Street crash which ushered in the Great Depression, Bill and George were doing quite well. Peg remembers having paid elocution lessons as a small child, which indicates financial security. It all went pear-shaped when the Depression hit. One of Peg's earliest memories was coming home from school one day to find every scrap of furniture in the house had been changed:

> *There was not one thing in the house that was the same between the time I left for school one morning and by the time I returned home that afternoon. The furniture would*

have been on a time payment system and Dad would have auctioned it off. He knew he was going to go broke and you couldn't keep furniture on a time-payment arrangement if you went broke. If he had not done anything, he would have lost the furniture altogether. Dad's job was to seek out debtors and he ended up in this situation himself. Creditors would have simply come and taken the furniture.

John Molony, an eminent Australian historian, sums up the impact of the Great Depression on both the ordinary Australian and the well-off in these words:

The poor, the unemployed, the small businessman whose economic base was shattered, the shopkeeper who no longer had customers or who had to extend credit beyond his resources, the professional whose services could not be afforded, the entrepreneur who had gambled and faced unpayable debts, the farmer who had overcapitalised in hope and walked off his property in despair; all these suffered deprivation to a greater or lesser degree.

On the other hand, the rich, whose capital was safe, the employed whose jobs were not at risk and especially those in government services, the clever who had enough capital to take advantage of those who were forced to sell their home or a business, all of these survived and some prospered. Those on salaries could absorb cuts because the drop in commodity prices compensated. To such people the Depression was a stage on which they played a part,

but as mere observers, although some were not even that as
they remained sheltered in their affluent suburbs, with their
rounds of social events, where misery did not penetrate.[1]

Bill Hughes with his two daughters, Peg and Mary.

The Depression created the haves and the have-nots. Bill
Hughes was definitely confined to the latter category. It seems
that after the business went broke, the family moved around a
lot and their circumstances changed for the worst. Peg remembers beginning school at either McKinnon or Brighton and then
in Oakleigh. She still remembers being scolded by the teacher for
not having any writing materials.

---

1   John Molony, *The Penguin History of Australia*, 1988, p.257.

We were absolutely penniless and I had no pencil. There
was not much I could do about it. I never understood why
the teacher berated me as it was outside my own control.
I couldn't help it if I didn't have a pencil.

Gwyn and Carmel remember:

... walking three miles to and from school in the boots that
the sussos² gave us. Other children would pick on us with our
susso boots.

The Hughes girls weren't alone. At the height of the
Depression, Australia had the second highest unemployment
rate per capita in the Western world. Between 1930 and 1934,
the unemployment rate never went below twenty-four per cent
of the workforce in Australia, peaking at 28 per cent in 1932.
Germany was the only other country in the West to have a higher
unemployment rate.

It says much for Australian resilience and common sense
that there was no shift to the totalitarianism which took place
in Germany with the rise of Hitler.³

For the Hughes girls, early memories centred on Eltham. Their
father had incurred bad debts and wanted to relocate his family

---

2   Sustenance Support Program.
3   Molony, p. 258.

to a place far enough away from the pursuit of creditors. It seems they moved from Bentleigh to Eltham to start a new life. The oldest three, Peg, Mary and Gwyn, attended school there at Our Lady Help of Christians. They lived in a few different houses in the area, first of all in Pitt Street. Their father was unable to do manual work since one leg was considerably longer than the other. Physically he was quite restricted and he had to wear a special boot to help alleviate this imbalance. He therefore relied on the Sustenance Support Program for him and his family to survive.

> *During the Depression, there were bankruptcies and suicides, heartbreaks and anxieties, which bit deep into psyches, especially when the loss of work meant a loss of a home. Men, married and single, tramped the roads, rode the rattler between the towns, begged and hawked trinkets ... dole queues of men lined up for 7 shillings per week if single, 14 shillings if married and an additional seven shillings for each child. It was no longer a crime to dye an army overcoat and the government issued thousands of surplus coats left over from the war but now died black. Wearing one became an outward sign of misery and defeat.*[4]

Peg remembers a joyride on a motor bike that she had with her three younger sisters when she was a child:

---

4   Molony, p. 259.

In Eltham we used to get rides on this old chap's motor bike with a side car and he used to putt along. This day he was giving the four girls a ride but there was no room for me in the side-car so I stood on a board at the back. We were not that far from home and I managed to slip and fall back and hit my head on the road, and had one hell of a headache. I was taken to the Children's Hospital for my bad nerves, and the next day I vomited profusely. There was a boy admitted at the same time with pneumonia and there was only one bed and he was given priority over me. When I went home, I rested for three or four days with the headache. I had to be really careful the way I moved my head. I could so easily have been killed.

She was fortunate. We hear a lot today about king hit punches, and people falling onto the road and hitting their heads, and either dying or being seriously maimed for life.

All the Hughes girls seemed to remember the devastating 1934 floods. The little creek that runs around the perimeter of Eltham burst its embankment and totally flooded low-lying areas. Gwyn recalls:

When the floods came I remember a piano floating down the river and a toilet ... we were up on a rise out of harm's way.

Eltham in the 1930s was one of the preferred places for day trips for Melbournians. Some would take the train out there. The more affluent who owned cars would drive. With the floods, many trees were uprooted on the main road in and out of the town. Quite a few were stranded there for days.

Photo of floods in Eltham, 1934.

Peg and her three sisters contracted whooping cough in 1933. Bill's brother Ernie and his wife Cybil came to visit them one day in Eltham. This was still Depression time, and it was so hard for the Hughes family to make ends meet. To ease a little of the pressure, it was spontaneously agreed that afternoon that, as the eldest, Peg would go and live with them for a while in Glen Iris. As Peg recalled:

We would have been relying on the food ticket at the time. I stayed with my Auntie and Uncle for several months in Ferndale Road. Ernie and Cybil did not have any children of their own.

They married late in life. Ernie had his face blown apart during the First World War. He couldn't work and they lived on a war pension. They didn't instinctively know a lot about parenting but they were very good to me. They bought me a new pair of shoes to wear to school. I looked after the shoes and was careful not to damage them. My Uncle Ernie would inspect the shoes each night for any scuff marks. They were not Catholics; they were Salvation Army, but they sent me to the Catholic school and paid for my school fees. I used to walk to school at Our Lady of Victories in Camberwell. It was a fair old walk for a seven- or eight-year-old. I was staying with them when I made my First Holy Communion. It was such a special moment. Afterwards the little band of children who had just made their First Communion had a party up at the convent.

Ernie and Cybil would have gladly adopted Peg, or at least have her live with them. At some stage, they broached the subject with her, to gauge her feelings about possibly staying with them long-term. But Peg would not have welcomed that:

I was very homesick really. Although they were fine people, it was a little bit dull living with them and I just wanted to go back to Eltham. After all I was only seven or eight years old.

Cybil and Ernie most likely approached Agnes about this possibility, but nothing eventuated and Peg settled back in with her natural family.

Photos taken when Peg was staying with Ernest
and Cybil Hughes in Glen Iris, 1933.

The Hughes children remember that their life was tough, but
they managed. They remember their mother being a good cook
and that there was a lot of love around her. Agnes would often
remind her children that 'the longest life is only short'. Later in
life she mused:

I guess it is pretty short, but you can get kind of busy and pack quite a lot into it.

In childhood, the Hughes girls seemed to get along all right. Mary, Gwyn and Carmel gravitated towards one another easily. Peg was that little bit older. Peg, Gwyn and Carmel shared Mary's pain when their father mistreated her, and they rallied around their sister. Gwyn was a real pest because she was a tell-tale. Occasionally on the walk to and from school, Peg would take a detour to explore in and around the railway line and novel places:

It would sometimes take us a long time to get to school and Gwyn made our life hell. She was a brat of a kid. If we did anything wrong, she would tell. Gwyn was spoilt as a child.

Peg spent Years 5 and 6 at St Patrick's School in Lilydale:

I had a nun teach me. Sister Leo. She was all right at maths, but weak in other areas.

This was the time of the Spanish Civil War and the persecution of followers of the Catholic faith. Communism was a threat and it was gaining momentum throughout the world. It was a definite force in the Spanish Civil War. Many Catholics were executed in Spain simply because of their faith, and news of these atrocities filtered around the world.

Sister Leo talked a lot about the evils of Communism and her distaste for mixed marriages.

Behind the latter view would have been the understanding that a marriage between two people of the same faith and the same creeds meant a better chance of passing on the flame of faith, as children born to this type of union would have a greater likelihood of maintaining their allegiance with the Catholic faith. If only one party to the marriage was Catholic, there would be a greater possibility of the children having a weaker faith, and they would have to contend with their parents' differing viewpoints and values.

For eleven-year-old Peg, the content of certain aspects of faith isn't easy to understand:

> ... the nuns trying to teach me about Original Sin and a baby being born with sin on his/her soul and how baptism takes away the stain of this sin but not its effects. Original Sin has always been a difficult concept to get one's head around. In essence it means that when one enters the human condition, that person is a flawed creature oriented towards sin and selfishness. He or she is not born in a state of equilibrium but a structural bias towards sin. Every human being has to confront this reality as he or she grows older. We were taught that sin remains a powerful force in one's life, even after the cleansing of Baptism. At school at St Pat's I would wonder about this black mark on my soul. I thought it must have been like a black pimple on my back.

Noted Australian Church historian Patrick O'Farrell writes of Catholic life in Australia in the 1930s and 1940s:

> *The prevailing religious theme was simple piety, of which devotion to the Sacred Heart and the Blessed Virgin Mary were key elements. Devotional life stressed a childlike spirit of acceptance, and although there was an emphasis on sin as the soul's first and last enemy, this was outweighed in the balance by the teaching of the infinite love and mercy of God and of the tenderness of His Holy Mother. Australian Catholicism had little in it of tortured ... pessimism which might have generated some intellectual questioning – and consisted in the main of an optimistic estimate of the individual's potential for good, and of God's ready forgiveness if he (sic) was not.[5]*

The Catholic Church has always understood the family was the first teacher in the ways of faith. Catholic schools, dedicated clergy, religious sisters and brothers are important but they are secondary to the family, which is considered the primary influence in the passing on of faith. The Hughes girls received their Catholic faith from their mother Agnes. She was devout, solid and practical in the exercise of her faith. She saw to it that all her children were baptised and prepared for the sacraments.

Bill, who had ties with the Salvation Army, flirted with Catholicism when he agreed to marry Agnes. He was given

---

5   Patrick O'Farrell, *The Catholic Church and Community An Australian History*, p.355.

instruction in the Catholic faith by a German-speaking priest who was attached to the Immaculate Conception Parish in Hawthorn. Peg said that Agnes told her the priest was really hard to understand, and Bill would have probably been none the wiser after having attended these instructions.

Bill reverted to his allegiance with the Salvation Army soon after his marriage. He was also a Mason, and pretty soon after his recommitment to the Salvation Army he proudly produced his Masonic badge. According to Carmel, Agnes did not know about Bill's affiliation to the Masonic movement until well after they were married. This is not surprising, as members were sworn to secrecy.

Religion would not have been a topic of conversation in the Hughes household. Nevertheless, the four girls gravitated towards their Catholic heritage. It is often the case that the religion of the mother is the one that is handed on to children. Peg remembers walking her sisters, Mary, Gwyn and Carmel, to church on Sundays. As with the walk to school, it was a fair hike. Because of the distance and their mother's precarious health, it would have been left up to Peg to lead this expedition.

Peg attributes her strong Catholic faith first of all to the witness of her good mother, and also to the influence of the Mercy Sisters at St Patrick's. When the question was put to her about the gift of her own faith – not simply faith, but incredibly strong faith – she responded:

Well, of course there was my own mother and in some ways
I suppose, the nuns gave you a good grounding. I just thank
God for this gift. Someone must have been praying for me.

The Mercy Sisters were founded in Ireland by Catherine McAuley. She left her Sisters a legacy by which to live. They were to bring the gospel to life by mercy values. In 1846, just five years after Catherine's death, a group of Mercy Sisters arrived in Western Australia. The leader of this foundation community was Sister Ursula Frayne, who had known Catherine well and was present in the room when she died.

The Mercy Sisters flourished in Australia, spreading rapidly until by the early years of the twentieth century there were fifty-two autonomous Mercy congregations in Australia. Wherever they found themselves, whether in growing cities or towns or remote outback places, they endeavoured to respond by evangelisation, education, health care and welfare services. Their most famous establishments in Victoria were the St Vincent de Paul Orphanage for girls in South Melbourne and St Catherine's Orphanage in Geelong. They began their work at Lilydale in 1857. The Hughes girls, Peg in particular, were beneficiaries of their educational method.

Sister Leo was one of the strongest influences in Peg's life. She was born Mary Muriel Willis in Colac on 22 May 1889, and entered the Novitiate on 19 June 1914. She made her first profession on 10 January 1918, and chose the religious name Leo after the outstanding Pope Leo the Great from the fifth century. In 1932 Sister M Leo was appointed Principal at St Patrick's Primary School in Lilydale, and she remained in that position until 1939. So whilst Sister Leo was teaching the young Peg in 1936-1937, she was also the Principal. She was later appointed to Mount Lilydale Mercy College, where she remained until her retirement. She died on 24 December 1974.

Peg remembered the two years at St Patrick's school just as much for their extracurricular activities as for their spiritual life and scholastic endeavours:

I was a tomboy. I used to play marbles on the footpath after school and Eunice Murphy, a fellow pupil, would tell on me to the Sisters. She informed teachers of my misspent childhood playing marbles after school on the road. I cleaned up all the boys. I was the marble queen. We played for keeps. In other words, the winner kept the marbles. It was fair dinkum stuff. You had the tombola in the middle and whoever got closest to the tombola took all. I was scolded more than once for playing marbles with the boys.

Peg, back row first on the left. Peg's sister Mary is in the second row, second on the left; and Gwyn is front row, second from left.

Peg's reputation went before her. More than thirty-five years later, her daughter Mary attended Mount Lilydale College in

1973-1974. By then Sister Leo was well and truly retired and living in the Convent attached to the College, but she remembered Peg. One day in 1973, there was a parent-teacher interview and Peg was there to hear from teachers about Mary's progress. She inadvertently bumped into Sister Leo, who remembered her from St Patrick's days, and said to her:

I pray for all my students, I EVEN pray for you, Margaret (Peg).

Sr Leo, it seems, didn't have a great deal of faith or hope in Peg and obviously thought that Peg would not aspire to any great heights of sanctity or achievement. Her memory was coloured by the tomboyish ways, which belied Peg's innate giftedness and her desire to be the best person she possibly could be.

After her two years at St Pat's, the family moved to Silvan and this meant a change of schools. Peg's Catholic education ceased and she attended a State School as it was simply too far to travel into Lilydale from Silvan. She really flourished at school in Silvan, where she completed the equivalent of Years 7 and 8. Not only did she attend school, but after school she helped to deliver groceries from her father's shop on her bicycle. There was a basket on her bike and she would traverse the hilly streets of Mount Evelyn delivering the groceries. It wouldn't have been easy as Mount Evelyn is quite hilly.

Peg's two years at Silvan school culminated in her being offered a scholarship to continue her education. With the scholarship, books would have been supplied in addition to any fees.

Those two years were highly productive educationally and Peg obviously blossomed. In her own words:

> *I went from the bottom of the class to the top. My male teacher helped a lot with pronunciation of words, elocution and appreciation of Australian poetry. He was a jolly good teacher. The nuns at St Patrick's Lilydale didn't correct pronunciation when you were reading out aloud. As long as you got the words out, it didn't seem to matter. If you said one word individually without the natural flow of the poetry, prose, etc, you were not interrupted. One time, early on in Year 7 at Silvan, I was reading and the teacher pulled me up and said, 'Stop, stop, stop!' I was racing the words. By the second year I was his prized pupil. I could read well, putting the emphasis in the right place, reading with feeling. I became the teacher's pet.*

It is quite amazing what a good teacher can do, the response they can elicit from their students. William A Ward once said that 'the mediocre teacher tells, the good teacher explains, the superior teacher demonstrates, the great teacher inspires'. Good teaching draws from what is within a person. Galileo correctly understood that 'you cannot teach a man (sic) anything, you can only help him find it within himself'. This superior and possibly great teacher at Silvan recognised Peg's efforts and her commitment to improve herself. She drew from the wells within. He assisted Peg to read fluently, he gave her a great love of the Australian poets, and he helped her to appreciate the value of a broader education. Overall this was a much better learning experience than her primary school days. It was no surprise, then, that by the end of the year she was offered a scholarship.

But it wasn't to be. On reflection, Peg was not resentful that her father stepped in and terminated any further education possibilities by bringing her into the shop to work:

> *I would have loved to go on with my education. I did have thoughts at some stage of becoming a teacher but my parents told me to work in the shop. I simply dealt with the cards that were handed to me. I tried not to dwell on it too much. Education for girls wasn't deemed that important. I wasn't bitter about it. It is just the way it was.*

Gwyn added ruefully:

> *Peg got her Merit. She could have gone further. She won a scholarship which would have greatly assisted in her education, but she had to go into the shop and work for old Bill. It was a lot of work for Peg. Dad used to go home for a sleep. He really liked his siesta. He would have left Peg in charge. She definitely worked hard in the shop. Peg would have loved to have gone on with her schooling but they didn't have the money and she was told to work in the shop. She just got on with it.*

Carmel said quite emphatically:

Peg was the one with the brains. Oh, she was smart! There is no doubt about it. Continuing her education would have assured her of a really good job but family circumstances prevented that.

Peg was physically short, but strong and quite accomplished at sport. She excelled at marbles, was invited more than once to join the Tennis Club in Mount Evelyn, and she shone at basketball (netball):

> *I had a really good Physical Education teacher at Silvan State School. This instructor was a good communicator. She coached our basketball team. I played centre. I was in the local paper as the best player more than once. This would have been 1939 as I pretty much finished school by the time the Second World War started.*

Peg, fourth from the left. She played centre in Netball team.

Wandin School Sports Association

Basket Ball.

Matches played on July 21 resulted as follow:—

Seville d Silvan, 28 goals to 13. Seville's goal throwers were K. Priest
(11) and D. Priest (1), and Silvan's
Pat. Wallace (12) and Laurel Chapman (3). Hilda Read and Gwen.
Banlksby figured at Seville's best
players, and Edna Hooke and Margaret Hughes served Silvan in that capacity.

Wandin Yallock A. d Evelyn, 29
goals to 11. Goal throwers.—Wandin: I. Henderson (19), T. Rouget
(10); Evelyn: T. Thompson (7), E.
Rose (4). Best players.—Wandin:
Jean McGregor and Beryl Underwood.

The Wandin East-Wandin Yallock
B. match was not played.

With 10 points, Seville heads the
premiership ladder; next in order are
Wandin Yallock A., 8 pts.; Evelyn.

Lilydale Gazette, 29 August 1939. Note: Margaret (Peg) Hughes
as one of the best players for the Silvan team.

Before Peg settled to life working in the shop, there was one
further experience of note. She was asked to be a nanny for Sister
Leo's[6] brother in Hawthorn. Carmel and Gwyn recall this even-
tuality, but they are light on the details. They were both unsure
how long this arrangement was for, but it may have been a month

---

6   The nun from St Pat's Lilydale.

at most. Was it after she left school or the summer before? It is hard to get the facts right here, although the family did have two children. Peg never had fond memories of this experience. She was lonely, missed the family, and was treated subserviently. She never ate with the family. She had to wait until called to take away the dishes after the evening meal.

'The father was okay, but the mother was very snobbish. They would sit and talk over the day with their dirty dishes and I had to wait till later to enter the room and clean up.

It seems good old Bill may have put an end to the arrangement as he missed his star helper, and Peg was called back to live with the family and assist in the shop at Mount Evelyn. She was happy to return to the family, and over time she became the linchpin in the shop with her hard work, social skills and nous.

From childhood, Peg was always the first one out of bed in the morning in her family. She had the habit of making tea and toast for everyone – her parents and younger siblings – and delivering it to them whilst they were all still in bed. She simply took it upon herself to do that. She wasn't instructed to perform this daily ritual; she simply naturally aimed to please and to serve. It seems this facet was always part of her character.

Before she was married, Agnes attended classes specialising in making sweets. Early on in the Mount Evelyn days, she put her cooking skills to the test. To supplement the meagre family income, she would make sweets and goodies and sell them. Gwyn and Carmel remember their mother having a big drum of glucose to make sweets, toffees, lollies, peanut toffees, and a whole array of goodies. Carmel recalled:

> I can still visualise Mum cutting out the toffee into squares and then using coconut ice as a topping. She would not let any of us eat them as these were to be sold.

And Gwyn remembered:

> Mum would walk around the railway line and deliver the sweets to their shop. We had a double shop, sharing the premises. The shop was divided down the middle but eventually Dad took over the whole shop. Initially he just sold Mum's wares but later on expanded the business.

As well as selling Agnes' goodies, Bill also sold fruit and vegies. Peg remembers that even whilst she was still at school, she and Bill would meet the train each Friday and pick up the fruit and vegies, then set up the shop for Saturday, which was a really important day for trading.

Bill, from all reports, was quite a difficult character to get along with. He was socially awkward and emotionally distant. Peg managed to put up with him in the grocery shop for four years, day in and day out. It would not have been easy. Come the age of 16, she could easily have decided she was out of there, but to her credit she didn't. She stuck by him, and by inference, the rest of her family. At an early age she demonstrated the values of loyalty, patience, hard work, getting along with quite a difficult character, and putting her family first.

Peg was quite sporty and was invited to join the Mount Evelyn tennis club on a Saturday afternoon, but she wasn't given time off or encouraged to take up tennis. Bill demanded she work in the shop. A Saturday afternoon tennis competition would have interfered with his siesta, and his needs came first.

Peg's three sisters all struggled with their father. Mary had a very poor relationship with him. He was totally unreasonable in his dealings with her. He couldn't see any good in her and he chastised her for the smallest thing. Agnes compensated Mary for the harshness meted out by her father.

Gwyn, too, worked in the shop for a short time, after Peg left to marry Jack. She would tell her father what she thought. She obviously didn't possess Peg's patience, and she told Bill 'what he could do with his bloody old shop':

> He used to sack me. This happened more than once. The last time, I told him he can keep his bloody old shop and walked out.

Gwyn was quite capable of calling a spade a spade. She remembers Mr O'Connor, who ran the Post Office next door, telling her afterwards that he had overheard her having 'harsh words with her father'.

Later on, when Bill was off the scene, he had a shop in Fitzroy and Gwyn wanted to see what her father was up to. She entered the premises and Bill told her to get out and mind her own business. Later she received a letter from a solicitor forbidding her to go anywhere near the shop. It all got a bit unpleasant. At this point, her father had made a new life for himself and wanted nothing to do with the rest of his family.

Carmel also remembers working in the shop at Mount Evelyn, and she recalls her father's poor judgement of character. She used to ask her friend Marie to be there when a certain client came:

> He was a bit touchy and feely. He wanted to play with me. Dad said he was all right. I wasn't so sure. He used to make deliveries to the shop and I instinctively didn't trust him and wanted my friend Marie Jackson to be present when he came by. He was not punctual. He never turned up at the appointed time. My friend Marie would be an ally in this awkward situation.

Courtships in the 1940s were not what they are today. Often there was not much contact before marriage. Jack Rankin, who was to marry Peg, had quite a wealthy aunt, Annie Regan, who was Jack's mother's sister. She had done well in the hotel business in South Melbourne, and had paid a deposit for a house in Mt Evelyn for Jack's parents to live in. Jack, who was enlisted in the army at that time, maintained the mortgage payments and often spent weekends in Mt Evelyn with his parents. Occasionally Kate Rankin would come down to the Hughes' grocery store to buy things.

The Rankins and the Hughes met each other when walking to and from Mass on Sundays. Their houses were reasonably close and the Hughes girls and their mother would walk right past the Rankin house. Over time, the families got to know one another. The astute Herb encouraged his shy and reserved son Jack to woo Peg, so a courtship began. Peg remembers that 'Herb thought the sun, moon and stars shone out of me'. Jack would have needed some coaxing. None better than from his own father. It wasn't a long courtship, but it led to a proposal of marriage.

Mr O'Connor in the Post Office next door also encouraged Jack to do a line with Peg. Over four years, he would have seen at first hand Peg's work ethic, tenacity, honesty, common sense, and her inner beauty. Much later Peg recalled:

> *Whatever Mr O'Connor told Jack, Jack remembered his positive summation of my character. John O'Connor spoke in glowing terms about me to Jack. Jack never forgot whatever he was told. Jimmy Spears the local milkman, who was still unmarried himself told Jack after the announcement of the engagement that 'you have the best catch in Mount Evelyn'.*

Herb and Kate's granddaughter, Mary Rout (nee Gilsenan), stayed with her grandparents in Mount Evelyn in 1943:

> *I first met Peg when I was ten years old. I was staying with Gran and Granddad as our school had been closed due to lack*

of pupils. Gran had sent me to get messages at the grocer's shop where Peg worked for her father. Peg had pigtails. I don't think she was long out of school and she used to deliver groceries on her pushbike with her pigtails flying along behind her. Jack was in the Army and came home on leave to Gran's place. Jack went down to the grocer's to get smokes and met Peg. After he went back to the Army, Peg had her hair cut and looked much older. If I remember rightly they started seeing each other after that. Grandad used to tell Jack he was a cradle snatcher as there was a big difference in their ages. I remember Peg did a First Aid course as part of the war effort; I guess it came in handy with the kids on the farm. It was a romance that worked. They were still on their honeymoon until Jack died all those years later.

In late 1943 Peg spent some time in Fumina. She came up to this rugged place without any creature comforts or amenities, accompanied by her fiancé Jack. It must have been a bit of a shock to the young Peg, travelling up by bus and walking the last six kilometres in the pitch black dark. She would not have arrived in Fumina till well after 11.00pm. She stayed with Jack's sister Millie, her husband Pat Gilsenan, and their family. Although excited by marriage and the possibility of a new life, she must have pondered what she had let herself in for!

Kevin Kealy, a nephew of Jack's, was only 11 years old at the time, and he fondly remembered the newly engaged Peg helping Jack plant potatoes:

There she was, barely 18 years old, a city girl, standing behind an unfriendly horse in remote country, planting potatoes. It was hard yakka. What a way to spend an engagement. This was her welcome to Fumina!

There is an old Czech proverb which says: *Do not choose your wife at a dance but in the fields amongst the harvesters.* Jack may not have heard the proverb, but he would have quietly rejoiced in the work ethic of his bride-to-be. Kevin (Herb) Rankin, Jack and Peg's third eldest, maintained:

In planting spuds (potatoes) you stand behind the horse poking around. It is an unpleasant job, not easy, physically demanding. We all had a bit of a go at it with Dad as kids. I do it for fun now, but it would have been no fun then.

From time to time, Jack was challenged about the way he treated his fiancée. His response, true to form, was that 'you have to test them out'. Peg was tested, and once again was up to the task. She managed with great aplomb whatever was put in front of her, whether it was walking her three sisters some distance to school and Church, coping with a sibling who would tell tales on her, working with a difficult father in the shop, or was planting potatoes in Fumina with a reticent fiancé, Peg would rise to the occasion each time. Over that summer of 1943-44, Fumina was in fever pitch awaiting the arrival of this new couple who would soon make their life there.

When it came to Peg marrying Jack, Bill Hughes was not very encouraging. Peg would have only been seventeen when the wedding was being planned and it would have required parental approval and a parental signature. Bill was reluctant to sign the marriage papers. Initially he tried to persuade Agnes to put a 'kibosh' on the whole thing. Agnes, however, didn't deviate from lending her support to the marriage, despite Peg's tender age. 'I suppose he had a right to his say as admittedly I was so young,' she reflected.

Peg thought her father gave her away at the end, but this is not definite. Bill could possibly see the ramifications of his star worker leaving the nest and the effect on his business, and that she was the glue keeping the family together. Mr O'Connor from the Post Office was on standby to give Peg away at the altar if Bill didn't front up for the wedding.

By the time Peg married she was eighteen, so she was legally able to marry without permission of her father. It must be remembered that in Australia at the time it was common enough practice for an eighteen-year-old woman to marry. If you were still single at twenty-five there was the real concern that you might be 'left on the shelf'. What was unusual was the significant age differential between Peg and Jack – almost fourteen years. In the end Bill gave Peg away at their wedding on 12 February 1944.

Their wedding was the first wedding in the new Catholic Church at Mt Evelyn. Bill must have had a heavy heart that day. People of Peg's calibre are few and far between. Their paths never crossed again.

Wedding Day, 12 February 1944, Mount Evelyn.

Soon after Peg settled down in Fumina, Bill and Agnes's marriage fell apart and the business floundered. It is not as if it had been a happy marriage. Agnes and Bill didn't have much in common, and communication between them was never a high-point of their relationship. What compounded the difficulty was

31

Agnes' attitude to alcohol. Her father was an alcoholic and had died in an asylum. Sometimes if Bill came home and smelt of alcohol, as happened occasionally, the tension was palpable. Peg recalls that 'you could cut the air with a knife'. Agnes, it seems, was unreasonable and expected total abstinence. According to Peg, Bill had no problem with alcohol:

> *There was no dependency or abuse, but a bit of social time with friends on a Friday afternoon.*

A case could be made that Peg was the glue that kept both the marriage and the shop together. By this stage she could have run the business all by herself. When Peg married Jack and went away, it was such a wrench for Agnes to have her eldest leave her that she was bedridden for an entire week, and it appears that a serious bout of depression and anguish set in. Trauma comes in different forms. Peg's departure was traumatic for Agnes. Bill, it seems, would have lacked the empathy and emotional awareness to offer any assistance. Is it a coincidence that as soon as Peg left the scene, Bill and Agnes' marriage ended?

Fairly soon after Peg's departure, Bill had the shop extended so that it could also be lived in, and he moved in there with a housekeeper and her child. This is where the marriage ended.

Will Hughes died in 1956 and is buried in the Lilydale cemetery. He was Bill Hughes to the locals and when he worked at the 'sussos', he would have been called Bill. Agnes always called him Will, but Carmel can't remember her mother calling him anything.

Peg's older children remember the phone call to Fumina informing her of Bill's death. Terry recalls that when she heard the news:

> *The emotional impact on Peg was minimal; there was no hint of sadness or sentimentality, indicating perhaps there was no real closeness between the two.*

Peg would not even have attended the funeral if it hadn't been for Jack's insistence. Her natural instinct would have been not to go but Jack really pushed the issue. She was strong, resilient and self-assured, but in important matters she occasionally deferred to the judgment of Jack. He stayed home to look after the brood and Peg went off to Lilydale for the funeral.

Agnes and Carmel were apparently not happy about her attending the funeral. It seemed to them a betrayal of Agnes, whom Bill had treated so poorly when he walked out on her and their children. Peg was the only member of the immediate family who actually attended Bill's funeral. Gwyn was at the Salvation Army Citadel at the time of the funeral but she did not venture inside, and only witnessed the funeral from outside.

Agnes soldiered on. It wasn't an easy life for her. She was on her own and she had other children to raise. Jack and Peg's oldest daughter Anne lived with Agnes and Carmel and attended the Convent of Mercy Lilydale:

> *When I went to live with my grandmother Agnes (1961)*
> *I found life a great contrast to the noisy family life that I was*

used to. Everything was orderly, well kept, and quiet. Food was properly shopped for and prepared. Grandma was a good cook, leaning on her experience rather than experiment with new ideas. I am not sure how she spent her days. She did walk to the nearby shops and knew the shopkeepers. She did not go visiting and had few visitors in return. Family would visit from time to time. I am not sure whether she read novels but she certainly read the newspaper, read a certain number of Catholic periodicals, did the crosswords (cryptics included) and enjoyed a game of scrabble immensely. She taught me how to play. She listened to the ABC news.

I also remember her being very devoted to the Catholic Hour, a long-running 3DB radio series. I also enjoyed this program, which came on late on a Sunday night. Agnes went to church every Sunday, and really any day that she would have been able.

Agnes kept in touch by writing letters. I do not know to whom else she wrote to but she did write regularly to her daughters. She did not have a phone. In Mooroolbark the public phone was on the corner about a hundred metres away. Carmel did the ringing from this phone after 6.00pm for the cheaper rate. I do not remember my grandmother ever going to the phone box, but she may have. If there was any immediate news, Carmel received a call whilst at work.

Agnes was devoted to her daughters and their families and worried and fretted about them – Gwyn bringing up Michael on her own, Mary and her ill health, and Mum and her hard life on the farm. She said that my mother had the most beautiful skin as a young girl and lamented that she was not looking after it. She worried if anyone was ill and rejoiced in the glad tidings. She prayed for us all.

She knew and understood the Church. She was a loyal Catholic. She knew its laws, its history, its practices, I would say better than most. She had a quiet, strong undemonstrative faith in God. She had worked God out, you could say.

Agnes had a past. A child out of wedlock, the death of a baby and a broken marriage. She would have battled to keep up appearances, as we say. We did not talk about these things. As we played scrabble or washed the dishes the conversation was mundane. However, this was who my grandmother was and she did pass on her reflections to me in subtle ways. I clearly remember her telling me the stories of young women saying goodbye to their soldier boyfriends during the war. I am not sure whether she was seeking understanding or simply putting me on the path to keep an open mind on these subjects. Family history, the history of our emotions, our passions and our regrets, are part of us. This is who I see in my grandmother. To the world, a kind, quiet, ordinary woman, devoted mother and grandmother, someone who had seen very little of the world. This was her persona, but in reality she had experienced great drama with probably very little support or affirmation.

In her later years, Agnes spent a lot of time in bed; she didn't enjoy good health. To give Carmel a break, Agnes stayed in Drouin with Mary and her family. Carmel then holidayed in Sydney for a well-deserved break. Agnes got sick and ended *up in Warragul hospital. The plan was to bring her back to Mooroolbark with Gwyn and Michael, as well as Carmel. God decided otherwise. Agnes died in Warragul hospital on 9 June 1964. She is buried in the Brighton cemetery alongside her beloved son John Joseph, who died in infancy.*

Agnes Hughes, Mooroolbark, 1960s.

Peg's childhood and adolescence were no walk in the park, right up to her marriage. It wasn't easy for her. Her parents had managed to stay together for her entire childhood, but there was not a lot of love, laughter and joy in their home. There was endurance and a sense of duty, and perhaps not much more.

As the eldest, quite a bit was expected of Peg. She was responsible for getting her sisters to and from school, and to Mass on Sundays when they lived in Mount Evelyn. She achieved well at school and was offered a scholarship. She had dreams of becoming a teacher but was forced to spend four years working in the family's general store. She wasn't even given the time to join the local tennis club as it was all hands on deck in the family business from Monday to Saturday.

She was then wooed by Jack Rankin, a much older man who was quiet and reserved; she agreed to marry him with her father's reluctant blessing, and her mother's support.

Childhood and adolescence had taught Peg the value of making the most of each situation, giving your best, serving your family, the reality of sacrifice, and the capacity for hard work. All these values stood her in good stead as she embarked on a new life with her husband Jack, in a rugged place called Fumina. Bring it on.

CHAPTER 2

Jack Rankin

JOHN SIMON RANKIN (Jack) was born on 2 February 1912, in the small family home in Fumina. As was quite common at the time, there were no doctors or nurses around to assist with the delivery of baby Jack. Anne, Jack's eldest child, heard the story:

> *The family folklore has it there was no time for Grandma*
> *to get to the hospital and so her husband Herbert stopped his*
> *ploughing and helped deliver young Jack and then returned to*
> *his ploughing without fanfare.*

Jack was the middle child of a family of seven born to Herbert Rankin and Kate Gargan. They moved from Jindivick to try their luck in the newly opened Crown Land of Fumina.

Jack's father, Herbert Rankin, was actually born in Jindivick in 1878. He was the youngest child of Eli Rankin and Louisa Walker, who were both immigrants from England. Eli was from Essex and came to Australia in 1852, and Louisa came to Australia from Buckingham Shire in 1844.

Kate Gargan was born in Barkstead, just north of Ballarat, Victoria, in 1873. She was the fifth of ten surviving children born to Simon Gargan and Annie Gilsenan. Simon was born in County Meath Ireland in 1840; Annie was also born in Ireland, and lived in County Cavan. Both Simon and Annie emigrated to Australia as assisted passengers.

Simon arrived on the *Young America* when he was twenty, arriving in Melbourne in June 1860. He lived and worked there before moving to the Ballarat district. This was the time of the gold rush, and all roads led to Ballarat. Annie came later on the *Marco Polo*, which arrived in August 1863; she too found employment in the hospitality trade in Ballarat. The two met there, married in 1865 and had ten children. Kate was the second eldest. Her older sister, also named Annie, married Harry Regan, and together they managed the Union Hotel in South Melbourne and later bought and managed the Southern Cross Hotel in the same suburb.

Kate Rankin, 1950s.

Anne Kilner, great-granddaughter of Herbert and Kate, has written the family history. She reflects on how Herb and Kate may have met:

A likely scenario is that Herb was a sewing machine mechanic for the Singer Company. He travelled frequently and may well have taken lodgings at the Southern Cross pub, especially if he had to travel to Melbourne when dealing with the company, picking up sewing machines or parts. He would have met Kate as she was working at the hotel.

One story passed down is that Kate had rejected Herb's proposal to marry him because he wasn't a Catholic. The Gargans were strict Roman Catholics while the Rankins were of Church of England or Protestant background. Inter-faith marriages were discouraged and quite uncommon in those days. For Kate and Herb this was an issue, so Herb decided to convert to Catholicism in order to win his bride. As the story goes, one day he turned up at the pub and threw his hat in the door and said, 'You've got me!' So she agreed to marry him. They married in 1902 when he was 25 years old and she was a few years older, at 29. [It was] quite unusual for a woman to be still unmarried at that age in that era. She must have been a very self-sufficient and independent woman. As she was working and living with her sister in the hotel, she would have had no real need to marry, and could afford to be quite selective in choosing a husband. She certainly chose a good man in the end, although it would prove to be a life of hardship. Apparently Herb was not well suited to sales work due to his kind heart – he was known to travel to someone's home to repair a sewing machine and instead of persuading her to buy a new one, he would end up 'feeling sorry for the poor woman' and fix up her old machine instead. This meant he made very little money.

In 1906, Herb took up a land selection of about 80 acres in a small settlement called Fumina at the foot of the Baw

Baw Mountains. It was some thirty miles from Brandy Creek-Jindivick where the family lived. The land was heavily timbered with giant mountain ash, messmate, yellow stringy, silvertop gum, beech, and blackwood, that needed to be felled by hand. Over the next two years he worked hard to clear some of the land and build a slab and bark hut for his family to live.

When selecting his land, Herb would have had to find enough money to pay for a surveyor to survey his selection. Once the application for his block was approved, he would have to start paying the lease on his land within three years. This meant paying not just the lease costs, but also the costs to improve the land. However, as the land would not have been productive by then, given the density of the forest that had to be cleared and the lack of roads or rail to transport the felled timber, the family had no income. The story has been passed down that Kate had to sell her prize possession, her sewing machine, to pay either the surveyor costs or the lease costs. The sewing machine was most likely a wedding gift from Herbert when they married. Kate remained greatly saddened by the loss of her treasured sewing machine.

Meanwhile, by about 1908 Herb had built a little place for his growing family. His second youngest, Millie, claimed:

> *Once he got his little camp built, he built a hut of slab and bark, slab walls, bark for the roof and dirt floor. When he got things organised, he brought my mother and her three*

children, Dorothy, Bert and Nell up to the settlement. The eldest was only four. There was no water. They had to cart water from one little spring. There were no facilities what-soever. There were no power tools in those days and the land had to be cleared. The trees were over 200 feet high and 30 feet round the girth. The only tools they had were a saw, axe, maul and wedges. The only way of getting anything delivered was with the bullock wagon or on a pack horse.

Millie also described the living conditions in those early settlement days:

There was no dole (unemployment benefit) at that time. The Government gave you absolutely nothing. You had to fend for yourself and find your own food and clothes. What you couldn't grow or couldn't buy, you went without. The main diet was tinned meat, potatoes, rabbits, home-made bread, fresh milk if you had a cow, tinned milk if you had the money. Things were very hard. I don't know how they lived, really. The only way, if they had no money, was they could have a month's account and the grocer would allow them that month so they could pay their bill. It was a terrible time for them.

As time went by we got a little four-room cottage made of split palings and put a tin roof on it, then we got a tank and we had water at the house and things were much better. A kind of a road was made but it used to take from 7 o'clock in morning to 11 o'clock at night to go down twelve miles to get supplies from Noojee. The road was shocking. The wheels were right up to the axles in mud and the horses could only go at a walking pace. There was no such thing as cars in those days.

Jack wrote of his childhood:

My memory takes me back to about 1916. In Fumina, the land was covered with soggy mountain ash logs which were difficult to burn, and dead trees stood everywhere. On a windy day, I would sit on our doorstep and watch the tall trees being blown down one by one. Sometimes as many as twenty would fall in a day.

On one occasion, my father was driving his horse and cart along a track when a gale began to blow. Trees started to fall. He jumped from his cart and made for home, dodging falling limbs as he went. When the gale had abated, he went back to see what had happened to the horse and cart. He found them quite safe. Big trees had fallen in front and behind, and the horse couldn't go in either direction.

In those days, everybody in Fumina was poor. Cows lived mainly on scrub as rabbits ate the bit of grass sown among the logs and trees. Bracken fern four or five feet high flourished everywhere.

We lived in a four-roomed house built of palings and slabs which my father had split. He carried them on his back to the building site.

The dwelling was hessian-lined, and had slab floors with cracks through which the cutlery escaped when dropped. There was an open fireplace with a chimney of stones about five feet high. From there it was paling, and as the soot in the flue often caught fire, we had to be careful that the fire was out before we retired for the night. My mother did all the cooking on the open fire. She had a four-gallon iron boiler and a few iron pots. There was no stove. On washing days, she boiled the clothes in kerosene tins, and scrubbed the muddy clothes on the washing board in a tub of water.

The house had an iron roof, and an 800-gallon tank. Almost every summer, the tank would go dry, and washing and bathing had to be done at the spring which was in a gully about twenty chains away. We had to scramble over logs about four feet in diameter to get to the spring. In the drought of 1923, logs were sawn through, and a track cut through to the spring.

The dairy, the cow shed and hen house were built with slab walls and bark roofs. The pig sty was a big hollow stump, and the pig paddock was fenced in by huge logs. To clear a piece of land, the logs had to be sewn through with the crosscut saw, and jacked up into heaps. By 1916, my father had only about three half-acre plots semi-cleared. Many trees still stood and had to be ploughed around. He grew maize and potatoes on these clearings, but there was no hope of earning a living from these blocks. Work had to be found wherever possible, sometimes many miles away.

Although poor, we were never hungry, as there were pota-toes, milk, butter and eggs – if the foxes hadn't taken the hens. They would come in broad daylight as there were so many trees and logs for them to make their escape. When we couldn't afford meat, traps were set to catch rabbits.

The house where Jack was born. He lived there until the 1926 bushfires, when it was burnt to a rubble.

When Jack he was a child, clearing trees for farming purposes made slow progress:

The ringbarked trees were left standing and were so dense that one of the first schoolteachers at Fumina remarked that although he was a good shot, he could not shoot anywhere without hitting one of them. The only trees that were felled were the few around the house sites, for safety. There were logs everywhere – some eight feet in diameter – and we, as children, used to walk from one end of the settlement to the other without putting our feet on the ground. We walked on top of the logs.

Jack's parents, Kate Gargan and Herbert Rankin.

Unlike his older siblings, Jack had the benefit of some semblance of a primary school education. Part of his very early primary education was in the home of James Yates, a kilometre or so away. One teacher alternated between Fumina and Fumina South and when the teacher came to Fumina, school was initially in the Yates home.

The battle for a school in the area had been more or less won by the time Jack was a toddler. After a bit of toing and froing as to the best place for a school, whether that be in Vesper, Icy Creek or Fumina, the Education authorities decided that Icy Creek would be the most suitable place to serve the local community with a primary school. Jack used to walk the nearly three miles to school, which meant walking through scrub and crossing the Icy Creek, all in bare feet. One day Jack decided he wouldn't go to school so he walked some distance with his older siblings, well into the bush, and whilst the other children walked on to school he spent the whole day alone with Mother Nature. He would have been only eight or nine years old. After school he joined the throng on the return journey home and continued on as if nothing had happened.

Jack's oldest son, Terry, would have heard the story of the 1926 fires often enough from his father. This is how he remembered the story being told:

> I think the biggest day in Jack's life was the day of the 1926 bush fire.
>
> Jack and Jim Kealy rose early in the morning and walked to the Icy Creek to catch fish. They landed a sugar bag full of freshwater crays. It was hot and there was smoke everywhere

and they were aware of possible danger. They returned to the Rankin's slab hut, where Herb and Kate were in earnest discussion.

Herb: 'No fire's ever jumped the creek before!' He drew heavily on his pipe. Kate: 'I don't trust it. I'm taking the kids up to Bert Mitchell's clearing. No trees there to catch fire.' She looked around and gathered her brood. Herb: 'I'll stay with Jack and Jim, and if she [the fire] comes through, we'll save the house.'

Come through? You bet it did. The trees were two hundred feet high. The eucalypt-fuelled cloud was exploding another two hundred feet above the trees. The roar became more and more deafening by the minute. Jack's only inclination was to run. He did not believe his father, who barked, 'Our only chance is to stay put.'

'Like hell it is,' thought Jack. 'Do I obey my father or die? This is crazy, we can't just do nothing. We'll die and nobody will know what happened. The old bugger is mad.'

Jack took a deep breath and stayed. Be damned.

'Bugger the house, just look after ourselves!' yelled Herb.

Three frightened men held hands and recited the Lord's Prayer. The roar of the fire and wind tore their words away into the raging hell.

'Amen.' They threw themselves into the vegetable garden, face down, and gave themselves up to the mercy of the Lord.

How long did it last? Two minutes, thirty minutes or, as it seemed, a lifetime. When the roar subsided they stood up to inspect the damage.

The mighty eucalypts were black silhouettes in the haze.

The house was a smoking rubble.

The cabbages in the vegetable garden had exploded like firecrackers.

A huge tree had fallen just feet from where they had been lying in the garden. The noise had been so intense they did not hear it land, or feel the vibration.

All the animals were dead.

Hell!

Gradually the locals started to congregate in Bosse's cow shed area. There was concern for the McHughs. Dom, Mary and the four boys, Dom, Paddy, Jack and Frank. The boys were all young, probably under ten. They were not to be found at their house or Bert Mitchell's.

Fred Mitchell, a neighbour, staggered, dazed and somewhat lost with his trousers in his hands, into the group. His nakedness was never explained.

The McHughs turned up alive covered in soot, sweat and tears. I think they either found refuge in the Icy Creek or they used tank water and some old lino for protection. Old floor coverings come to mind. They may have evacuated to the farm dam. Everybody thanked the Lord the youngsters had survived.

If the story has a moral, it would be listen to your father, he knows best. A young man's instinct which told fourteen-year-old Jack to run would have resulted in certain death. There was no haven to run to. Herb's call was the right one. Jack's desire to run was folly, but natural.

In Jack's childhood, the most influential person outside his immediate family was undoubtedly his Catechism teacher, Larry Power. Every weekend this faith-filled man would trudge through the bush, with little or no tracks, to teach the rudiments of the faith to youngsters at Hill End, Fumina South and Fumina. It wasn't just what he said, but the witness of his lifestyle, which impressed Jack:

> *Larry Power was my Sunday school teacher soon after the First World War. He was Irish-born, and a man known for his piety and self-denial. He taught Catechism to all the Catholic children in the district in the pioneering days at Fumina. The roads were so bad in those days that the priest, Fr Shanahan of Trafalgar, would only come to Fumina South to say Mass once a year. Thus the saintly Larry Power certainly kept the faith alive in this isolated area in those days.*

From the following poem we glean the austerity of the man, and his shunning of the world and what it had to offer. Larry Power's true home was in heaven and he wanted his charges to keep heaven front and centre and not be swayed by putting too much emphasis on this passing world. The lure of the world, the flesh and the devil features in the poem, and one is challenged to hold steadfast with the heart fixed on the kingdom of God.

Jack wrote about his early and significant mentor in the following words:

LARRY POWER

On Larry Power muse awhile
Was he a sage or ass?
The man who practised self-denial
And died attending Mass.
He always carried Rosary beads
His medals and his cross.
His was a life of goodly deeds
Which many would endorse.
The coarsest clothes he always wore
He loathed the filthy pelf.
Whate'er he earned he gave the poor
And scrimped upon himself.
He lived upon the meanest fare
Most rancid food he'd eat
And thanked his God with many a prayer
For giving such a treat.
His motto was "In every deed
Our flesh we must control,
For pampered flesh will always lead
To death traps for the soul"
He'd navvy, slosh, or toss the shears
From sunrise till it set:
From Monday morn till Sunday eve
He'd labour, pray and sweat.
He'd walk for miles on Sabbath's Day

To teach and catechise
The children so they would not stray
From God – and Paradise.
He'd trudge o'er tracks of mud and slush,
In rain and snow and rime
Through soggy overhanging brush
Up hills so steep to climb.
For children he especially loved
In them, he saw no guile,
And constantly his soul was moved
To greet all with a smile.
Now you who have scholastic brains
Who've excelled at the schools,
But have not curbed your flesh with reins
Are you the wise, or fools?
And you the most astute tycoon
Who've amassed a pile of pelf,
Are you the wise, or just the goons
In gratifying self?
Now in this life of joys and stings
With many an up and down
Did Larry choose the cream of things
In choosing next life's crown?

Jack, it seemed, was always quite devout as a youngster. He liked praying, enjoyed solitude, read the scriptures, was interested in history, mulled over things; he had a compassionate streak. His father Herb was originally an Anglican and well versed in the scriptures, before he became Catholic to marry Kate Gargan. Catholics at that time were not known for their knowledge and love of the scriptures. They seemed more interested in sacraments and tradition. Herb gave the young Jack a love for the Word of God. When he was in his mid-teens, Jack expressed a desire to become a priest. His family did all they could to support him in his vocation. It was decided that he would attend St Kevin's College in Toorak, to qualify him for entering a seminary to train for the priesthood. Aunt Annie Regan, his mother's sister, paid for his school fees. Annie and her husband were in the hotel industry and ran a successful business. Jack lived with them in a hotel in South Melbourne and commuted by tram to St Kevin's.

There is no doubt he'd had a deficient and interrupted education in Fumina, with little or no secondary education till this point; and now he found himself attending a reputable college in Melbourne with middle class lads. Although he was a bit older than his peers, to his credit Jack successfully completed his Intermediate examinations. He passed external exams in French, Latin and History. This was quite a feat really, considering his earlier limited educational opportunities. On the strength of his Intermediate results he was admitted into the Leaving Certificate program. Successful completion of the Leaving Certificate at that time was a prerequisite for entrance into the seminary.

It was in this second year at St Kevin's that Jack lost interest in becoming a priest. It was never clear what transpired that year to change the direction of his life, but he no longer had the passion for a priestly calling. It seems that he possibly could have passed his Leaving Certificate, but with his heart no longer in the priesthood he left St Kevin's before the final exams. Jack thought his time at St Kevin's was a failure, but his children thought it was an amazing feat for him to actually pass several Intermediate external examinations with his limited educational background. One of his undoubted gifts as a student was his ability to memorise and store information. It would have held him in good stead when it came to examinations.

Between school and meeting Peg more than ten years later, Jack tried his hand in a variety of jobs. He would have come home to the farm at Fumina to work for a while and to reassess his options. Henry Thoreau once said that 'an unreflective life is one not worth living'. At some point, Jack left the farm and became what was known as a bush carpenter. He was working with a company that were making secure storage huts to stand alongside tents. He didn't last very long with this firm.

Jack told the story against himself on a few occasions. His boss apparently said to him:

> *I have seen some rough bastards (sic) in my time here, but you would undoubtedly be the roughest. Your work is just too shoddy. You had better try something else.*

Those who have seen Jack's carpentry skills over the years would not be surprised at that comment. Jack spent some time working as a Surveyor's Assistant in and around the Healesville area. He was working as what was known in the industry as a 'chainman', which was someone who held and positioned a chain while the surveyor was taking measurements.

At the beginning of the Second World War, Jack volunteered to join the Army but did not meet the physical requirements. When he was twelve years old he had suffered a nasty incident in which a falling tree broke his leg. It took days for him to get to the hospital and the leg never healed properly. Five years afterwards the leg still oozed fluid and Jack was deemed unsuitable for military service. After the bombing of Darwin, the sighting of Japanese submarines in Sydney Harbour and the dominance of the Japanese in South-East Asia and the Pacific, Army selection by necessity became less rigid. The Australian Government enlisted further personnel into their armed forces to meet this new threat. Since Jack's work as a surveyor was not considered an essential service, he was enlisted for military duty. He performed a few different tasks at this time, which included working at a Detention Centre in Maribyrnong, Melbourne (Germans, Italians and others were interred around the country). Towards the end of his time in the war he attained the rank of Sergeant.

Dennis, Jack's eighth child, slightly bemused, wrote:

> *Surprisingly enough, he reached the rank of sergeant and he was in charge of hygiene. This is quite funny as cleanliness was not his forte.*

Jack and Peg might not have met at all if it wasn't for a drinking mate. Jack wasn't a really big drinker but he enjoyed a quiet ale with friends and colleagues. When he was working as a surveyor, he had a few drinks with workmates in Bethany near Healesville, perhaps more than he usually would have. They were staying in a hotel, and when Jack came back to his room and lay down with a cigarette in hand, he may have dozed off; the cigarette set his mattress on fire. Luckily, one of his drinking buddies came to call on him to continue with the drinking session and when he came into the room found Jack's bed on fire. If he hadn't come to find Jack, there is every chance he would have been burnt to death. A salient lesson was learnt, as Jack never smoked in his bedroom again.

Jack met Peg in 1942. The Rankin family and the Hughes family met on the walk to and from Sunday Mass, as their houses were not far apart. Jack's mother occasionally came into the shop to buy groceries and Herbert encouraged his son to pursue Peg. Jack presented a fine figure in army uniform, short, tanned and fit. He owned a clear title to a small farm and a modest home, with his sparkling blue eyes and great posture, Peg was hooked. After a short romance, the couple married and forged a life together in Fumina.

There is a saying that opposites attract, and this was certainly the case for Jack and Peg. When they married on 12 February 1944, Jack was thirty-two and Peg was eighteen. Jack was the introvert, Peg the extrovert. Jack was the thinker, Peg the doer. Jack was the procrastinator, Peg the initiator. Jack was the pessimist, Peg the optimist. Together, however, they made a formidable couple. They played to each other's strengths, gave space to each other, and didn't press each other's buttons too often. They didn't try to change one other.

Their eldest child, Anne, reflected on their relationship:

Mum was a remarkable, lively, sociable, capable, energetic, generous and beautiful woman, who at eighteen married my father who was introverted, lacked social graces, scorned an extravagant lifestyle, a dreamer with a deeply philosophical and religious approach to living. He was thirty-two. I never doubted that Dad deeply loved my mother. Not that he ever showed it in any outward sense. He grew to rely on her in many ways and instinctively trusted her. To the outside world, it was our mother who made all the decisions, who ruled the household, ran the farm, organised the children, but their children knew without quite realising it that their mother did not do anything without our father's approval. Not that she sat around waiting for his approval or even that he demanded approval; it went beyond approval to the complexities of love and respect. Our father loved and admired our mother. He was quietly proud of her prowess and her beauty. He loved her vitality and exuberance, so different from his own introverted ways. She also brought the world to him. People loved talking to our mother and she was able to share all her musings (mostly uninterrupted) with our father. Whatever they were as individuals, together they were remarkable. Full of faith and strength of character, they carved this life together. What is the essence of this life? We do our best. I was privileged to

hear my father's last words on this earth and they were simply
'I love you', spoken to my mother – words she rarely heard.

Much of the complexities of their relationship as we see it
can be summed up in my brother Terry's Foreword to Dad's
Anthology of Poetry written in 1994.

Terry reminisced about his father:

He was a colourful and shy character, but was held in high
regard by almost all that knew him for his gentleness, wisdom
and enduring sense of humour. It was Peg who supported him in
his desire to pen poetry, although it could be argued there were
more pressing and immediate chores to attend to on the farm.

Anne mused:

My first memories of my father were when he built us a
playground, a slide, a swing, and best of all a rocking horse
which I think I would have claimed as my own. I was about
four years old. This rocking horse would have been made
from a branch of a dead tree and with a bit of imagination
somehow the top of it resembled a horse's head. I remember
being extremely pleased with this and my father would have
been amply rewarded by my enthusiasm. All his trade work
was very shoddy; the sheds that he built, the fences and gates,
all left a lot to be desired. They were not the neat and careful
sight that some of the handy work of neighbouring farmers

were. So looking back, this rocking horse would have been a bit rough and ready, but the chosen bit of wood was just perfect. I loved it. It must have worn well as after I had outgrown it the rocking horse was still being used by my siblings.

Older children remember the bushwalks, the stories, the laughter, the silliness, and Jack making things. He could memorise portions of the work of great poets, and he loved to quote Shakespeare, Chaucer and Keats. He had a workable knowledge of the scriptures, and had an ingrained belief that the end of the world was fast approaching. He wrote poems for his children and they would learn them and recite them at school. When there were social functions at Icy Creek and Fumina, Jack was invariably called upon to recite some poetry.

Jack getting ready to recite poetry at Icy Creek Hall in 1971.

He was well renowned in the district for his recitation of poetry. He was in his element in this setting and really entertained the throng. He would recite poems which had a connection with people's lives. Some of his favourite recitations included material from John O'Brien's *Around the Boree Log*, and his own compositions. He never had a script in front of him. He had a real gift for memorising poems and texts and making them come to life.

Then, in 1964, Jack developed a stomach ulcer. Peg recalled the time:

> Surgeons used to cut away most of the stomach. When I saw him for the first time after he came out of surgery he looked like a scared rabbit. The operation certainly changed his personality. He wouldn't have gone out and murdered anybody. I was never scared that he would be violent with me, nothing like that, but it affected his personality. After the operation he became touchy, you couldn't criticise him in the slightest way. He wasn't like that before. I had a new husband. Life took some adjustment; it was much easier to simply accept Dad's situation than challenging him in any way.

Bernard was ten at the time of the operation, and this is how he remembered it:

> In those days, an ulcer operation was major surgery. Dad took months to recover from the operation; it seemed to me

he sat huddled over the kitchen stove for months, and did not go out of the house. Looking back, he was probably severely depressed, a common by-product of an operation like that.

This of course meant Peg took on the entire workload of the farm. She was amazing like that; she had these inner reserves of strength that enabled her to step up. Talking to her about this in later life as an adult, her explanation was someone had to do it; there were no real alternatives, it was up to her. She never seemed to complain, although she must have felt like telling Jack to get over it. She is one of the most resilient people I have met in my life.

It is probably an amusing footnote, but Jack was even too sick to smoke after the surgery. Peg saw that as a great opportunity to get him off the cigarettes and weaned him down to one packet of tobacco a week (from the previous four). As he got better, Jack decided it was time for the rationing to cease. From memory, he rang the grocer himself to get extra packets included in the week's food supplies. Peg was ropeable; it was one of the very few times I heard them argue. She stormed off, and didn't return for hours. Jack stood out the back of the house with a forlorn look on his face; he was probably worried she wasn't coming back.

Jack was only fifty-two, but his world came crashing down around him. He became more withdrawn, more introspective, less engaging. He was depressed and moody. He could no longer handle any criticism. Peter recalled this time:

He would often boast that he didn't break anything, ie crockery etc. He wasn't amused when I told him that was because he did nothing. In the evening after arriving home from school he would never ask, 'How was your day?' The only interaction seemed to be the demand of 'hush' when the 7.00pm ABC news came on. If you persisted in talking you would receive a painful knuckle on top of the head. We were all chastised if we left a light on, or if I hadn't cut enough wood for both the stove and open fire for the next day. It wasn't much fun at that time with Dad.

Mary was one of the younger children but also a strong extrovert, and she had a different relationship with Jack. Occasionally she was able to draw him out of himself. In these years, Jack became less inclined to work on the farm as it seemed more drudgery than anything else. The last ten years in Fumina were certainly not Jack's best years.

Jack at work on the farm, 1960s.

Most of his children witnessed the following at some stage. Fridays were the main delivery day for groceries. Peg would put her order in each Friday morning. Always included in the order were four packets of Havelock Fine Cut tobacco (in later years it was boosted to five). That was Jack's weekly quota and it had to last the week. Too bad if he ran out of tobacco before the week was up, as the groceries didn't arrive till after lunch each Friday. Later in his life he would boast that he had smoked three-quarters of a ton of tobacco – he gave up smoking four years before his death.

Some Friday mornings, the Rankin kitchen was not a pretty place if Jack had exhausted all of his tobacco supplies. Paul remembered the scene well:

He would be sitting on a chair hunched over with arms outstretched and fingers pointing towards the floor, literally groaning. This was his classic withdrawal symptoms pose. I was only 13 years old at the time, and more than once he asked, 'Have you got a smoke for your little old father?' I usually had a few cigarettes stashed away. After Mass each Sunday at Noojee, whilst Peg was chatting away, I would run up to the milk bar and get my cigarette supplies for the week and run back and Mum would still be talking about life, the world, the universe and the price of cattle at the market. I often had a few smokes left by the end of the week and Dad would put the pressure on to hand any smokes over if he had run out of his tobacco. When Dad was in this predicament,

and observing him in such a sorry state, I would reluctantly
hand over any cigarettes I may have had to my poor suffering
father.

It was a blessing for the younger siblings when Peg and Jack sold the farm and moved into Warragul at the beginning of 1976. Jack certainly lightened up, and he became his old self again. He became more fun, more engaging, and relationships with his younger children were rekindled. His connections with the older children didn't need much strengthening because their earlier memories were more positive. With a modest house entirely owned, money in the bank, Peg working, and only two children to support, understandably the financial pressure was no longer such a burden.

In 1976, Kathleen attended boarding school at St Martin's in the Pines at Ballarat, and Paul began Year 9 at Marist Sion College in Warragul. Whilst Peg was working at the hospital, Jack found things to do. In these years, he walked a lot, pondered a lot, read a lot, wrote poetry, pottered around in his vegetable garden, and visited people he knew. He also became more involved in the church. Fairly soon after Peg and Jack moved into Warragul, St Joseph's Church was rebuilt and Jack spent many hours cleaning bricks from the partially demolished building to be used in the construction of the refurbished church. It was here that he renewed acquaintances with the likes of Laurence Murphy, a retired farmer from the Neerim area.

He also became involved in the Legion of Mary. The Legion

of Mary is an association of Catholics who serve the Church on a voluntary basis by performing some active work each week, such as visiting homes in the parish, visiting hospitals, nursing homes and prisons, and providing instruction in the faith (catechesis) to both children and adults. The focus was generally on people who were remote from the Church's influence. All work was carried out with the approval of the parish priest. The members came together once a week to pray, and to report on the work they had done during the previous week. The weekly meeting was of utmost importance in the Legionary program, providing formation for its members. This was done primarily by the reading of the Legion Handbook and a short talk, or Allocutio, given by the Spiritual Director (usually a priest). Members strived to grow in holiness. Legionaries placed themselves at the service of Mary and wished to help her in her mission as Mother of the Church.

The Legion of Mary has as a high ideal: the sanctification of its members. Through the carrying out of works of mercy and attendance at the weekly meeting, members strive to grow in holiness. The Founder, Irishman Frank Duff, was just 26 years old when he wrote a booklet called *Can We Be Saints?* He also wrote most of the *Legion of Mary Handbook*, which is one of the great spiritual classics of the 20th century.

When a person became a Legionary, in practical terms it meant attending a weekly meeting and visiting Catholic folk street by street. As in the gospel, these Christian foot soldiers visited homes in pairs. George Avon, a retired policeman, was Jack's main apostolic partner for visiting homes. Visits were a way of connecting people to their church and encouraging them to be part of it. Since the visits were usually in the daytime, often enough no-one was home. Dad took his Legion work seriously and was a most reliable and conscientious member of this valuable arm in the Church's mission.

In those early Warragul years Peg was working most days, and the close friendship with Mary and Paul Lindau and bonding with their children, Shane, Monica and Therese, provided a really valuable social network for Jack. When Monica was just a toddler she used to call Jack 'Ranks' (abbreviation of Mr Rankin). Therese followed suit and the name stuck. Monica and Therese have fond memories of Ranks singing the words 'dancing with the dolly with the hole in her stocking and the knees kept a knocking'.

The Horan and Rankin families were always close. Jack had taught Mary Horan Catechism back in the late 1950s and early 1960s. Mary and Paul lived in three different houses in Warragul North over that time, all within easy walking distance to Jack and Peg's house. Jack used to look after their vegetable garden when they lived in O'Dowd's Road.

For most of the time, the Lindau family lived in Princes Street, just a couple of houses away. Jack would pop over nearly every day for a short visit and usually a cuppa. He would tap on the window with his forefinger and alert Mary he was there. When Jack died in 1994, Mary could still see the fingerprint marks on her kitchen window from when he would announce his arrival. She never wiped them off.

Monica Shane and Therese Lindau, early 1980s.

There is an old saying that we are what we eat. We are also what we read. Jack went through a religious transformation in 1977-1978. For some time now, his relatives had tried to convince him that the Catholic Church had taken the wrong path in renewal. Jack initially brushed it off as nonsense. His father came from the Anglican tradition in which the liturgy was celebrated in the local language, and he couldn't really fathom the reason for continuing the liturgy in Latin. Jack would often say his own father would have rejoiced in the revised liturgy that was prayed in the vernacular, with the priest facing the people.

If you get badgered long enough, your attitudes can change. For some time Jack had been receiving literature by mail from his sister Millie, who was living in Bribie Island at the time. The literature was critical of the reforms in the Catholic Church instigated by the Second Vatican Council (1962-65). Previous Church Councils had a much more condemnatory tone but Vatican II ushered in a more conciliatory approach with the world. Rather than condemnation, the new *modus operandi* was dialogue with the world. Significant changes followed. The Mass was now celebrated in English, new ministries opened up to lay men and women, the Word of God received more attention, and the Catholic Church now recognised that truth existed outside its own walls.

The material Jack was receiving from his relatives opposed this new thought and practice within the Church, and he was beginning to think the Church had taken a backward step in accommodating the world and some of its movements. In a series of letters written to his son Peter, who had recently joined the Salesians of Don Bosco (one of the largest religious orders in the Catholic Church) there was a gradual shift in Jack's religious thinking. In May 1978 he wrote:

> *I went to the Tridentine Mass in Hardware Street in the city on Thursday and went to Nell's (his sister Nell Maloney) at Middle Park and returned home by train on Friday. I wonder should the Church had changed to the modern Mass. I have my doubts when I consider the fall away of attendance and less dedication to it. I think you have joined a good Order where you will do much good so 'pray and obey' and you'll get there.*

At this point, Jack was 'wondering' and 'doubting'. By mid-July he was firmer in his position that the Church had taken a seriously misguided step in its decision to reform itself. In a letter dated 13 July 1978 he wrote:

> *There are three things wrong with the Church today, firstly our compromising attitude towards Communism, secondly our Church's surrender to Modernism and thirdly the way the Protestant doctrines have been allowed to infiltrate our Church. These things have been vehemently condemned by former Popes and I believe the former Popes were right so I am going to 'hold to my traditions' as St Paul writes to Timothy.*

By September 1978, Jack was convinced that the Church had erred in taking a new path towards renewal. He felt the Church would have been better off without the Vatican Council, and with things left as they were. In other words, if 'it ain't broke, why fix it'. He saw no positive signs since the Council, but only fewer people in the pews each Sunday, a plurality which never led towards unity, dissent from Church teaching in morality, and a compromising attitude to the world which was contrary to the Christian gospel.

Again in a letter to Peter, dated 9 September, he wrote:

> *It was through the help of six high ranking Protestants that the Novus Ordre (Vatican II) was introduced. Pius V in 1570 commanded unequivocally that the Latin Mass was to*

be said for all time and that Cardinals Bishops or any lower ranked clergy would incur the wrath of God and of Sts. Peter and Paul if they altered it.

For Jack, who accepted the teaching of Papal Infallibility – which was endorsed at the First Vatican Council (1870-1871) – this meant what it said. If the Pope spoke in the area of faith and morals, he spoke definitively, and what Popes said mattered for all time. This would have been drilled into Jack in his childhood Catechism classes with Larry Power in the 1920s. So when Pope Pius V in 1570 promulgated that the current Mass was to be celebrated for all time, and with no deviation under the pain of mortal sin, that was deemed an infallible proclamation. Jack never quite understood that every papal statement is a situated utterance: it has a context, it has a history, and it is limited. He just couldn't fathom that any truth or anything of real value could originate from our Protestant brothers and sisters. It must be said, though, that he stayed with the Church and nearly always attended a mainstream Catholic Mass; but deep down, and if push came to shove, he wished the Church had never ushered in the second Vatican Council.

Dennis (child number eight) and Jo married in 1982. They always lived in Warragul and had three children, Sarah, Luke and Katie. Jack saw a lot of Jo and the three children, and they brought a lot of joy to him. Jo reflects:

Jack always had a great relationship with our children, Sarah, Luke and Katie.

Sarah never liked to go near Jack in her first year, and Jack never pushed the issue. That was until her first birthday. Jack would sit in the lounge chair in our house and watch her from afar. On this day, she decided to walk over to Jack, and just back herself up to him where he picked her up and put her on his knee. No words were spoken, but the bond had been created and never ended. He used to sing to Sarah constantly. Luke used to love getting down in Grandad's garden with him, or creating 'masterpieces' with lumps of wood and nails that Grandad would help with, or he would go to the school oval and play cricket in the nets with him. Katie was really funny with him; she used to want to get his 'medicine' for him at 9.00 am in the morning, only to be told by Nana that it was too early. His medicine was a stubby of beer which he used to tell her was his medicine. When she went to pre-school, she never wanted to go home after it until she had been to 'Drandad's' (sic) for tomato soup. So poor Peg had to have a ready supply of tomato soup for them both. His garden was a real lever for us, as Katie wouldn't eat anything unless it was grown in Drandad's garden. Well, he grew everything in our house, even sausages and pasta!

The three of them always knew where Jack hid his lollies, heading straight to his bed side table where they would find Violet Crumbles or Minties. He would say to them, 'Don't tell Nana you found them, it's our secret.' Little did they know it was Nana who bought them and put them there! Who could forget the hand whistle every Sunday morning at 8.00 am when he walked up our driveway on his way to Mass to see if the kids were up ready to go. They spent every Sunday morning breakfast practising their hand whistle so they could show Grandad when he arrived.

Sarah, Luke and Katie Rankin, 1996.

The Warragul years were good for Jack. He regained some zest and enjoyed his family visiting. He had enough interests to occupy him and maintained pretty good health until 1990. He continued to write poetry, and towards the end his thoughts lingered on the next life, judgement, death, damnation and salvation. One of the last poems he composed was simply entitled *Rocks*. He saw his whole life, both temporal and eternal, through the image of rocks.

ROCKS

I was born on the rocks, I have lived on the rocks,
I have toiled on the rocks all day.
I have broken the rocks, I have buried the rocks,
I have carted the rocks away.
I have been on the rocks, the financial rocks,
These rocks that rock men into ruin.
And these rocks of despair, they have lurked everywhere
On the pathways I've trod thickly strewn.
And when I shall die 'neath the rock I shall lie
For a rock shall be placed o'er my head,
With my name on that rock, which will tell all the flock,
That another old crony is dead.
I shall sleep 'neath that rock
Till the echoing shock, of that final great trumpet shall call.
And from under that rock I'll be called to the dock
To give an account of my all.
And I pray that my God, calling me from the sod,
May my fears and offences dispel,
And I'm spared from the shocks of the damnable rocks,
Jagged rocks in the chasms of hell.

Photo depicts the problem of rocks on the Rankin farm.

Jack digging up rocks on the Fumina property.

Jack's health began to deteriorate in 1990. Mary tells the story:

It was early evening in the winter of 1990 when sitting at home Dad's surgeon called me to say, 'Your father has prostate cancer.' He told me Dad's prostatic specific antigen was twenty-five. Though a nurse, I knew little about prostate conditions. I didn't know how high above normal this was but he assumed I did. The phone call was all a bit of a blur with comments about hormone therapy and bone scans. I was too shocked to ask the questions – Why are you telling me? Why aren't you telling Dad and Mum? What does this mean? I got off the phone with a sinking feeling in my stomach. How do you tell your parents one of them has cancer?

The following evening I sat my way through dinner with Dad and Mum trying numerous times to pluck up the courage to tell them Dad had cancer. I couldn't do it; the words just would not come out. So it wasn't until a few hours later when Mum and I were making my bed that I blurted out to Mum, 'The surgeon called last night and said Dad has cancer.' She stopped making her side of the bed and looked at me quite shocked as she took it all in. Mum was amazing, though understandably upset she was also calm and grounded. I couldn't tell her much as I didn't know enough to tell about how long, what the options were, what to expect. After a time, we went together to tell Dad – he was sitting at the end of the table and she put her arms around his shoulder as she sometimes did when there was something important to say, and just told him. Truth be told, he picked up significantly for a couple of years. As a sign of his improvement was his ability to take long walks around the town. Only nine months before his death Jack was successfully completing a nine kilometre walk around the town a few times a week.

Dad's health started to decline some three and a half years later – not long after the Back to Fumina centenary celebrations in late 1993. It was a gathering to celebrate 100 years since the settling of the Fumina area (the whole district initially was called the Parish of Fumina and later the names of Icy Creek, Vesper and Fumina came into vogue). Dad was really excited about it and talked about it for many months leading up to the event, encouraging us all to attend.

Once the celebrations were over, Dad slowly started to deteriorate. Mum and I had made a decision that whatever happened and whenever the time came we would look after Dad at home. Dad hated hospitals and I'm not sure why. Maybe it was his experience when, as a twelve year old he suffered a compound fracture of his leg (bones visible externally) and then had to travel in a horse and dray to hospital. The journey took two days in terrible wet muddy weather conditions on unmade roads. The dray was mud up to the wheels so by the time Dad got to hospital he was a sorry mess. The complications associated with the fracture and delays in getting to hospital meant Dad had to stay in hospital for six months. Dad's second hospital experience was when he had surgery for a stomach ulcer. This was a life changing and negative experience in terms of Dad's spirit.

So with the decision made to care for Dad at home, Mum looked after Dad lovingly over the next six months – as she had always done. Though Dad wasn't eating much, she went to great lengths to cook him things he liked. She showed incredible kindness and patience. I travelled home most weekends to support her and in the last couple of months during the week as well. My brother Tim would often accompany me, to offer support, encouragement and humour and keep me awake on the journey.

During that six-month period Mum rarely left the house and when she did it was only to stock up on medicine supplies and food. Late in Dad's illness she was encouraged by a family friend to go to the footy. She was reluctant to leave Dad and I must say I prayed that nothing would happen to Dad while she was gone.

That same day my brother Herbie called and asked could he bring anything. I said, 'Yes a bottle of wine.' He laughed as it was only 11.00 am. I remember that evening having the extra glass – maybe on purpose – as thankfully I stayed the night.

I woke at 2.30 am to hear Dad in severe respiratory distress and Mum somewhat anguished and calling out my name. 'Mary, Mary come quickly!' I was already awake, but couldn't move. I was frozen, not wanting to get up and face whatever I was about to face. Dad was having trouble breathing and finding it difficult to cough. He was really very distressed. I was trying to help him breathe, to percuss his chest and give him the strength to cough. I sent Mum outside to get some bricks to raise the foot of the bed to help drain his chest. We talked about calling the ambulance, but through shortness of breath Dad was adamant that he wasn't going to hospital. It was all a bit scary, but as usual with the strength of my mother we got through the night. By morning Dad was calm and his breathing was more settled.

The following morning Dad told Mum and I that he had had enough; that it was time to go, that he didn't want any treatment and he wanted to be fed only if and when he asked for it. It was a rational decision made by Dad and one Mum and I both respected, as would all the family.

We called the GP to get advice on palliative care and pain relief. When the GP came he tried to talk Dad into going to hospital. Dad said a firm no – he wasn't going back there!

The GP took Mum and I aside as he was concerned about the enormity of the task of us nursing Dad at home. It wasn't a very common practice in the early 1990s to do this. We assured the GP that we would be okay and that we would call if we needed anything. My mother as stoic as ever, told the GP, 'We promised Jack we wouldn't put him into hospital if we could help it.' The GP reluctantly organised home District Nursing services and we couldn't believe it when an old family friend turned up as the district nurse – Heather Colbert. How fabulous was that! She was like an extended member of our family from our younger days in Fumina.

Mum and I then rang everyone to tell them of Dad's wishes. Of course the questions about: How long has he got? Should we come now? Questions that we had no answer for. Everyone was encouraged to pay a visit while Dad was conscious, and eerily cheerful about his decision – telling people, 'I have told the women folk to stop force feeding me.' Over the next few days all the family filed in to see Dad; there were moments alone, laughter, blessings for new babies, tears and words of wisdom and comfort for each one of us. There were little children running in and out of the bedroom laughing; it was in many ways a very joyful family experience!

While Dad's voice had been weak, on the Tuesday night with all the family gathered around, we prayed the Rosary. Dad's voice was strong and melodic as though he had a second strength, his eyes shone brightly, he beamed, he radiated love and something beyond our understanding, a presence that seemed ethereal, it was amazing and incredibly beautiful.

The following day Dad lapsed into unconsciousness, though just before he did he had a visit from an old family friend, Mary Horan. We were teasing Dad saying that his girlfriend was here – Mary is a much loved friend of the family – we were all laughing and joking. Dad all of a sudden pointed at Mum and said, 'I love her!' Mum wept as Dad wasn't a great one for expressing love for her. He soon lost consciousness. Dad only awoke for a brief moment one more time. He gave us a kiss, trying to say something, and then slowly slipped into permanent unconsciousness.

Later that afternoon, I was sitting beside Dad in his little single bed while Mum took a nap in the marital bed. I couldn't bear it when I looked over at Mum and saw the rise and fall of her little body wracked with grief, noiselessly sobbing. That kind of broke me, this strong resilient little woman who had held it all together for so long, silently breaking.

The night before Dad died was absolutely freezing. It was as I say a beautiful experience. We all spent the night with Dad; Mum, siblings, in-laws, nephews, nieces aunty and friends all gathered around talking, reminiscing, laughing and just being plain old sad wondering how long Dad would hang on. It often happens that when people die those closest to them are not in the room. Mum had slipped out of the room when Dad took his last breath at 7.00 am on 1 July 1994 ... we all kissed and cuddled and said our individual goodbyes to our Dad.

Mum's bravery needs to be noted. She called those family members who couldn't be there, the GP and local priest. As a family we washed our Dad, each washing and drying a little part of him. It was if I may say a very moving and lovely way to farewell our Dad. When the remaining family members arrived at the family home there was a long procession to the bedroom. We were in no rush for Dad to be taken away. Siblings, nieces and nephews, in-laws, friends all came to pay their respects to Dad. We had prayers led by Peter (the priest in the family). The older boys later sat on the double bed reminiscing, drinking beer, telling Jack it was his turn to shout. Cracker, one of our nephews, coming into the kitchen said, 'You should see all the uncles, they're all drinking beer with Grandad with tears running down their faces onto their sandwiches – it looks really funny!' All the little kids running in and out of the bedroom laughing, being their usual selves, looking at grandad and talking to him and it all seemed so normal!

A credit to both our parents really. It's amazing that we can go through such an experience and all family members (some fifty of them!) did their little bit. While this story was written from my experience, every family member had his/her own journey. There was so much love and generosity from every family member. From our beautiful brother Peter who conducted our Dad's funeral, our nephew Doug buying a heater for Dad's room, to Anne and Herbie and Jackie stocking up the fridge, Dennis and Jo always there for anything, Bernard physically helping where he could. Paul and Brigette and their little girls who gave us much humour ... And Gerardine and Kath with new little babes and children made it a few days before Dad died; and those that couldn't be there right at the end, they were there with us in spirit. There was not one argument or disagreement over how things should be done or who needed what or who should be doing what or how. There was only unconditional love and care shown by all. That is the great parenting we received from both Peg and Jack to make it all happen! Jack had said towards the end of his life that one of his many blessings was that all his children loved one another. It was most evident at the time of his death.

So our wonderful mother fulfilled her commitment to her darling husband that she would look after him until the end and she did so with all the love, bravery, care and patience a woman could possibly muster. Her husband Jack had been part of her life since she was 16 years old. Jack died a beautiful death surrounded by Mum, our family and close friends. Not once in that six months of caring for Dad did she ever complain or mention that she couldn't do it, or seek sympathy. She was stoic to the end. That was always our mother. Wow, what a woman!

A photo of Jack taken towards the end of his life, 1994.

CHAPTER 3

Fumina – The Early Beginnings

THOMAS HOBBES COINED the saying that life is 'solitary, poor, nasty brutish and short'. The pioneers who ventured into the wilds of the recently opened-up Crown Land in Fumina Parish certainly found life solitary, poor, nasty and brutish, to say the least. Fumina comes from the Aboriginal word *eumenia* meaning repose, but was far from it. It was more likely to be heartache and misery.

Before the turn of the 20th Century a number of pioneers had settled on the flats around what was later named Pennyweight Creek. William Bride, John Green, Sam Wolstenholme, just to name a few, were trying to make a fist of a new life on virgin land. They had to carry provisions for approximately twelve miles, and there were no roads at all. A year or so later, those making roads were paid five shillings a day. When these men had built a home and brought their families up to Fumina (present-day Vesper), they came by dray from Neerim South, camping overnight at the Latrobe River. Everything was unloaded and carried across the river, then reloaded. It was a tough gig in those early days. The mail came one day per week, usually on the Sunday, and whoever brought the mail waited for a reply to letters before traversing back towards Warragul.

An early traveller describes the last part of his trip from Warragul to Fumina after crossing the Latrobe River (later called Noojee) and heading further north:

> *Off again in the cold wintry night. Now sliding down into a creek or steep gully and clambering up the other side, or again forcing our way through the dense undergrowth, so as to get around a recently fallen tree. At last our goal is reached after nine hours in the saddle, to do a journey of twenty five miles from Warragul. After the tired horses had been tended to, then, despondent, weary and worn, to bed, and there to dream not of the El Dorado of the South, with its perpetual spring and summer, and evergreen trees, but of a God-forsaken land.*[7]

Herb Rankin was one of the earliest settlers. He came to Fumina in 1906. This is how his daughter Millie heard the account of her father's arrival in Fumina:

---

7   Graeme Butler, *Buln Buln A History of the Buln Buln Shire*, 1989, p.626.

The settlement was about twenty-eight miles from a railway station. My father caught the train, arrived at Neerim South and had to walk the rest of the way across a bullock wagon track. He got halfway there when it became dark and he had to sleep the night. In the morning he only had a little bread and a little jam for his breakfast and set off to the settlement where he knew there was another family (possibly Mitchells) and he thought he would be able to get a meal there. When he arrived the people did not have anything in the house to give him. The father had gone to the store and would not be back till late. So he had to go down to his little settlement, pitch his tent and then set off three miles across the country (to Mitchells senior at Fumina south) to get enough supplies – tinned meat, flour and so forth. When he arrived back at the camp after walking that long distance, a wild cow had invaded his tent and pulled it down. He had to set out to build it again before it got dark.

Land tenure was a risky business. Immediately after the 1890s Depression, unqualified people were handling land grants, village settlement and land sales in newly opened-up Crown Land. One early settler sarcastically reflects:

We find our far-seeing Lands Department heads establishing a village settlement in the heart of a forest, where in part 50 trees grew to the acre – for the Melbourne unemployed, some of whom could not even tell us as to whether a steer

or a heifer would eventually supply the household with milk
and butter. They were allotted 50 acres each and 50 pound to
clear the blocks of land. When the 50 pound was spent, and
wallaby and wombat flesh with an occasional parrot stew,
became unpalatable, the ephemeral village settlement ceased
to exist. Applicants for land can be seen pacing to and fro in a
corridor of the Lands Department, awaiting the call to appear
before a Departmental official. The call comes. 'Well, what is
your business? You wish to select in Noojee (Fumina).' A map
is laid on the table. The would-be settlers point out where they
wish to select... No advice or information is given as regards
the nature of the district, for the simple reason that the offi-
cer-in-charge knew absolutely nothing about Gippsland.[8]

The critique of settlement in such an inhospitable place
expressed his view with these words:

And the results today of heeding that practically ceaseless
cry of 'Go on the land' would have been far different had it not
been for the ignorance, stupidity or indifference to the welfare
of settlers, or perhaps the three combined, of our 'Bourbon'
Lands Department. Unfortunately it was not the settlers who
alone suffered by the action (or inaction) of the Department,
for the whole State has suffered an incalculable and irretriev-
able loss in making available for farming pursuits extensive

---

8   Butler, *Buln Buln...*, p. 609.

areas of forest country, with the inevitable destruction of the
one crop that such country could produce; timber.[9]

Jack Rankin, who was born in Fumina in 1912 and married Peg in 1944, lived there most of his life. He heard the stories from his own father and others and echoes the above sentiments in verse:

And now deep inside me it gives me much pain
to think that their hardships and labour were vain.
It may have served man in a much better way
to have left that fine forest to thrive and to stay.
Had it remained forest – not cleared up and farmed,
could it have survived its opponents unharmed
The raging inferno that's never a stranger
which places Fumina in imminent danger
I doubt very much if it could have remained
with its exquisite beauty that nature ordained.
But the laws of our country are grossly unfair
That forced men and women to struggle back there
As long as land-hogging tycoons are around
The poor must go further afield to get ground.

Again I turn to Jack Rankin, who captures the decision-making of the powers that be and the hardship of those early years in his poem etitled *The Birth of Fumina*. Here is an extract:

---

9   Butler, *Buln Buln...*, p. 693.

The Depression still worsened, small banks were closed down.
No money for business in city or town.
And workmen were tramping each road and each street
entreating employment or something to eat.
The Government grieved to see men in such plight.
It talked and discussed how to set things right.
There was much idle land needing men and their tools
that was listless as snakes when the winter wind cools.
Nearby to the cities, but dared not to touch,
it was owned by the gentry and well in their clutch.
They had legal entitlements, stamped, signed and sealed,
so the men wanting land must go further afield.
They must go out beyond where there's barely a track,
where the dense forests grow, on the land further back.
So the motion was passed – to relieve the distress
to open up land in the wild wilderness.
Rush land for selection, land rugged and torn,
so in came the settlers, Fumina was born.
They came, though the land near the main city routes
was unused and idle as rubbish dump boots.
There were thousands of blocks in monopolists' grip,
Which no-one could touch without gold on his hip.
So the needy were driven to pioneer the blocks
on the dense timbered ridges, all covered in rocks.
Then the ranges soon rang with the axes' loud sound,
and the crash of the giant trees striking the ground.
One gallant young bridegroom, escorted his bride

to this rough, roadless block, on the rough mountain side.
They had ridden since dawn, and while daylight expired,
'How far to our cottage?' she coyly enquired,
'This is it,' he replied with a short little laugh.
He dismounted and gave both the horses their chaff.
'The walls as you see are these tall sapling spars,
The roof is the tree tops, adorned by the stars.
The kitchen is here, near this rock we will cook.
The bedroom is there, and the bathroom's the brook.'
I guess that the bridegroom erected a tent,
and their first month of marriage within it was spent.
The pioneers soon settled this land away back.
A few days of toiling, then up went their shack.
Then their homesteads were built with a hastening rush,
concealed and well screened in the heart of the bush,
where barely a sunbeam would enter or stray,
except at the very high noon of the day.
For the forest was tall and the trees grew quite dense,
For mountain ash trees have proportions immense
And some of them here had a forty feet girth.
This land was the hardest to clear on God's earth.
The pioneers felled some with the axe and the saw
Then split up the logs into palings galore
Into bearers and scantling, so long and so straight
For uses like this – well this timber was great.
In construction of homes, they bought little from stores,
except glass and nails, and the hinges for doors.

But they had to earn tucker, so much of their time,
Was spent seeking gold in the mullock and grime,
Or fully depend on the wallaby snare
To fill their own bellies, and those in their care.
The big hollow stumps served as sheds very well,
And fences were logs that were used where they fell.
When the pioneers got settled, some cattle were bought,
And into that jungle of forest were brought.
The wilderness stirred as some cows wore a bell,
To ring loud and long, and their whereabouts tell.
The cows were fed mainly on wild oats and scrub.
They were milked, and their milk conveyed to a tub.
The cream was skimmed off and then churned with a clutter,
And walloped and pummelled till it became butter.
Then they hawked it twelve leagues to retail it in town,
At fourpence a pound, or for eight the half crown.
If a settler had ailments, he had a rough spin.
He could not get out and no leech would go in,
For to venture those tracks, it was madness to try.
He had to get well, or remain there to die.
One pioneer was ploughing a patch he had cleared,
And speeding towards him a housewife appeared.
A female came running o'er roots and the rubble,
'Come quickly,' she cried, 'For the woman's in trouble.
She's travelled for hours, and laboured in vain.
She's almost unconscious, she doesn't feel pain.'
The ploughman at once left his team there to stand,
And sped like a hare o'er that rough scrubby land.

Though childbirth to him as a trade that was new,

He soon took command as a doctor would do.

In cows' parturitions he'd learned a great deal,

And this was a breech he could tell by the feel.

He told those around where to push and to squeeze,

And after some time had its feet then its knees.

A little while later a baby was born.

A fine healthy fellow of muscle and brawn.

The mother she rallied to toil and to pray,

And the boy, I am told, is still living today.

The ploughman, thus ending his midwifery job,

Left the scene to the housewives, to clean and to swab,

While he, himself quickly returned to his team,

And ploughed until Jupiter cast his first beam.

These pioneers were hemmed in by trees and huge logs,

Where from twilight to dawn was the howl of wild dogs.

And the nerve-wracking loneliness sapping their life,

With their toil and hardships and harassing strife,

Along with the bitter ordeals that they had,

Which left some eccentric and others went mad.

These scenes are all facts I have written in verse.

The condition out there could have hardly been worse.

Just a decade or two ere the time I was born,

What I say is authentic – don't treat it with scorn.

I witnessed these happenings when I was a child.

I was born there, and lived in this heart of the wild.

I know to what hardships pioneers were subjected,

When land in this forest was firstly selected.

By the early stages of the twentieth century, more and more families were settling in the Fumina district, and there came the need for schooling. Some children who were reaching double figures in age had received little or no education.

One of the early drivers in acquiring a school for the district was Arthur Turner. He informed the Education Department of the growing number of children in the settlement, and calculated projected enrolments in the immediate future. Because the Government was reluctant to build a school due to shortage of funds, Arthur Turner offered the front room in his own house for a small rental fee to serve as a school, and his offer was accepted by the Education Department.

Initially the teacher had to commute between what is now Icy Creek and Fumina South, with Icy Creek operating for two days, and Fumina South the other three days each week. This arrangement was better than nothing, but far from ideal. A continual problem was finding and keeping teachers to serve this far-flung community. There was also the distance involved for the children. Those living in Fumina had a three-mile trek skipping over logs, crossing creeks, traversing steep gullies and contending with scrub and undergrowth, simply to attend school.

In less than forty years, Fumina suffered from three major bushfires. At the time of the 1906 fires, temperatures in northern Victoria reached 51 degrees. The hardest hit area in terms of life lost was in South Gippsland, where seven members of one family perished at Mount Best. In Fumina there was a loss of property but thankfully no loss of life. Nicholas and Eva Penny and their three children, George, May and Charlie, lost their house. Their response to this predicament was novel and creative – their new dwelling was a tree.

> *It was so big they could make a fire in the centre and sit around it and have their family beds in the hollow roots.*[10]

It was twenty feet across at floor level and had twelve feet of head room. Above that there was storage area. The Penny family lived there for almost a year until their more permanent home was completed. The tree was destroyed in the 1926 bushfires.

The Penny family lived in this tree after the 1906 fires.

---

10   Butler, p.700.

Fumina was relatively new, but it had packed a lot into its short history since the time of white settlement. On 25 February 1921, a young man armed with a shotgun broke into the local Post Office and shot the post-mistress, Amy Beale, and her step-daughter Edith.

The perpetrator was Conrad Ballantyne, the son of respected Fumina pioneer Albert Ballantyne and his wife Wilhelmena. It seems Conrad used to tag along with Jack and Penn Yates, two First World War veterans, on their hunting expeditions. Apparently, the two brothers were expert marksman who taught Conrad the basics of gun use, and they allowed him to borrow one of Penn's guns. In late April 1920, on one of these trips in and around Fumina with the Yates brothers, Conrad became separated from them and remained lost for 14 days.

He survived without food and weathered two snowstorms. The Yates boys and other locals searched continuously for him until May 13 when he was found starving and delusional and was carried back to his home. When asked about the time he was lost he stated that he remembered nothing.[11]

Nearly one year later Conrad in what a Court would later say was a state of delusion, entered the Beale household and shot Edith Beale and her step-mother Amy with a borrowed gun. It seems that Conrad's unusual manner and temperament was more than just that of a sullen youth. When the case went to Court, Conrad was proven to be mentally unsound and sent off to the Ararat Lunatic Asylum. It seems that Conrad believed that he was a bushranger and wanted to be famous. The gun that he used belonged to Penn Yates, who blamed himself for many years afterwards. Edith and Amy spent months in the Warragul Hospital but both survived the ordeal although they carried the scars for the rest of their lives. Four years later, young Edith married Penn Yates, the brother of her step-mother and the man who owned the gun that shot her.[12]

---

11   Google.com: *The Shootings at Fumina.*
12   *Ibid.*

Herb Rankin, Chris Bosse, Bert Mitchell, Penn
Yates, Jack Yates Fumina, 1920s.

Only a few years later came the 1926 bushfires. Nature once
again wreaked havoc on this fledgling community. Every building,
apart from a shed owned by Chris Bosse, was totally destroyed,
and people gathered around Bosse's shed afterwards. There was
one casualty. Mrs Mitchell went back to her house to retrieve a
couple of precious family photographs, particularly of her son
who went to war, and she was burnt to death. Paul Collins, in his
book *Burn: The Epic Story of Bushfire in Australia*, writes:

> *Another family the McHughs ... took refuge under wet
> blankets in the open. Dom McHugh and his wife and four
> children, including a baby, survived for three hours as the fire*

burnt around them on a clear patch of ground. McHugh was badly burnt on the face, neck and arms. Stranded for seventeen hours, they survived on a loaf of bread and some milk from a neighbour's cow which happened to wander by in the chaos.[13]

Peg's future father-in law, Herb Rankin, penned the following words a few months into the aftermath of that tragedy. The poem speaks of compassion, healing and hope. It is quoted in its entirety.

THE 1926 FIRE

'Aye, times the healer,' quoth the sage
To one who thought life's joys were o'er
'Time brings a healing in its wings
No matter what the grief and sore.'
Who has not seen some kindly friend
Entombed among the lowly dead
And thought the world had changed for him
And brightness with that spirit fled
The years roll on, he don't forget
The loved one long since laid to rest
But time the wound has slowly healed
New aims and ties his life has blessed

---

13   Collins, Paul, *Burn: The Epic Story of Bushfire in Australia*, p.97.

And so you see us here today
In naught else but a happy mood
The sorrows of a few months passed
No longer make us sit and brood.

When fire like hell itself unloosed
Swept up across our little ridge
Destroying all that we possessed
We thought the loss we could not bridge

It was a night of anguish sore
We spent amid that hellish flame
And none so hardened but he called
For mercy on the Father's name

We knew not how our friends they fared
For we were scattered far and wide
We feared that ere the sun should rise
We'd find some loved ones who had died

The night like all things had an end
And when the morn in sadness broke
Oh! What a sight beheld our gaze
On peering through the pall of smoke

These places which we called our homes
On which we'd toiled for twenty years
Were nothing but black rubble heaps
No wonder that our eyes showed tears

Sad, burnt and sore and almost blind
We gathered down at Bosse's shed
A few potatoes for our food

The earth itself our only bed
But soon there through the clearing came
A band of men to give us cheer
They told us that our plight was known
And all things needful now were near
They took us down a fire swept hill
One woman said, 'I'll not come back'
We trudged along with tearful eyes
Through forest timber burnt and black
We reached Fumina South that night
Before the blood red sun went down
And cars all packed with food and clothes
Were on their way from Moe town
The people took us to their hearts
Like parents take a much loved child
Their love soon banished care away
And loving gifts upon us piled
And soon the tale was blazened forth
From north to south from east to west
And nobly grand the people rose
And gave us of their all – their best
They put us back into our homes
And each and ev'ry one may hope
That all the struggles on life's road
He may with courage seek to cope
So time again has helped to heal
The sorrows of that hellish night

And love and sympathy has helped
Our heavy burdens to make light
Herb Rankin

As well as compassion, hope and healing, one other positive outcome of the 1926 bushfires was the clearing of trees for
farming. The fires made it easier to cut down burnt timber and
dead timber, and created easier access to fallen logs and timber
lying on the ground. This was in the time before bulldozers and
chainsaws, when farmers had limited implements. They relied on
axes, cross-cut saws, sledgehammers, wedges, chains and horses
to remove the timber, and burnt-out scrub made timber removal
more accessible for them. Sometimes good comes from bad.

Once land was cleared, a major difficulty for farming in
Fumina was containing the bracken fern.

> *Were these the good old days ... the grass, mainly ... white*
> *dutch clover was sown on the burns beneath the tall trees and*
> *among the logs. At first the grass did well, but not for long.*
> *Charcoal and shade, it seemed, was an ideal home for the*
> *bracken fern and it soon flourished, five or six feet high, and*
> *smothered the grass. The ferns had to be cut several times a*
> *year or there was no grass.*[14]

---

14 Butler, *Buln Buln...*, p.712.

Then came the disastrous bushfires of 1939.

Victoria suffered a Black Sunday in 1926, a Black Saturday in 2009, and a Black Friday on 13 January 1939. The 1939 fires, which devastated a lot of Gippsland, had their origin in Kinglake East and swept ferociously across mountainous Victoria. The town of Noojee was almost totally wiped out, apart from the local pub and one or two other dwellings. The pub became a haven of hospitality, which was offered by the owners Bill and Rita Chamberlain. Despite being burnt herself and obviously in some distress, Rita provided meals and accommodation. The *Argus* newspaper said of her:

> *Suffering from blisters on her face and with one eye bandaged she has been on her feet for sixty hours giving assistance to all who have requested it. She has provided scores of refugees and volunteers with excellent meals and has resolutely refused to accept payment for any of them. Nursing babies so that their mothers could rest and comforting sufferers from smoke blindness, she has won the admiration of the district.[15]*

---

15   Collins, Paul, *Burn – The Epic Story of Bushfire in Australia*, p.7.

Noojee Hotel, a place of hospitality after the 1939 bushfires.
Photo: 1940s.

On Black Friday a train service from Noojee was authorised to leave an hour and ten minutes earlier than scheduled. The train, carrying mostly women and children just made it over the trestle bridges to the northwest of the town before fire destroyed these unique structures.

When they got to the cobweb ladder as the 102-metre long and 21-metre high number seven trestle bridge was called, the driver stopped the train. He ran ahead to try to check the state of the structure by leaning over the edge and peering through the dark and choking smoke to see what was happening at the base of the wooden piles. It seemed safe enough, although there was burning vegetation down at the bottom of the bridge. Gingerly, the driver eased the train across.

Remnants of Trestle Bridge at Noojee after the 1939 bushfires.

Others took refuge for hours in the nearby Latrobe River. Although nobody lost their life in Noojee itself, to the north the saw-milling town Tanjil Bren suffered nine casualties. Mill owner Ben Saxton, his wife Dorothy, and mill workers Michael Gorey and Arthur Poynton all perished. Nearby the entire Rowley family, Ben, his wife Agnes and their three young children, John, Ben and Agnes, were also killed. Ben Rowley had survived the 1926 fires and thought he had the wherewithal to withstand another fire, but he wasn't prepared for what nature unleashed this time.

Yet again, fire wiped out the nearby hamlet of Fumina and left only one house remaining, the mud-brick house built by Pat Gilsenan a few years earlier. This is where survivors congregated and spent the first night after the fire. Nell Powell (nee Kealy), who was twelve years old at the time, vividly remembers Black Friday in Fumina on her family property:

The bushfires came along. Dad got up that morning and said the mountain is alight on the right hand side. I think we are going to get burnt out. We prepared ourselves. We filled up a 44-gallon drum with water and dragged it over with the horses and sledge. There was a big heap of rocks near the house and we took comfort behind them, we broke up the horses. It was important to know what to do with the horses. Grandad Rankin (Herbert) was there. We took some valuables out of the house as we knew we might lose it. We took blankets and dunked them into the drum to keep them wet. The fires were approaching us from the other side as well... For a while everything was okay. We kept wetting the blankets and putting them over our heads and then the wind changed. At one point we realised that the Sacred Heart picture was still in the house. I ran back to the house with my brother Bill to retrieve the picture of the Sacred Heart. I remember Dad saying to Grandad, 'Well Herb, I think we might be gone if the wind stays in this direction.' Then the wind changed again, possibly a half hour later, sending it all back. We took the blankets off our heads and we were all looking around. The entire mountain looked like a giant birthday cake with candles... as kids we were more interested in that than survival. Dad said we were right again and we were only kids and removed the blankets from our heads. We had the blankets over our heads when the house burnt. I don't remember feeling scared, although every move you make is risky. You have to rely on the adults and as the wind kept changing you were not sure of your next move. In the meantime the water level in the drum was diminishing and the fire was coming closer. It was all quite an ordeal. After it was all over we went back up to the house again which was gone of course; we were rummaging around all the rubble and we found whole cups in one piece. As soon as you touched them, they broke into bits. For the kids, it was novel and in a sense exciting but for the poor old parents, they must have worried themselves sick. It was pretty much the same all over Fumina. Only one place was left still standing and that was the Gilsenans'. We all went and stayed the night there. They sent a bus out to get us and I remember staying in Noojee for a couple of days. They handed out food and clothes and rations at Noojee. After we returned, we stayed in a big tent for a while until Mum and Dad built their house. You had to paddle your own canoe after that.

Joy Rankin was a baby at the time of the 1939 fires and survived the ordeal in Fumina. This is how she remembers the story being told:

At the time of the 1939 fires there were three babies, Joy Rankin, Jimmy Gilsenan and Jack Kealy. The story is that in the aftermath of the fires all three babies were breastfed by Dorrie Kealy. I was the oldest of the three children at six months. My mother had smoke inhalation and a really bad headache. She would have been de-hydrated. Eric and Linda (my parents) were there at the time of the fires. They had moved there in October 1938 and the fire came through the following January. A cluster of people congregated near the Mitchells' place with big cream cans of water and blankets and sat in the paddock. Mum who had no experience with bushfires was specifically instructed that she must not run when the fires hit and so she followed directions to a tee. She sat low to the ground nursing me. There was Eric, Linda, Fred Mitchell, Sarah Mitchell, Daphne Mitchell and me.

Anyone who has experienced at first hand bushfires and survived to tell the tale talks of the roar of the eucalyptus trees exploding and the power of the wind. The instinct is to run. The men apparently ran and in the process of getting up on their feet knocked over the can of water. Apparently they ran into a barb wire fence and realised the folly of their actions in doing the very thing they told Linda not to do. Immediately folk ran back to the place where they were before. Those gathered sat there for the entire afternoon in the pitch black dark inhaling all this smoke. Fred Mitchell in semi-darkness watched a pile of cow manure burning and thought it was Joy. He wasn't going to say anything to Mum for fear of upsetting her any more for he thought the cow dung smouldering was the remainder of human flesh. Imagine his relief when he heard or saw the child for the first time afterwards. We all gathered over at the Gilsenans' as this was the only house to survive. The McHughs, Rankins, Mitchells and Kealys all congregated there. Since there was little or no water some went down to Kenny's creek to fetch water. It took a few days before emergency services were able to make their way through to Fumina. There would have been many trees fallen down during the inferno. Police came and shot all the horses and cows that had been burnt.

Pat, Millie, Kath and Mary Gilsenan, 1930s.

Gilsenans' house in Fumina. This was the only house in the hamlet to survive the inferno of the 1939 bushfires. Folk gathered here immediately after the fire. The house was made of mud-brick and built by Pat Gilsenan himself.

'Cometh the moment, cometh the man' the saying goes in sporting parlance. One could also say, 'Cometh the years, cometh the woman.' Barely five years after the 1939 bushfires, newly married eighteen-year-old Peg Rankin and her husband Jack settled in the hamlet of Fumina.

This is where she and Jack raised their brood and eked out a livelihood. It is where Peg demonstrated practical faith, extraordinary resilience, great resourcefulness and loads of common sense. Fumina could easily break a person, but not Peg. She was made of tough stuff. She stamped herself just as much as those earlier pioneers, albeit in a different way. This was where Peg really made her mark, where she rose to the occasion. These years, in a sense, defined her and set her apart from others. The almost thirty-two years in Fumina are pivotal to Peg's story.

CHAPTER 4

Raising a Family
Part 1: 1944-1960

To all who were born in the 1940s, 50s and 60s:

First, we survived being born to mothers who smoked (or who inhaled smoke for years from their spouses) while they carried us and lived in houses made of asbestos.

We took aspirin, ate raw egg products, loads of bacon and processed meat, tuna from a can, and didn't get tested for diabetes or cervical cancer.

Then after that trauma, our baby cots were covered with bright coloured lead-based paints.

We had no childproof lids on medicine bottles, doors or cabinets and when we rode our bikes (if we were lucky enough to have one) we had no helmets or shoes, not to mention the risks we took hitchhiking.

As children, we would ride in cars with no seat belts or air bags.

We drank water from rusty tanks and piped up from springs, not from a bottle.

Take away food was limited to fish and chips; no pizza shops, McDonalds, KFC, Subway or Nandos.

We shared one soft drink with four friends, from one bottle, and no one actually died from this.

We could collect old drink bottles and cash them in at the corner store and buy toffees, gob stoppers, bubble gum and some bangers to blow up frogs with.

We ate biscuits, white bread and real butter and drank soft drinks with sugar in it, but we weren't overweight because we were always outside playing!

We would leave home in the morning and play all day, as long as we were back before dark. No one was able to reach us all day. And we were okay.

We would spend hours building our go-carts out of old prams and then ride down the hill, only to find out we forgot the brakes. We built tree houses and dens and played in river-beds with Matchbox cars.

We did not have Playstations, Nintendo Wii, X-boxes, no video games at all, no 999 channels on SKY, no video/DVD films, no mobile phones, no personal computers, no Internet or Internet chat rooms.

We had friends and we went outside and found them!

We fell out of trees, got cut, broke bones and teeth, and there were no lawsuits from these accidents.

Only girls had pierced ears!

We ate worms and mud pies made from dirt, and the worms did not live in us forever.

You could only buy Easter eggs and hot cross buns at Easter time.

We were given air guns and catapults for our 10th birthdays, we rode bikes or walked to a friend's house and knocked on the door or rang the bell, or just yelled for them!

Mum didn't have to go to work to help Dad make ends meet.

Footy, cricket, tennis, netball, all had tryout. Not everybody made the team.

Those who didn't had to learn to deal with disappointment. Imagine that! Getting into the team was based on merit.

Our teachers used to hit us with canes and leather straps.

The idea of a parent bailing us out if we broke the law was unheard of. They actually sided with the law.

Our parents didn't invent stupid names for their kids like 'Kiora' and 'Blade' and 'Ridge' and 'Vanilla'.

We had freedom, failure, success and responsibility, and we learned how to deal with it all.

If you were born in the 1940s, 50s or 60s, YOU are one of them.[16]

When Peg and Jack arrived back in Fumina after a short honeymoon in Bethany, a new life began in earnest for them. Jack had fond memories of Bethany (near Healesville) when he

---

16   Adapted from the internet.

was working as a surveyor, so that is where the newly married couple spent their first night. Again the long haul back to remote Fumina beckoned. It was always quite an ordeal, requiring a bus trip from Lilydale to Turner's Bridge on the Icy Creek on Sunday evening, which meant travelling with the timber workers from Tanjil Bren who were returning for work the next day. After they alighted at Turner's Bridge, Peg and Jack had to walk over six kilometres in the pitch darkness carrying suitcases, plus dreams and hopes for a bright future. Herb, Jack and Peg's third eldest, heard the story a few times. He maintains:

> There was a bus service that operated between Lilydale and Tanjil Bren. The bus was known as 'Goldie'. The operator was some kind of miracle man. He made his own fuel and his own tyres, and did his own maintenance. He dug himself out of a bog, patching things up. It was a miracle if you arrived at your destination; roads were bad and passengers were travelling in this derelict bus. The owner would have been out in the middle of the night with a blow torch often enough patching up the radiator. This was the 'limousine' that brought Mum and Dad back to Fumina from their honeymoon.

It wasn't a case of the newly-weds settling into their little farmhouse and living happily ever after. Nothing was ever that simple in Fumina. Jack's older brother, Bert, who was farming the family property, had a good thing going. He and Katie had children who were school-age, and to ensure the school was viable he had a tenant with a number of school-age children living in the house Jack and Peg were to move into. Maudie Pledger, a war widow, had a brood of children and the rent would have been a steady source of income for Bert and his family. So for several weeks, Jack and Peg lived at the Kealys' (Dorrie Kealy was Jack's oldest sister and she was married to Jim Kealy) until their own place became available.

The financial arrangement and the legal transfer of the farm into the hands of Jack are slightly unclear. Peg, all of 18 years old and a new bride, was not privy to the settlement details. What is known is that for a few years Jack was managing the mortgage repayments of his parents' house in Mount Evelyn. Although the deposit for the house would likely have been put up by Aunt Annie Regan, the deeds of the house were probably in Jack's name. As a trade-off it seems likely that the house was transferred to Herb and Kate and the bulk of the farm in Fumina then given over to Jack. When Peg and Jack arrived, however, Bert was still farming part of the property and living in another dwelling a few hundred metres away with his wife and children.

Although there was no prolonged ill feeling between Bert and Jack, there were a few unpleasant moments in this transitionary phase. After Maudie and her brood departed the scene and before Jack and Peg moved in, the curtains and the bath were taken out of the house. Jack had eyed some good timber and informed Bert that it would be ideal to make a sledge. Later, when he wanted to start work on building the sledge, the timber was gone. Bert, it seems, always farmed the best part of the ground and left Jack with the least productive part of the property. Unlike most of the farm, Bert's paddock had few rocks, and it was most fertile. This patch of ground was planted with potatoes and yielded a rich harvest.

Despite this minor hiccup in the early weeks and months following Jack and Peg's arrival, there was generally a lot of cohesion in the hamlet of Fumina. Eric and Linda Rankin (no relation) were well ensconced in their property a kilometre to the north. At that stage they had two children, Joy (aged five) and Ian (a toddler), and a third on the way. Further away, Dominic and Mary McHugh were still farming; all their children were grown up and had flown the coop. Pat and Millie (Jack's younger sister) Gilsenan and their three children were still there. Pat Gilsenan was a builder and he built their house which survived the 1939 fires. He also built the hall which was to become a school, and the house which Jack and Peg were eagerly looking forward to moving into. Fred and Sarah Mitchell, an older couple, were farming there, and their one and only child, Daphne, was well and truly grown up. This couple had the Fumina school teacher boarding with them most of the time they lived in Fumina. Fred's brother, Bert, a World War 1 veteran, lived on his own near where the hall/school were located. To the south, the Kealys – Jim and Dorrie (Jack's eldest sister) – still had quite a few children at home: Kath, Kevin, Peter, Jack and Pat, some of whom attended the school in Fumina. Bert and Katie and their children were the other family living there. From all reports, it was a pretty close-knit community, bonded by blood ties and a common effort to raise a family and forge out a livelihood in this remote part of Gippsland.

Peg and Jack moved into their home on 4 April 1944, a date which stuck in Peg's memory. It must have been exciting to finally have a place they could rightfully call home. At that stage, little did they know just how the future would unfold in this humble abode. So much would happen here – the laughter, friendships, the twists and turns of life, the happy moments and occasional sad ones. It has been said that life is what happens to us when we are making other plans. In this home, Peg and Jack raised their twelve children and continued to live there until January 1976, when they moved into the town of Warragul.

From the outset, there needs to be a word on friendship. Peg always had that special bond of friendship. She had the gift of putting people at ease around her. She was always good company. She knew how to start a conversation, a gift undoubtedly developed in her four years in the grocery store with her father. A Swedish proverb says that 'shared joy is double joy, shared sorrow is half sorrow'. Right from her early days in Fumina, Peg befriended the women in the hamlet and they all became life-long friends – Linda Rankin, Dorrie Kealy, Millie Gilsenan, and later Clarence Potter, Phyllis Batchelor, Kath Kilner and others. In all of these friendships there were shared joys and sorrows. As the Dalai Lama[17] said, 'without the human community, one single human being cannot survive'.

---

17   Spiritual leader of the Tibetan monks.

Anne was conceived during Peg and Jack's honeymoon. Linda Rankin was four months pregnant with Lindsay when Peg and Jack settled there, and she would have been a good sounding board for Peg throughout her first pregnancy. There were no doctors on standby to consult during pregnancy, and women's business was no doubt on the conversation agenda for these two formidable women. Peg wasn't overly concerned during her first pregnancy. She believed with some conviction that 'women have been giving birth since the world began so it wasn't something to fret too much about'. Anne was born in Warragul.

Mum went to stay with Phyllis Malady both before Anne's birth and in her time of recuperating. Phyllis was another woman who became a life-long friend, and Peg stayed with Phyllis and her family many times over the years. The only time Peg left Fumina in those early years was to attend the funeral of a dear relative, to give birth to a baby, or to attend to the Easter duty.[18] One cannot underestimate the importance of friendship in Fumina for Peg's sanity and well-being.

---

18   This required going to Confession and receiving Communion between Ash Wednesday and Pentecost Sunday in any given year.

Peg and Linda Rankin (back left), friends in arms, Fumina, 1950s.

Peg's children came along very quickly. Anne was born on 11 November 1944. This was a great opportunity get out of Fumina for the first time since Peg and Jack settled there. Peg and Jack made the trip to Mount Evelyn to share the joy of their first-born with their parents and families, and to show Anne to the relatives. Anne was baptised in Lilydale and then there was the long trek back to Fumina beckoned. Peg recalls it vividly:

> *Some of the Kealys were holidaying in Melbourne and were on the same bus. We had a seven-week-old baby, our suitcases, and the Kealys brought back a large bag of plums. So there was no rest. Peg and Jack were always carrying someone or something as there was no let-up on the six kilometre walk.*

Peg thought to herself: 'The Kealys should dice the bloody plums onto the side of the road so as to give the adults a break from carrying something or someone.'

They would have arrived home very late. When the mailman came the following morning, Peg and Jack were still in bed. That would have only happened once!

At this time in Australia, local community halls were important centres for civic responsibility, voting, meeting places, dances etc; they became important for the fabric of a local community, even more important than the local pub. Attached to the Fumina community hall (which served as the primary school) was a tennis court, and it was a hub of regular social activity in the mid-1940s. This was before most of the locals switched from growing potatoes to dairy farming. Milking cows seriously interfered with a social life, and growing potatoes gave some respite. During this period, many Sunday afternoons were spent around the tennis court.

Tennis in Fumina has an interesting history. Jack Rankin penned a poem about Fumina folklore, in which farmers earlier in the century used creative instruments for tennis racquets:

> *They built a court, they had a ball*
> *But had no tool to whack it,*
> *So Ted Beale got his frying pan*
> *And used it for a racquet.*
> *Herb Rankin, too, was very keen*

And his ideal was novel,
He went into his garden patch
And fetched the garden shovel.

Joy Evans (nee Rankin), who was a small child at the time, remembers the Sunday tennis afternoons:

> *I remember as a pupil at school preparing the tennis court with a big concrete cylinder. These cylinders were left-overs from making the roads and were useful in flattening out the stones on a tennis court. Sometimes a child would lie in the cylinder for a bit of fun. Tennis didn't last a long time, perhaps a few years. Eric (Joy's father) did not play much. Linda (Joy's mother) certainly did. We had to weed the court during school time and prepare it for the weekend. Peg and Jack were certainly there, Millie and Pat Gilsenan. Tennis games were more social than competitive, a 'bit of a hit and giggle'.*

Maybe a bit of hit and giggle, but also a great occasion to catch up, share news, and have a bit of a fun. Maybe there were a few tennis racquets around by that stage, and the folk didn't have to resort to using frying pans and shovels!

Terry was born on 5 December 1945 – a little brother for Anne. Peg was told he was born so close to midnight between 5 and 6 December, she could choose his birthday. She chose the 5th.

At the time the Trafalgar Hospital had a little annex designed as a place for mothers to give birth. This is where Terry was born, and fifteen months later on 3 March 1947, Kevin (Herb, child number three) was born there. The birth of children always gave Peg a rare chance to leave Fumina for a while, which also gave her an opportunity to meet up with friends and relatives. Bert and Katie provided hospitality on both these occasions. Bert was still working in the timber game at that time. It must be noted that there was no time for holding onto grudges and resentments. Even though, as mentioned, there were some hurtful moments for both families in the transition of the house and farm from Bert to Jack, Fumina was no place to harbour resentment. It says a lot that Peg stayed with Bert and Katie while she was waiting for the birth of these two children.

Terry and Anne, 1947.

Peg always had the capacity to move on quickly, as did Jack, it seems. And Bert and Katie opened their home and heart to Peg as she prepared to give birth to her second and third children. It was the usual practice for Peg to have her children baptised before she returned to Fumina after giving birth. Both Terry and Herb were baptised in Trafalgar on the return journey.

All the children had different personalities and temperaments. According to Peg:

> *Anne was placid. She was a good baby. There was no sign of resentment when Terry came along. She once said to me, 'I don't like being smacked, Mummy.' Anne had been playing in a puddle of water; I gently rebuked her but she continued to jump in the puddle and so I smacked her, and she was none too pleased about it. Terry was boisterous, handsome, lively. And Herbie, it took a lot to upset him. He yawned a lot.*

Peg and Jack were lucky in that all their children had the opportunity to complete their primary schooling in either Fumina or Icy Creek. Not long before their arrival, the Fumina school was closed for some time and at that stage there was no bus transferring children across to the Icy Creek Primary School. Three of Jack's siblings children, who were living in Fumina in the late 1930s and early 1940s and attending Fumina school, had their education interrupted with the occasional school closure. Although Fumina was a one-teacher school and often the teacher was young and inexperienced, at least Peg and Jack's children had school every day. Nearly all of the teachers who came to Fumina were straight out of Teachers' College, and in one sense there was little of the accountability and mentoring that is normal today. Some went to Fumina even before they officially graduated from Teachers' College. Gary Muller, who taught in Fumina, reminisces:

I was four months short of my twentieth birthday when I commenced teaching at Fumina in late April 1957 and I taught there until the end of 1958. Having completed Leaving Certificate in 1954 and attended Bendigo Teachers College in 1955-56, I had to sit two Exams to attain the TPTC (Teacher Primary Training Certificate). Afterwards I undertook three months of National Service at the beginning of 1957 and was posted to Fumina School following that stint. It was not uncommon for trained teachers to begin their careers at twenty years of age. In that year there were eight pupils. Six of the students were Peg and Jack's offspring. The other students were Janet and Lindsay Rankin. An entire school of Rankins! Two families in a small hamlet and not related. Amazing!

These young teachers had their work cut out for them when they arrived to begin their careers in Fumina. It certainly was some initiation, a no frills experience. There was no electricity, no mentors, no guidance, no creature comforts. It would have been quite a lonely time.

Fumina Hall, location for the school until 1960.

Fumina School students 1958. L-R back row: Herb,
Anne, Lindsay Rankin, Janet Rankin, Terry and
Tim.Front row: Barry and Gerardine.

In the mix, there were some good teachers at both Fumina and Icy Creek. For Jack and Peg's older children, the likes of David Coe and Roger Gibbard stand out as very competent educators. They were both a bit older, and Roger certainly had considerable teaching experience behind him.

David Coe was English. He had an interesting initiation in Fumina. He was asked by the Education Department to move from Geelong to Fumina, and arrived in a taxi. This caused intrigue in the local community, who surmised from his grand arrival that he must have been quite a wealthy man. In fact, he was a person of modest means, but he was given only a day's notice to commence teaching in Fumina and the only way to get there in time was to hail a taxi. The fee would have been astronomical – equivalent to about a month's wages – and he sent the bill to the Education Department, which apparently reluctantly paid it. Coe was told not to do this again!

During Coe's teaching stint in Fumina, the place was covered with snow, which reminded him of his beloved homeland. Lindsay and Joy Rankin both remember the thick blanket of snow that year. Lindsay recalls:

> *The whole place was covered in snow, Fumina was trans-formed into a fairyland. I thought it was wonderful and exciting. I remember going down to the Mitchells' and my feet sinking into the snow. It was stunning, magnificent. We were at school when it started. It seemed to snow for three days. I remember our teacher, David Coe, was in seventh heaven being from England and all. It obviously reminded David of home.*

Joy remembers the snowstorm too. She puts it this way:

> *Mr Coe thought the snowstorm was great. He was rubbing*
> *his hands. This is like home. But after a day or two, he was*
> *over it.*

Back at that time, the Fumina hall was little more than a shed with exposed rafters and a corrugated iron roof which was exposed from below. After the snowfall there would have been at least a foot of snow on the hall's roof. When corrugated iron is covered in snow it tends to drip a lot of water. In this case, the dripping water was covering every of piece of paper in the hall/schoolroom, including Mr Coe's personal papers. Again Joy reminisces:

> *There would have been no supplies, no mail, no warmth.*
> *David Coe came to school the following morning and he*
> *trudged through the snow, face downcast. This time he*
> *was talking about the 'wretched snow, the wretched snow'.*
> *Sometimes the firewood wasn't the best and it took quite a*
> *bit to heat the big empty hall. It was up to the men of the*
> *hamlet to keep us in stock with firewood. The kids helped with*
> *stoking the fire.*

Peg remembers the snow too:

> *In around 1951 there was a heavy snowstorm. We had a*
> *foot of snow around our house and further up the road on*
> *higher hills they may have had fifteen or sixteen inches. Snow*

didn't occur very often. It started falling about lunchtime on a Thursday and the older children, Anne and Terry, had to walk home in the snow. It wasn't easy for a five or six year old to push through in a walking stride in a foot of snow. Terry got stuck in the snow. He was only five. Fred Mitchell went to get them. He could see they were in some distress, the little tackers with arms in the air crying out for help. Anne and Mary Kealy were together lifting their legs high up in the snow. It took some effort. I think Fred may have seen the little tackers and accompanied them home. In hindsight Dad should have gone up to the school and met them whilst I stayed home to look after the three younger children. Sometimes on the way to school or on the way home you might give the Mitchells a billy for the next milk collection. Maybe this is how Fred saw Anne and Terry in a bit of bother. They were left to fend for themselves. This seems to have been the biggest dumping of snow in Fumina's post-war history.

David Coe was quite a cultured person and was frustrated at the students' lack of culture. Terry Rankin got the strap on his first day because he wouldn't sing. That evening Terry went home and said to his mother, 'I can't sing, can I Mummy?'

I have two final anecdotes regarding David Coe. Terry tells the story that this well-mannered English gentleman used to ask the students sometimes if he could remove his jacket. One day when he popped the usual question, Peter Kealy told him 'No' and to everyone's amusement, Coe left his coat on all day. At the end of the year Coe apparently failed everyone in the school and described the children in Fumina as 'unteachable'. They couldn't sing and had no culture.

One teacher really made a difference to Anne's education. She writes:

> One important person that I would like to remember is the arrival of our teacher Roger Gibbard. Roger came to Fumina in 1954 to teach at the local Fumina State School. Roger had a great zest for life. He was an exceptional teacher. I remember that he added gymnastics to the curriculum and taught us all to do cartwheels, walk on our hands etc. We also had time out of the classroom going on bushwalks taking in the beauty of nature. Roger was an experienced bushwalker who joined the search for a missing walker in the Baw Baws. He opened our eyes to a broader world and made learning fun.

Roger Gibbard with students at Fumina school, mid-1950s.

In terms of the safety requirements in motor cars, the 1950s were a vastly different era than today. Many risks were taken without thinking too much of it. Gary Muller, the teacher in 1957-58, would occasionally pile all the children into his old Chev. Mary was born on the 15 August 1957, and when Peg came home after having the baby, school was out. Tim remembers:

> ... *sitting on this convertible with our backsides on the back of the chairs. So here is this car, a great long row of us, going down to see our new sister Mary. We were sitting on cloud nine.*

Anne remembers one day Gary Muller was in the Chev with a heap of kids on board and when he turned a bend, all the doors flew open. Obviously at that time there were no seat belts in the car. Luckily no-one fell out. Another time the whole school population of Fumina with their teacher were in a car which didn't have brakes.

Sometimes the students went into Noojee to see the mobile school dentist or receive injections of some sort. Lindsay Rankin tells the story of one of these trips into Noojee:

> It was down at Blacker's place. There was a cowshed near the road and cows were crossing the road near the Tooronga Falls turnoff. The teacher came down the hill with a carload of kids ... we used to go to Noojee from time to time to have injections or to attend the mobile dentist. We were all in this car in the late 1950s. Anyway the brakes were not functioning in this old Chev and we needed to pull the car up. It was quite tricky to drive and braking was done by dropping down to lower gears and pulling up the car that way. As he is working down the gears and we are fast approaching the cows, Mr Muller revved the engine, doubled the clutch and shimmied the bloody thing into reverse. The engine groaned and gyrated, but he was actually able to jam the Chevvy into reverse gear ... it didn't go in easily. The clutch would have taken up the strain and the car definitely made a funny noise, but it came to a halt. I was in the front seat and I swear this

is what happened. I know a bit about cars and although mechanics will tell you it is not possible to jam a car into reverse whilst it is in forward motion, I tell you we did it.

Gary Muller's Chev. The whole Fumina school crammed into this car on more than one occasion!

Gary Muller, a young teacher, who taught at Fumina school in 1957-1958, and his beloved Chev car stripped to its chassis. All the students at the Fumina school crammed into this car at the one time.

Babies kept coming. Tim was born on 31 March 1949, Barry on 29 May 1950, and Gerardine on 23 March 1952. Herb reflects on the ritual of pregnancy for Peg:

> *When you are pregnant and it is 40 degrees in the shade, and this is in Fumina, it can be a bit tough. You can't even get yourself a cold drink. Everything is lukewarm. Mum didn't breastfeed for long. Her breasts would have got a bit dry. There were absolutely no creature comforts for a woman several months pregnant.*

These babies were born in Warragul, and Peg stayed with her good friends Phyllis and Joe Malady. Peg described them this way:

> *Phyllis was the quiet and reserved type, but a very good person. Her husband Joe had a good sense of humour and again a very good man.*

(L-R): Barry Gerardine and Tim, 1953-54.

Their daughter, Barbara Malady, remembers Peg coming to their home before she went to hospital to deliver the babies, and returning there afterwards:

> We used to wait and wait and wait for Peg to come home from the hospital with the new baby. She usually had the child baptised on the way home from the hospital. This was usually arranged with the priest beforehand, although it may have been spontaneously administered on some occasions.

Barbara Malady reflects on Peg's arrival back at their house in Bowen Street, Warragul, after the birth and possibly the baptism of the newborn:

> Peg would be knitting all the time and her children had the best of clothes. She didn't buy cheap stuff. She used to be knitting every night making jumpers for her children. She would be going ten to the dozen with the knitting, not baby clothes, just for the other kids. She would worry if it was cold, and the kids being cold and she would be in a house that was warm and cosy. She would be worried about the kids freezing and always wanting to be home in a hurry. Sometimes she was away for a fair while, a couple of weeks. This was obviously a long time with toddlers and many youngsters back at the ranch; she just wanted to get back there.

This is the Maladys' house in Bowen St, Warragul, where
Peg stayed prior to giving birth to eight of her children.

Peter and Barbara Malady have fond memories of Peg coming to stay
with them both before and after the birth of many of her children.

Knitting was in the family. Grandma Agnes would post jumpers and things for the kids. Terry remembers:

> *Grandma would knit jumpers with animals on the front. I remember one with a koala bear. Mary (Peg's sister) was a fine knitter also. Knitting was in the family. Mum probably taught herself to sew. She always had a sewing machine and most likely mastered it herself. Mum was good at picking up new skills. She had quite a remarkable skill set.*

Much later, Peg hand-knitted her grandchildren's school jumpers. As well as working full-time doing her bit for the Church and her community, she found time to knit in the evenings. Anne and John had four children, Isaac, Olive, Dominic and Adrian. Peg maintains that all these children had their school jumpers hand-knitted for the entirety of their primary schooling at Our Lady of Lourdes in Bayswater, east of Melbourne. They all realised their jumpers were slightly different from their peers', and it was because Granny had personally knitted them.

Queen Elizabeth II was crowned in June 1953. She and her husband Prince Phillip made an extensive tour of Australia in 1954. Anne remembers:

> *Mum was pretty laid back about the Queen's visit until the newspapers reported it and it was receiving a lot of media attention, and so Mum started to get a bit excited. She went to see Mrs McHugh and invited her to come along. And so off they went, first of all on the school bus and then the special train.*

The children from the district who were attending primary schools were all invited to see the Queen when she visited Gippsland on 3rd March 1954. Anne, Terry, Herb and Tim and all the children from Fumina Primary School caught the special train that ran from Noojee to Warragul. Bernard was born on Australia Day 1954, and so was only five weeks old at the time of the Queen's visit. Anne tells the story:

> *Mum and baby Bernard sat in the part of the train reserved for adults whilst the children were in the part allo-cated to school children of the area. When the train stopped at Rokeby, Mum passed Bernard to her sister Mary McHugh (daughter-in-law of Mrs McHugh) who minded him for the day. It was quite a drop out the window but that is what happened. It meant that she could enjoy the moment without having to worry about her baby. Gerardine and Barry would have been left with Dad.*

On the Gippsland tour, there was a special Royal Train which went as far as the Latrobe Valley, stopping at towns along the way. On the return trip, Warragul would have been one of the last stops before the train arrived back in Melbourne. The Royal visit to Warragul centred on the Showgrounds. Anne picks up the story:

> *When Mrs McHugh caught sight of the Queen, with her and Mum just a few metres away, she said, 'You lovely, lovely lady,' and the Queen beamed at them. The Queen was only in*

Warragul for about half an hour, but that was certainly a bit of local history which every school child who was there would remember. Dad thought the whole thing was overrated and a waste of time and effort. He was amused by Terry who told his father that he saw the back of the Queen's head. He joked about it afterwards. Mum, however, got into the groove and enjoyed it.

There was further history made on that grand day. This was the last time the passenger train ever ran from Noojee to Warragul. One of the major trestle bridges on the train line just southwest of the town of Noojee mysteriously burned down a short time later.

The Royal Train during the Queen's 1954 visit.

Trestle Bridge, Noojee, 1934.

The house in Fumina where Peg and Jack raised their family was pretty basic. In 2012, Dennis gave a talk to the Hill End Historical Society. He was child number eight and was born on 13 March 1955, more than ten years after Anne. The house and its contents hadn't changed much in that decade. It was still pretty much the same. This is part of what he shared that evening:

> *My early days of childhood were spent entirely at Fumina. We didn't have a car so we rarely went anywhere and with so many kids we needed a people mover which was not an option back then. We only had the very basics in our home, which my kids find very hard to believe.*
>
> *We had one tap in the kitchen, no sink; we used to use a large dish for dishes with the hot water coming from a big cast iron kettle on the stove. That same dish would then be used to wash ourselves in before we went to bed. The fire was always going so hot water was never an issue.*

We had the old drop toilet away from the house – that was a scary trip in the dark so if you were a boy and only wanted a wee you would usually stop halfway.

We had no electricity until I was 12 years old, so even something as simple as cooking a piece of toast was done on the red coals of the stove. Our fridge ran on kerosene and every now and then it would start smoking. I'm not sure why, but when it happened it meant the kerosene flame had to be put out and the fridge then defrosted!

Our lighting consisted of pump-up Tilley lanterns in the living room run on kero again, with a couple of other lanterns we would use to carry around the house. We occasionally would break the glass and end up with glass everywhere in the dark. Even our iron was heated by a kerosene flame.

All our cooking was done on the stove or in the oven. On a Sunday when we eventually went to Noojee for Church when some of the older kids with their cars were home, Mum would put a casserole or roast in the combustion stove and it was ready when we returned home. In our haste to get home to rescue our Sunday lunch one day, Mum forgot to check how many kids were in which car and we realised that we had left my youngest brother Paul behind – we found him walking up the road towards home. He would have been five years old and had already walked at least five kilometres of the twenty kilometre journey home before my older siblings caught up with him. He just seemed to take it all in his stride.

The bathroom laundry/wash house was an interesting set-up in our house. Sunday was bath night. As a young-ster the bath was made of galvanised iron and by the time I started to use it, a couple of the soldered seams had given way. Today we would just fix it with a few pop rivets and a tube of silicon, but no, not us, we would seal it up with Velvet soap that had been left in the tub, to make it seal. The hot water for the bath was obtained from a large copper boiler which would hold about 40 litres, and with a fire underneath. As each child climbed out, more hot water was added. The hot water from the copper was also used for the laundry.

One can't underestimate the importance of rabbits for poorer Australians as a food source. Eminent Australian historian Geoffrey Blainey reveals:

In 1859 the Victorian squatter Thomas Austin imported in a sailing ship from Liverpool in England some twenty-four live rabbits … Released onto his sheep run beyond Geelong the rabbits flourished beyond all his dreams, but the price of their meat was still high. Within one decade, the descendants of the rabbits had escaped his fences and entrenched themselves like an invading army in the rich soil of his neighbouring proper-ties. Each year they occupied more and more Victoria.[19]

---

19   Blainey, Geoffrey, *Black Kettle and Full Moon*, pp.208-9.

Rabbits became a very important food source for poorer families. Peg was a quick learner and after watching the men trap, kill and skin rabbits a couple of times, she mastered the art very quickly. To kill the larger ones, she had a rabbit stick which entailed breaking their necks with a single stroke. For smaller rabbits, she used the 'rabbit whack' – breaking the neck of the rabbit with her bare hand in a slicing action. In most families this task would have been the responsibility of the husband and father, but not in the Rankin household. Often it was left to Peg to set traps, kill the rabbits, skin them and cook them in a variety of ways. Rabbit was a plentiful and tasty food source, and it was on the menu of a lot of families in those days.

Lindsay Rankin remembers Pat McHugh, Dominic and Mary's son, returning to Fumina to see his family. This is how Lindsay remembers Pat telling the story:

> *I was going home to Mum and Dad's (Dominic and Mary) and I dropped in to see the Kealys. Dorothy and Jim invited me in to have a bit of rabbit stew. So I tucked in and enjoyed a bit of good old rabbit stew. I stopped by next at Jack and Peg's and they were having braised rabbit and I was invited to sup with them but after a quick chat I was on my way. I called in to see Eric and Linda Rankin and Linda was about to serve a baked rabbit and when I got home, slightly further up the hill and walked in, my mother said, 'Just in time for a nicely baked rabbit!'*

This little incident would have occurred in the early 1950s.

Older children remember eating rabbits. Some of them got sick of the sight of them, but Terry enjoyed them. Kids would fight over the kidneys. Rabbit stew was a much cooked meal in Australia, and it certainly was in the Rankin kitchen in the 1940s and 1950s. It was easy to cook as the basis of a stew, but harder to bake. Peg mastered the latter.

Jack Rankin penned the following lines in the 1950s:

> *Come to Fumina where the grass is always green*
> *where a meal without a rabbit is very seldom seen;*
> *and if you have a palate that craves for something new,*
> *then you may snare a wallaby and eat him in a stew.*
> *The Scotsmen love their haggis, the Chinese love their rice*
> *but for those who love the rabbit, Fumina's paradise.*

Now, from rabbits to snakes. Henry Lawson captures something of the fear and menace of snakes in rural Australia in his short story, *The Drover's Wife*. The plot centres on the wife of a Drover who is confronted with a five-foot black snake nesting under their two-room house. She is alone with her four young children and a dog called Alligator, eighteen miles from nowhere. Her husband has been away this time for six months, droving sheep. She waits patiently through the night, reminiscing on happier days, vigilant in case of the snake's re-emergence, with a stick nearby and Alligator ready to pounce if the snake is sighted. One can detect the suspense as Lawson wrote:

It must be near daylight now. The room is very ... hot because of the fire. Alligator still watches the wall from time to time. Suddenly he becomes greatly interested; he draws himself a few inches nearer the partition, and a thrill runs through his body. The hair on the back of neck begins to bristle, and the battle-light is in his yellow eyes. She knows what this means, and lays her hand on the stick. The lower end of one of the partition slabs has a large crack on both sides. An evil pair of small, bright bead-like eyes glisten at one of these holes. The snake – a black one – comes slowly out, about a foot, and moves its head up and down. The dog lies still, and the woman sits as one fascinated. The snake comes out a foot further. She lifts her stick, and the reptile, as though suddenly aware of danger, sticks his head in through the crack on the other side of the slab, and hurries to get his tail round after him. Alligator springs, and his jaws come together with a snap. He misses, for his nose is large, and the snake's body close down on the angle formed by the slabs and the floor. He snaps again as the tail comes round. He has the snake now, and tugs it out eighteen inches. Thud, thud. Alligator gives another pull and he has the snake out – a black brute, five feet long. The head rises to dart about, but the dog has the enemy close to the neck. He is a big, heavy dog, but quick as a terrier. He shakes the snake as though he felt the original curse in common with mankind. The eldest boy wakes up, seizes his stick, and tries to get out of bed, but his mother forces him back with a grip of iron. Thud, thud – the snake's back is broken in several places. Thud, thud – its head is crushed ...

Snakes were always a threat in Fumina. Peg remembers:

Tim having an afternoon nap as an infant and I saw a snake slither across the floor of the room. That was the only snake I ever actually saw inside the house, but it was always a worry, snakes and children. Snakes would usually only respond to threat. If you accidentally stood on them they would try and bite you. This is what happened to Ian Rankin who lived just up the road. The snake was under the house; he was only two, I think. He must have stood on the snake when it came out from under the house and it bit him. He came into the house saying, 'A snake has bit me.' He was taken into Warragul Hospital with either Jack or Frank McHugh. His mum put a tourniquet around the wound (it doesn't seem to be the practice anymore). The tight bandage was in vogue then, to prevent the poison travelling through the bloodstream to the heart. There was talk of Ian losing the leg with the tight tourniquet in which they had wrapped the child.

For Peg, snakes were a constant menace in the summer and one had to be on guard:

There was also the snake that loved warming itself near the front veranda. We didn't want to disturb the snake. It had been around the house for a couple of days. It hid under the house. On a sunny day, it was lazing around and Jack crept up on it and killed it before it awoke. Another time there was a snake resting under our bedroom. I couldn't get near it but threw a kettle of boiling water through the vent in the general vicinity of where he lay. I must have killed it because the stench coming from the spot in the next couple of weeks or so was noticeable. Our cat pretty early on broke the back of a snake and dumped it under the kitchen table still alive. Gerardine was only about four when she had an encounter with a snake in the cowshed. Hens would lay eggs there and it would have been a nice warm spot for a snake to snuggle into. Gerardine and her little accomplice Bernard had the task of collecting the eggs. A few days after collecting the eggs one day she said, 'Mummy, a snake bit me.' Gerardine showed Peg her index finger and there were two little black spots a few centimetres apart. When Peg quizzed her a bit more Gerardine said the 'snake bobbed up and then bobbed down'.

To quote Peg:

We have certainly been blessed along the way. God has been looking after us!

One winter the menfolk were grabbing a few bales of hay to feed the cattle; they were more than ten feet high in the shed and discovered a snake hibernating.

Auntie Gwyn, Peg's sister, was in Fumina in 1955, helping out whilst Peg was in Warragul giving birth to Dennis and she recalls:

A snake came into the kitchen through the back door. It was obviously looking for water. I grabbed Bernard the baby and headed for the nearest exit. I called out to Jack who was nearby and I have never seen Jack move so fast. He raced to the back veranda, grabbed a long stick which was strategically placed for these sorts of situations, and killed the snake.

In the drought of the summer of 1967-1968, a five-foot tiger snake in search of water nestled under the tool shed, just a few metres from the house. Some of the children had seen the snake and it was clear it had taken refuge under the shed. The two dogs, Paddy and Smokey, loved digging holes and they had dug what seems like a trench under the rear of the shed, and the snake thought it had found a safe haven in this little patch of dirt. Peg, however, had her game plan. She gave clear instructions. She wanted all the children out of the way. She wanted quiet, to lure the snake out of its comfort zone – it was no good having excited and noisy children around. The younger children were ordered to the cowshed, some distance away. It was time for milking the cows anyway – about 4.00 pm in the afternoon.

Tim was 18 years old and had just finished his matriculation at boarding school in Sunbury. He was already an accomplished marksman and during holidays on the farm, he had shot many rabbits. He was told to get the shotgun and wait for the snake to make its move, and then nail it with his straight shooting. Barry, a year or so younger, was strategically positioned at the other side of the shed to be alert to any plans of escape. The game of patience began. After a stalemate, possibly an hour or two, Tim became more proactive and crouched under the door of the shed, and with a torch he was able to locate the snake. Knowing pretty much where the snake was and without the aid of any torchlight, he took aim and true to form, struck it with his first shot. The snake was not done with and tried to escape, but as quick as a flash Barry grabbed it and struck it a fatal blow. Afterwards the dead snake was wrapped over the fence nearby, a prize on display for all to see.

Dennis remembers another incident involving a snake:

> As kids, we entertained each other, building cubbies or playing with sticks etc. One year the boys decided to dig a cubby into the side of the road area, a dungeon so to speak. It had two rooms that we covered from the top with sticks and dirt. We could access it through a door we put in. It used to be great to spook people coming along the road too, as we could hear the cars coming and would all stick our heads out of this hole to see who it was. The drivers got a hell of a shock to see six or seven heads sticking out of the side of a hill. It was great fun until we found a big snake curled up in the second section of it. We fell over each other trying to get out of there.

In Fumina, snakes were an ongoing challenge, but they weren't the only problem. It required a certain amount of resourcefulness to survive in Fumina, with limited water supplies, no electricity, harsh winters, long summers, few appliances and groceries only being delivered once a week. Water was always a precious commodity, especially in the long hot summers. Most families just had one thousand-gallon tank attached to their houses. To save water, there were expeditions down to the Icy Creek to do some serious washing. Joy Rankin remembers this:

> In the summer they gathered up the washing in bundles in sheets, kids and all, they would light a fire and boil the water from the creek in a large kerosene can, wash the clothes and lay them out on the bracken to dry. Sometimes they would take rope or wire and run a line between a few trees and hang out the washing on these makeshift clothes lines. They would have lunch by the creek and come home again. They might go down with the horses and bring back a 44-gallon drum of water.

Joy also remembers when Peg acquired a motorised washing machine in 1955:

> She was the first to have one in Fumina. When Peg acquired the engine-driven washing machine, that was a big thing. It must have been such a help for her everyday life. You kick started the engine like a motorbike.

It was petrol-driven and after a few years of constant use, Herb reflects:

> The noise and the stench and filling the thing up with petrol were something else. The copper fire was only a metre

or two away, so how the hell the whole lot never burnt down is beyond me. I set fire to it once and tried to get the machine out the door and it wouldn't fit through easily. Gwyn was there, Mum was away.

Herb was concerned about the danger of the washing machine causing a fire. When electricity came to the district in November 1967, he bought Peg a new washing machine that was guaranteed to last for five years, and according to Herb 'it lasted five years and one day'.

Meat was delivered three times a week. Prior to 1955, when a kerosene refrigerator was purchased from relatives who opened an electrical store, there was no refrigeration. There was a meat cooler, but its capacity to preserve the meat was limited, so when meat was delivered it had to be partially cooked to preserve it. In parts of Asia today, and elsewhere where there is no refrigeration, meat is still purchased and cooked straight away. Terry remembers the days before refrigeration:

We had a meat mincer. Before we got the fridge, I remember having a lot of mince, sausages, chops, corned beef. In the summer wet bags were placed over the meat. Obviously in the winter the meat lasted a bit longer. There was never any hint of food poisoning in Fumina; we never got sick. We only got sick when a sibling went down to Drouin and came back with the measles or mumps, or school sores.

Peg had a kind heart and did not brood over things; but if she felt she was wronged or treated unfairly, she would stand up for herself. She certainly had her own pride and could be quite assertive if the situation demanded it. A case in point was her dealings with a local butcher in Trafalgar. Sometimes she just didn't have the money to pay for the meat which was delivered, and the meat bill would have been piling up over a long winter. One day the mailman arrived with the usual mail, newspapers, bread and groceries, but the standard order of meat didn't appear. The mailman simply told Peg the butcher refused to give her any more credit.

Herb was in the room when she called the butcher to tell him what she thought of the way he did business:

> *Mum got onto the blower (telephone) and asked for the manager and proceeded to tear strips off him. This is not how you do business. How dare you do this in a public way? There is a way of doing things and I am never ever going to buy a piece of meat from you again. She must have paid the butcher out with an overdraft the next day and searched out a new butcher. That shows spirit. The bill would have been significant and the fellow would have been surprised but Mum was adamant there was a way of doing these things and a way not to do them. A phone call to her would have been a more appropriate tactic rather than a message and no meat delivered through the mailman. Mum learnt from experience. She*

knew about bad debts. Her own father was caught up in bad debts. Bill had to do the occasional 'midnight flits'. Bill went broke and they had to come and live in Eltham after accumulating debts and people chasing their money. She would have known bad debts in the shop at Mount Evelyn.

The main grocery delivery was on Friday. Jimmy Rees, who ran the General Store at Hill End, was the supplier for virtually all of the time Peg and Jack were in Fumina. He was a generous man, and supported the Rankin family and many others through the winter months. When the cows were dry for those seven weeks, there was literally no income apart from the meagre income from running the Post Office and child endowment payments. Bills would not have been paid until two months later. Jimmy Rees just docked the bills up, knowing they would be paid in good time. He would have done the same for many other families in the district. How he could afford to keep this up is difficult to comprehend. He had his own bills to pay, yet he never forced the issue with his clients. After a long winter, he waited patiently and expectantly for the cheque in the mail. He must have been owed a lot of money come the end of July. Joy Rankin remembers:

He would send us broken biscuits and not charge us for them.

Every Friday morning, Peg would ring through to the grocery store with her order. If by some chance the phones were out of action or Peg was away, Jimmy would just second guess the order and send it through as per normal. If he didn't have in stock what was ordered, he would send the next best thing. When Peg rang and when the phone was picked up at the other end, she would begin with these or similar words: 'My order please, Mr Rees.' She would have started saying that as a young mother in the 1940s, and he was given the title of Mr Rees until the very last grocery order in January 1976. For thirty years, it was part of Peg's ritual every Friday to put her grocery order in before the delivery that afternoon.

When Peg and Jack left Fumina, one of the last things they did was to visit Jimmy Rees and personally thank him for his generosity, loyalty and trust. Life would have been vastly different for the Rankin family without his ongoing generosity.

J.L. Rees' General Store in Hill End.

Peg was a real marvel when it came to food. Some children in the hamlet of Fumina would have gone hungry from time to time, but Peg always found a way of feeding her brood. She was resourceful, knew how to utilise any ingredients she had, and could whip something up quickly. She taught herself to cook through trial and error. She had come a long way since Jack mocked her when he came in from the farm and saw her with a cookery book following recipes – one of the best things her mother gave her was a really decent cookery book. Because there was a main grocery delivery only once a week, she had to follow the Boy Scout motto and always be prepared. Visitors were given a hearty welcome with freshly made scones or a cream sponge whipped up in no time, Peg all the while engaging with her visitors. Occasionally visitors would drop by unannounced, and if it was close to mealtime Peg would offer them some of her wares. Anne remembers:

> There was a time when Mum baked her own bread, made her own butter, worked the meat through a mincer, had a few chooks and home grown vegies. Visitors would occasionally pop in, sometimes from Willow Grove, Hill End area, sometimes relatives of neighbours, relatives of the Kealys, Gillespies, maybe friends of the Mitchells or the Webbs. They would be given a warm welcome and offered some country hospitality. We were thirteen miles from the nearest milk bar so you couldn't just pop down the street and get an extra loaf of bread or a few vegies. Not that the visitors would have been

expecting much, but Mum was quite amazing with food and could quickly size up what was in the cupboard/cooler needed to rustle up a decent meal. Anyway in no time on this one particular day Mum had whipped up a hearty meal with fresh bread, meats, salads etc, for a sizeable group of guests. They would not have been expecting a gourmet meal, perhaps a cup of tea and a biscuit, but they sat down to a really high quality freshly made meal prepared in next to no time. Mum herself was feeling pretty satisfied about what she was able to whip up for her visitors and said something to that effect after the visitors had gone and it was at this point that Dad piped up, 'But there were no spuds!' This little incident says a lot about both Peg and Jack.

Terry recalls that Mum always did her best to deck us out properly if she was able. Neighbours noticed how nicely the Rankin children were dressed for special occasions like the reception of sacraments, such as First Communion and Confirmation. She knitted with quality wool. She didn't buy the cheapest clothes. She wanted her children to look nice.

Mary Horan, a neighbour from Icy Creek who was about the same age as Herb, would often hear her own mother Phyllis comment on this:

Mum would always admire Mrs Rankin (Peg) for whoever was making their First Communion, or whoever was being Confirmed, everyone seemed to get new clothes for the occasion. That was easy enough when you only have a small family, but Peg had a brood to clothe.

Monday was often washing day. Peg boiled the clothes and nappies on the stove, and that really helped to keep them nice and white.

Frankie Hoffbauer was a travelling clothes salesman. He had a little green van and would travel through country Victoria selling clothes to people who lived in far-flung places. He was a regular visitor to Fumina right up until the 1970s. His father came to Fumina before him. Fumina folklore has it that Frankie Hoffbauer senior used to buy rabbit skins off the farmers, and in turn sell them to a furrier. Skins would have been used for coats and making Akubra hats. Joy Rankin tells the story:

One time he apparently fleeced Katie Rankin in what was considered an unfair price for the rabbit skins. The next time he visited Fumina, Bert Rankin who attempted to get fair recompense from the previous visit was not having any success. In a moment of exasperation Bert apparently ventured to the back of the van, grabbed a pair of trousers and he and Frankie became involved in a tug of war for this pair of slacks, and after an intense battle the trousers ripped in half and they are both left holding one leg of the trouser pants each! Rankin children remember Frankie's visits. He would rattle off what clothes he had in the back of his van. Peg usually bought workpants and the occasional pair of boots for Jack

as well as clothes for herself and the children. He had good
quality clothing in his little van. After some small talk and
concluding his transactions he would depart to visit the next
family, usually saying, 'Time is money.'

The district had its fair share of alcoholics and lonely men. Often lonely, broken men were guests at dinner or simply visited. In the early 1950s one of these men, Paddy Kane, came over to visit the Rankins from nearby Vesper. He lived on his own and supported himself through 'picking up spuds' and general farm work. Paddy Kane was a mad Irishman, but a generous man; the demon drink had taken a stranglehold on him. His one loyal friend was a big white Alsatian dog which accompanied him everywhere. By that stage Peg and Jack probably had five or six kids, all under the age of eight – Anne, Terry, Kevin and Tim, Barry and possibly Gerardine. On one visit to Fumina, Paddy's Alsatian dog mauled Terry quite badly. Terry, only a youngster at this stage, was scratched and bruised and his face was a sea of red. He carries marks on his face from that incident to this day.

Paddy was mortified when he saw what his beloved Alsatian had done to the 'little tacker'. He quickly took out a ten-pound note and offered it to Peg by way of compensation, to pay for any medical expenses and so on. At that time it would have been the equivalent of a couple of weeks' wages for the average person. Peg refused the offer, but Paddy was quite insistent that she take the money. Peg was just as strong-willed in her reluctance to accept the offer. In a moment of exasperation, Paddy apparently said to

Peg, 'If you don't take the money, I will bloody well throw it into the fire.' It seems that Peg wasn't going to budge, so in a rush of madness Paddy threw the tenner into the blazing open fire!

Peg has the capacity to blot out disappointments, unfortunate experiences, setbacks, frustrations. Letting the bad things that happen wash off her has been one of her many coping mechanisms. When she was asked for her recollections of this incident, she remembered Paddy Kane and his dog, and when it bit Terry, but not the money aspect of the story.

Photo taken inside Peg and Jack's lounge room, 1950s.

Peg had a vivid recollection of a very frightening incident of a different kind:

It was quite early on in the piece. Dad (Jack) was worried about white ants. To prevent the problem exacerbating, he had a potion of arsenic and treacle which he kept in a tin. He would wipe the timber with it to prevent the spread of white ants. I deliberately put the tin what I thought would be high enough, out of harm's way from the children. I was having a nap one afternoon as we had had a late night the night before, and thought that the tin of arsenic was well out of Terry's reach. I panicked when I woke from a short nap and found a chair positioned near the table and discovered the tin of arsenic and treacle on the table. Terry, it seems, was unable to open the lid. If that was not scary enough, there was a further twist in the tale. Many years later I discovered Gerardine and Bernard had got hold of the same tin and taken it outside and were seated in a grassed area not far from the house, this time with the lid off. Talk about panic. Maybe they had tasted it. It would not have tasted very nice. They would not have come back for seconds. I remember seeing some white powder around one of the toddler's mouths. Neither of them had enough poison to do any damage, if indeed they had tasted it. That arsenic tin would never see the light of day again. I well and truly buried it in the ground.

Guy Fawkes night, as it was called then, was a social highlight on the yearly calendar, and Tim had many memories of it:

> It can be stated that Mother really did seem to enjoy the bonfire night. In the 1950s the bonfires were usually built at Eric and Linda's place and out the front between their house and the road. Usually they would take a week or so to build. Jack and Peg's tribe would also pick up bits of wood and twigs on the roadside and toss them on the pile on their way to and from school. There are stories of Ron Potter stealing his father's car to go and get wood for the fire. One year apparently there was a fire at Mrs Sulcas' mailbox site instead of the usual place at Eric and Linda's. Bert Mitchell, a World War 1 veteran, was not at all fazed by crackers going off under his seat, which was pretty impressive. It was thought it might bring back horrible memories of wartime experience. Mum always seemed to really enjoy bonfire night and was always the one who stood the skyrockets in the beer bottle and lit them. From memory she didn't care much for the standard bungers, but she loved the prettier ones such as the skyrockets and Catherine wheels. Joy, Ian, Lindsay and Janet Rankin would always make an effigy of Guy Fawkes but we were never involved in that. Dad did not care much for bonfire night. We would always get a lecture about it not being right to celebrate someone being burnt at the stake. After our lecture at about dusk we would walk up to the other Rankins' place and the host family would wait for us before they lit the fire. Dad would normally stay at

home. From memory the crackers were always ordered from Jimmy Rees and delivered by the mailman. Cracker night was a bit like Christmas, on reflection, as there was never much money about but we never missed out.

Ian Rankin adds to the mix:

It was such fun everyone would come, and they would have a bundle of firecrackers and skyrockets. I have to say it was a miracle that no-one got hurt. We would spend weeks and weeks before the event collecting firewood to build the bonfire and it would end up being more than six feet (two metres) high. Guy Fawkes was made out of a few branches of wood and then dressed in old clothes. The whole lot would burn with great gusto.

Community cooperation was everything in Fumina. There was a definite bond between families. Lindsay Rankin captures something pretty special in the intertwining of families with one another:

It was quite amazing really, as a little kid growing up in Fumina. Although the two Rankin families were not related, I always viewed the other Rankin children as my brothers and sisters just because of the way we grew up in Fumina. There was a certain closeness, a certain bond between us. Truly, if I was playing with kids of the other Rankin family and hurt myself, I wouldn't run home to my own mother, I would just go and see Peg and she would patch me up. I had the same attitude towards her as I would my own mother. She would treat me as if I was her own son and that in itself warmed me to that branch of the Rankin family. Bandaging me up after a scrape happened not just once but a few times. The positive feelings towards the other Rankins haven't altered through time; they have stuck with me all my life. Relationships are everything to me and I think very, very fondly of the Rankin family – they are indeed an extension of my own.

The primary school in Fumina had a radio, and so did Eric Rankin and his clan. But Peg and Jack did not have one until the 1950s. Anne recalls how their family got a radio from Leena, a second cousin on the Rankin side:

Leena Britain, a relative of Dad's, gave us a radio, probably in 1954 or 1955. She came to Fumina and discovered these poor people haven't even got a radio. She said I have a lovely radio at home. I wonder who can bring it up to you. She was most insistent.

Herb adds:

It ran with a six-volt battery in the back, with a twelve-inch speaker. We used to charge the battery up at Eric Rankin's.

3UL had the Top 40 every Sunday morning. *Radio Market, Dad and Dave, Tarzan, The Life of Dexter and D24* became part of the lives of the older children.

Terry says:

> We were Argus (newspaper) people. We also had The Weekly Times delivered.

Anne remembers the magazines:

> Grandma (Agnes Hughes) used to send up the Women's Weekly every month or so in a big bundle. Dad always had a dream of writing the National Anthem. There was a competition in the Woman's Day to write the National Anthem so we subscribed to this magazine for a while. Once the contest was over Dad suggested we withdraw our subscription. Mum said she would like to continue with the subscription, which we did. Us kids liked it as it had juicy bits in it like Dorothy Dix.

She also remembers Mrs Potter, a neighbour up the road, who had a different magazine:

> She used to subscribe to True Confessions or some raunchy magazine. I am sure Mrs Potter wanted to educate me in the ways of the world. Mum used to let them in the house. We used to receive copies of this publication with a great deal of relish.

Sometimes the meat and bread were wrapped up in the *Truth* newspaper. Terry remembers an incident around this:

> I asked Mum, 'Why did this man keep this lady in a wardrobe for thirty years?'
>
> Mum asked him, 'Where did you read that?'
>
> 'I saw it in a newspaper which wrapped up the vegies which were delivered to us.'
>
> Mum thought it might have been written in the True Confessions magazine and she may have suggested to Mrs Potter not to hand over these risqué publications anymore.

Christmas was an important occasion. The Fumina School had its Christmas ritual every year. It meant sprucing up the hall, decking out a Christmas tree with ribbons and streamers, and giving presents to all the children. It was a real community event and a highlight of the year. Joy Rankin has vivid memories of Christmas in Fumina:

> Auntie Nell (my father's sister) would be the one delegated to buy Christmas presents. She would have been given a list of the children, their names, ages and gender. She would have been given money to go and buy presents. Nell lived in Ashburton (eastern suburbs of Melbourne) and often went into the Vic Market to buy the presents. She would catch the train into the city and disembark at Flinders Street. It was then a matter of catching a tram up Elizabeth Street, alighting at

Victoria Street and there you are, in one of Melbourne's most famous institutions, Victoria Market. These were the days before shopping trolleys and everything would be carted home in a string bag. We had this Christmas party every December in the school hall. We cut down a tree and decorated it – one of the Dads played Santa Claus. Auntie Nell would get extra fruit and lemonade, you name it. We made ourselves sick on Creamy Soda, Ginger Beer etc. My Auntie Nell had a car, a Morris Cowley. The car would be packed to the ceiling with presents. This was quite an ordeal, quite an effort, something she just did. She got presents for all the children. There would have been a meeting or phone call between Lyn and Peg and Mrs Sturtevant and Dorrie Kealy. The school Christmas party was a red letter day in the Fumina social calendar.

Joy Rankin's Aunt Leena Britton, who would bring up Christmas presents for all the Fumina children from Victoria Market.

Linda Rankin, Peg Rankin and Mary McHugh after the
annual Christmas party at Fumina, enjoying an ice cream.

Peg was insistent that her children have presents at Christmas.
There were no birthday presents but Christmas presents were
deemed important. In addition to the presents given out at
the school Christmas gathering, Peg organised presents for her
children on Christmas morning. Other children in the neighbourhood may not have received presents, but to Peg gift-giving
at Christmas was an expression of faith. Children were to share
the joy of God entering humanity and dwelling amongst us with
the receiving of presents. Getting presents for so many was a big
job in itself, and she would have gone shopping for Christmas
with people around the area who had a car. Community members
were so generous. Jack Beale, Foster Potter, Jack Spears, Frank

Horan and others would have driven Peg into Warragul so she could buy the presents for her brood.

By the late 1950s, the Rankin children and others in the hamlet were ready for secondary school. The Education Department had made provision for immediate post-primary opportunities at the Neerim South State School, when it expanded to what would be called Neerim South Higher Elementary School. This catered for students undertaking Forms One, Two and Three. It was all pretty makeshift, with classes in a couple of rooms next to the sports pavilion. However, the teachers weren't trained adequately to teach these classes. Most of the students involved would have sad memories. Anne reflects that her year at Neerim South was the worst educational experience of her life:

> *I worried about my future. I felt I was lagging behind my peers.*

Mary Horan, who was a year or two younger, said:

> *I hated it. The days were so long.*

Terry maintains:

> *The first year was okay as I had companions; after that I was on my own. I haven't good memories of the last two years there. It was as if I was in a broom cupboard. I spent so much time on my own in this pokey little room.*

Schooling at Neerim South meant hours of travel for Peg and Jack's older children, but at least they were able to further their education and remain living with their family.

Neerim South Higher Elementary School excursion, 1961.

In a further note on the temperament of her children, Peg reflected:

> *Tim and Bernard both had sense of justice and fairness. If they reckoned they were right they would stick to their guns. They would both let you know if they thought a situation was unjust. Barry was always careful with his possessions. He was fastidiously tidy. If he was playing with something and it was time for his afternoon nap, he would take that something to*

bed with him. Barry had a loud voice. Gerardine was a good
helper with the younger kids. She was a natural leader. She was
a really good storyteller. Bernard always had a book in his school
bag. He was quite independent. Dennis told us occasionally, 'We
have too much (sic) kids.' He was cheerful and resilient.

By the beginning of 1960, Peg had had ten children in sixteen years, and she was pregnant with her eleventh child. She managed all this without electricity, running water in the kitchen, or any creature comforts whatsoever. Despite these hardships there was always a ready smile, a helping hand to a neighbour in need, and the capacity for work.

One of the strengths of Peg's personality was that she could put the deprivation aside, ride the bumps, forget the setbacks, not focus on what might have been, and deal with the present. She had the knack of moving forward and not dwelling on the past. This trait was most evident when Peg was interviewed for this book. Peg has a really vague memory of when her little brother died as an infant, but her younger sister Mary has a much more vivid memory of this sad occasion. And a reliable source remembers that Peg alighted from the Tanjil Bren bus earlier than she should have, which meant an extra four-kilometre walk with a newborn child – but Peg doesn't remember it at all. She doesn't remember the ten-pound note going into the fire, although she does remember the dog biting Terry. She has been able to block out certain hardships, meanness and deprivation.

Anne put it this way:

She let all the muck go through to the keeper. She let things wash off her, and got on with the next thing. She moved on quickly. She just got over disappointments, all the hardships. When someone was a little bit nasty, she just got on with it. She didn't dwell on it. These were incredible gifts, these gifts of resilience and forgiveness. When she got really angry or hurt, she was able to give a serve when necessary. When this occasionally happened, within a few minutes she had forgotten it. She could have steam coming out her ears, but was quick to get back on an even keel. She was made of extraordinary stuff.

CHAPTER 5

Raising a Family
Part 2: 1960-1975

Babies kept arriving. Kathleen, child number eleven, was born on 27 June 1960. Her birth was quite eventful. Peg tells the story:

> At that time Neerim South Hospital did not have a good reputation. Although it was the closest hospital, I preferred to have my children in Warragul. The Doctors at Neerim South were hopeless and unreliable. The hospital itself and nursing care were good. Kathleen was born in Neerim South Hospital. Foster Potter, a neighbour, took me to Noojee to meet the ambulance which was manned by volunteers. In the process of being transferred from Foster's car to the ambulance there was the realisation that someone had milked the ambulance dry of petrol. It took some time to organise petrol and by

this time Kath was on the way. There was no time to get to Warragul for this birth. Kathleen was on the edge of being born. The contractions had begun.

The best laid plans of mice and men! The way to prolong delivery and slow down the actual birth is to puff and pant. On the twenty-minute trip from Noojee to Neerim South, there was a lot of puffing and panting.

Two gorgeous English nurses were there for Kathleen's delivery. She was born a bit blue and with a long umbilical cord. I could easily have lost her.

Because of this positive experience, Mum had no hesitation in voluntarily going back to Neerim South for Paul's birth two years later.

By 1962 Peg had had twelve children, but there was never a moment when all twelve children were living together in Fumina on a full-time basis. By the time Paul was born on 6 May 1962, Anne was at Kildara Teacher's College in Malvern, and Terry was boarding with his Kealy cousins in Drouin and studying at Drouin High School. In holiday time, all the family would have been home living in a small three-bedroom house.

For some years, a house owned by Peg's brother in-law Jack McHugh was sitting idle about two kilometres away in the north of Fumina. It hadn't been lived in for almost a decade and it was thought at the time that the McHughs owned the house but not the land it was sitting on. Between them, the two Jacks decided to transfer the four-room house to Peg and Jack's place, in effect giving four extra bedrooms for the agreed sum of one hundred pounds. It seems that Jack McHugh never cashed in the cheque, so the only cost incurred was in the relocation. In fact, it cost about the same amount (one hundred and twelve pounds) to transport the house and set it up in its new position on the eastern side of the Rankin farmhouse.

Herb tells a funny story in the lead up to the relocation of the house:

> Logging was taking place up at the back of Fumina. A timber company was transporting a very large bulldozer down the road past our house. Dad decided to stop the truck driver and ask him if he could move the house up the road for him. This was all fine except that Dad had no idea how hard it might be for the truck to stop when he walked out on to the road. He didn't seem to comprehend how difficult it was to pull up a load of twenty ton weight hurtling down the road. Dad had a really impractical side. I am sure the driver must have wondered what he had struck! The upshot was he asked the driver about moving a house and was told to ring Fowlers in Trafalgar.

So Fowlers Home Removal was entrusted to relocate the McHugh's property. In less than a day a group of about ten or so men had dug by hand about fifty holes, placed the fifty concrete posts in the ground, installed the bearers, secured them, relocated the dwelling and laid the building in its new surroundings. Not bad for a days' work! The extra rooms certainly added much needed space to the Rankin home.

The house on the left was relocated from Fumina.

Every one of Peg and Jack's children continued at least part of their secondary education in Neerim South, at Neerim South Higher Elementary School (1960-1962) or Neerim South High School (1963-1975). They were long days, as the school bus came to the front door at 7.25 in the morning and returned at 5.30 in the evening. A smaller bus driven by John Danks transported students from Icy Creek, Vesper and Fumina to the outskirts of Noojee, where they transferred to a larger bus. The larger bus, for most of the time driven by Frankie Fallon, picked up students in Noojee, Nayook, Neerim Junction and Neerim, for the journey to Neerim South.

In its infancy Neerim South High School was the smallest High School in the State of Victoria, but it served the local community well with its sound leadership, quality teaching and engaged learning. Every one of Peg and Jack's children who went there would have at least some positive memories of their education at Neerim South High School.

Installation ceremony of Neerim South High School, 1964.
Gerardine Rankin in the front row, fifth from the left.

With the closure of Fumina Primary School at the beginning of 1960, a downside to the school bus arrangement was that the primary school-aged children living in Fumina had to catch this early bus to Icy Creek School and wait around for an hour and a half before school commenced, and again in the afternoon before the return trip. During this period before and after school, the Rankin children spent time with the Findlays, Flemings and Horans. Once the primary school children alighted at Icy Creek, the little Dodge bus driven by John Danks would head south to Noojee to meet the larger bus bound for Neerim South Higher Elementary school.

Dennis was only five years old and for a time he was leaving home at 7.25 am and returning at 5.30 pm. Peg was obviously concerned about the toll this was taking on her child, and she suggested to Dennis he might take Friday off school. Dennis, however, would not have a bar of that and dutifully and cheerfully readied himself for school each day.

Thankfully, this bus arrangement changed after a year or two. Mr Tom Carse, the local district School Inspector, lobbied the Education Department to fund an additional bus service. He could see the impact this one-bus schedule was having on the smaller children who had to leave their family so early and return home so late. It was duly arranged that a second run to Fumina would pick up the primary school children and take them across to Icy Creek. The bus punctually arrived at 8.30 am and children were home again at 3.50 pm. This proved to be a very satisfactory arrangement, particularly for the younger children.

Danks family. Mrs Pat Danks holding Rodney in her arms,
Norman and Pamela either side of her.Middle row L-R: Glenda,
Gordon and Ronise. Front row L-R: Ernest and Kelvin.

Mr John Danks transported school children from Fumina to
either Icy Creek or Noojee for more than twenty-five years. This
was the first bus he used. His son Gordon (centre) continued
the service after his father retired (photo early 1960s).

The local school hall was the venue for the Icy Creek Primary
School until 1963. Toward the end of that year, a new purpose-
built school building was transported to a site about seventy-five
metres to the north-west of the hall. This more functional
building served the Icy Creek district for thirteen years.

Max White stands out as the best teacher on this site. He
taught there in 1965. In his first year in 1967, Eric Barton was

most dedicated. In vogue at this time was the setting up of parent bodies to assist parental involvement in the education of their children. Peg served on the school committee in the mid-1960s.

The school closed at the beginning of 1977 due to insufficient enrolment numbers to warrant a school. The school building was relocated to another area and from that time any primary school students in the Icy Creek, Vesper, Fumina district attended Noojee Primary School. Peg and Jack's youngest child Paul completed Year Six in 1973.

The NEW GUARDIAN, Tues., Dec. 24, '63.—Page 13.

MEMBERS OF ICY CREEK SCHOOL COMMITTEE.
Left to right : Mr Geo. McDougal of Vesper, Mr Geo. Findlay (president), Mrs J. Rankin of Fumina, Mr John Danks of Vesper, Mrs R. Turner (secretary and treasurer), Messrs P. Brock, F. Findlay and F. Horan.

There is no doubt that Peg and Jack valued education. They were united in giving their children the best education they could offer them. Peg would have liked to continue her own education when she was awarded a scholarship at the end of Year Eight at Silvan School, but family circumstances prevented her from fulfilling her early dreams of becoming a teacher. With all the limitations of a primary education in Fumina, Jack found himself at St Kevin's Christian Brothers College in Toorak for some time. To his credit, he passed the Intermediate external examinations. He had a desire to become a priest and his aunt, Annie Regan, gave him board and lodging and paid for his school fees. None of his siblings were given the opportunity of secondary schooling.

In deciding what was best for their children in their later years of secondary education, Peg and Jack didn't have the attitude that one size fits all. Options depended on the child's needs, family circumstances and what was realistically available at the time. Of their twelve children, ten had at least two years, if not more, of Catholic education, and eight attended boarding schools in various places across Victoria including Sunbury, Sale, Lilydale and Ballarat. The eldest three children stayed with relatives to continue their education in a variety of locations. Peg always took charge of determining who went where and when, and Jack fully supported her in whatever was decided.

Tim at boarding school, Rupertswood, Sunbury, leaning
on his cousin Michael McFadden, 1965. Ten of the twelve
Rankin children spent some time at a Catholic school.

Peg's day began around 5.30 am. At her busiest, she made eight
school lunches each morning, including one for her nephew
Michael McFadden, who stayed with the family from time to
time. After preparing the lunches, Peg's routine was to round
up the cows for milking and start the milking. Often she would
return to the house to ensure everyone was up and ready for
school, especially those catching the early bus. She recalls that:

All the children were pretty good at getting out of bed except for Gerardine. Barry sometimes had the task of getting Gerardine on the move.

Some sort of drama was never far away. Bernard was probably only about six years old when Mary came close to death. He tells the story:

Mary was only small; from memory she would have been about two or three years old. We kept drums of petrol and kerosene in the timber shed at the rear of the house. It was common on the farm to leave a hose hanging from the 44-gallon drum of petrol for syphoning purposes. On this particular day, a drum was sitting on the ground outside the shed with hose inserted. I remember I was outside playing with one or other of the siblings, and when I was coming around the back corner I saw Mary sucking on the hose. She had obviously swallowed a significant amount of petrol, had turned blue in the face and was gagging. The kids all screamed for Mum, who came running outside. As I recall it, Peg rang the local doctor at Neerim South, Dr Burles, and got instructions as what to do. My memory is Mum had to induce vomiting to get the petrol out of Mary's stomach. Peg got a terrible fright and wept with the stress of it all. We were all locked out of the house for some time whilst Mum had a good cry and composed herself.

Mary tells a great story of her childhood:

When I was four years old and my brother Dennis was six, we were keen to get a fire going outside. We had seen Dad and Mum doing the burning off and thought this could be a fun thing to do though we knew it was naughty. I was not able to reach the matches so Dennis kindly got them down for us. Matches in hand we excitedly wandered down to the back of the yard to the roadside, where there was quite a high embankment and some good grass and bushes.

There Dennis and I got our fire going. We were really chuffed with ourselves because there was an embankment, no one could see us, no one would know. We got ourselves a great little grass fire going not too far from bushes and bushland across the road!

Before long our mother came hurtling along with chaff bags and was running around frantically to put the fire out. Once the job was done she quietly took us back to the house and sat us on the long stool behind the kitchen table.

She then went to the phone and pretended to call Mr Brown, the local policeman, who resided an hour's journey away. 'Oh hello, is that you, Mr Brown? It's Peg Rankin here from Fumina. I'm afraid, Mr Brown, I have two very naughty children here who started a fire and it could so easily have got out of control and caused a large bushfire. Thankfully, Mr Brown, we were able to contain the fire.'

We sat there – I am sure white-faced. Then we heard Mum

say, 'No, Mr Brown, please don't come and get them and take them away; they are usually good children and I'm sure they won't light a fire outside again... Yes, Mr Brown, I'm sure... Thank you, Mr Brown...'

The next day Dennis and I were playing on the front veranda of our home and who should show up but Mr Brown the policeman!

Dennis and Mary, culprits in starting a fire in Fumina.

We couldn't run as he would see us! So we quickly made our way and hid behind an old sofa lounge sitting on the veranda! We crouched down like a pair of little criminals while Mr Brown knocked on the front door. We seriously thought he was going to take us away.

Thank God Mum opened the door to let Mr Brown in, and as soon he was safely inside we bolted as fast as our little legs could carry us down the road where we hid in bushland and there we stayed until we heard Mr Brown's car move off.

Well, we found out later that Mr Brown only visited the house once a year to do the annual cattle census and it just so happened this was the day! Good on you, Mum, we didn't light another fire!

After Jack had the serious stomach operation in 1964, he was never quite the same again. There is an old saying, that 'when the going gets tough, the tough get going'. Peg was amazing at adapting to new situations and never seemed to play the 'poor me' card. 1964 was a difficult year for her. Her mother died, Jack had his operation, and her sister-in-law Dorrie Kealy passed away. But as in other times in her life, she didn't brood. She simply stepped up to the plate, saw what was needed, and responded accordingly. Those that know Peg well must admit that she is an extraordinarily resilient person.

Bernard remembers more drama!

It was a night during the school year when Mum was out. I believe it was prior to Tim going off to Rupertswood (boarding school in Sunbury). It was certainly dark. From memory Mum had been into Warragul or somewhere. Tim went out to the shed and had to change the hand pump from the petrol drum to the kerosene drum or vice versa to get fuel for some reason or other. There was no lighting in the shed. Tim struck a match to enable him to see what he was doing. The lit match ignited the residue of petrol on top of the drum which immediately flared up. Dad was in the kitchen, he ran outside, and threw a couple of buckets of water over the flames which managed to extinguish it. Tim ferried the water to him by bucket load. The little kids were alerted by the panic and shouting. I remember standing with Gerardine and Dennis in the old lobby watching Dad throw water over the flames. We were terrified and I remember going back inside. Even though we were young we knew there was a fair chance the drum could blow sky high. If the fuel inside the drum had caught fire, there would have been a terrible explosion. Thankfully the flames were restricted to the fuel on top of the drum. Knowing what I know now, Dad and Tim would not have survived if the drum had gone up. I think someone was looking after the family that night. I was in bed awake when Mum got home. I heard Jack relay what had happened earlier whilst she was out. Peg found it incredible that Jack had stood there and thrown water over the flames. I remember her saying we would have all been out of the house and left the drum to its own devices if she had been home. Peg's pragmatic view was the house and shed were replaceable, and in hindsight she was certainly right.

Some sort of excitement was never too far away. When Gerardine was about eleven, she thought it would be a good idea

to take the 'four littlies' – Mary, Peter, Kathleen and Paul – for a
bit of adventure:

> *As the middle child I felt as though I did a great deal of
> the caring for my four younger siblings. My job was to feed
> them and put them to bed before Mum and Dad came home
> from the cowshed. Not only was it my duty to provide for
> their basic needs but I always felt a sense of responsibility for
> providing fun in an environment where toys were not plen-
> tiful and other kids did not live nearby. I read books each
> night and would often make up scary stories to get us all to
> huddle together. On one such evening in the summer it was
> still too light to put the four little kids to bed so I thought we
> could have a bit more fun outdoors. I found the old pram and
> packed the four kids into it and pushed them around the yard.
> Whilst fun it soon became a bit mundane, so in my wisdom
> I decided to take them to the top of the hill where the joy of
> speed and action would be found. It was a big climb to the top
> of the hill but we all agreed it would be worth it. We finally
> got to the telegraph pole and positioned the pram for take-off
> down the hill. The excitement was palpable, the anticipated
> thrill was there for all to see. 1-2-3, and I let go with a shove
> and a shriek of joy thinking I was about to give them the thrill
> of their lives. My shriek was quickly followed by one from
> Mum who had witnessed the event from the cowshed. She
> could see the danger, the gathering speed and the barbed wire
> fence waiting for them at the bottom of the hill. She cried, 'My*

babies, my babies!' and with that the four kids stood up in the pram and screamed. They also immediately felt the threat of danger and wanted their mother. Of course by standing up, the pram quickly overbalanced and Mum's four babies were thrown out crying and bruised across the paddock.

Mary, all of five at the time, remembers it too:

Our sister Gerardine (Ged) aged ten decided to take the four youngest children aged from 5 years to 1 year on an adventure. She packed us all up and led us up a very steep hill located between the family home and the cowshed. Pete and I, aged 5 and 4, pushed the old pram and Ged carried the baby. At the top of the hill she popped us all in the pram and let us go... except for the baby. We were all going yippeeeeeee, yippppeee and then all of a sudden out of the cowshed we could hear the screams of our mother and see the frantic swaying of her arms as she yelled – my babies my babies! We were suddenly so frightened that we stood up in the pram and started crying and screaming out – MUUUUMMMM!!!!!!!!! – as though we all sensed the near and present danger. As we frantically screamed, the pram overbalanced and tipped over ... we all tumbled out on top of each other ... just moments later and we would have hit the barb wire fence at the bottom of the hill.

A memorable family event in the mid-1960s was the wedding of Peg's sister Carmel to John Fahey from New Zealand on

Saturday 12 February 1966, exactly the same date as Peg and Jack's wedding twenty-two years earlier. Up until 1964, Carmel had devoted her life to working and looking after her mother. Following Agnes' death she went on a holiday to New Zealand and met her beloved John. The wedding took place at St Ita's Church in Drouin.

This was John Fahey's first trip to Australia, although he had met many Aussies when he lived in Fiji. Kathleen and her cousin Therese McHugh were flower girls. Reminiscing on the 30th anniversary of their wedding, John Fahey wrote:

> *Who had ever seen the twelve Rankin children dressed up in their finery and looking the part. What an effort it must have been for Peg and Jack to get the cows milked, kids fed, everyone to be washed, hair groomed, shoes polished and to get to the Church on time. Not an angry word was spoken.*

1966 was a memorable year. Australia's longest-serving Prime Minister retired in January. The six o'clock swill was abandoned with the extension of opening hours for hotels. Two days after Carmel and John's wedding, decimal currency was introduced in Australia. There are only two surviving photographs of Peg and Jack with all their twelve children. This is one of them:

Photo of entire Rankin family taken at the wedding of
Carmel Hughes and John Fahey, 12 February 1966.

Something that made a difference to the family was when Peg acquired her driver's licence, in early 1966. She already she had a car, a Hillman van purchased from Jack's brother Bert, who ran a store in Moe called Rankin's Radio. When Bert upgraded his work van, the Hillman became available for a small purchase price. At all of nineteen years old, Herb was Peg's main driving instructor himself. He was practical, easy-going, and knowledgeable with anything mechanical. Occasionally Ian Rankin, who was a bit older and more experienced, also helped teach Peg to drive, and Peg practised driving on her own in Fumina. Herb recalls:

I showed her the very basics, had a few lessons with her and she pretty much taught herself by driving up and down the roads around Fumina.

When it came to the practical driving test itself, Alice Spears (neighbour and Herb's future mother-in-law) accompanied Peg. During the test, there were three people in the front seat – Peg, Alice Spears and the local policeman, Mr Brown. Peg remembers it well:

I got my licence in the Hillman van. Mr Brown asked me to drive out towards Neerim. We didn't go very far and when I was in the process of turning the car around to return, it stalled. Mr Brown didn't seem too fazed and actually compli-mented me on my driving! I now had my licence.

On the same day Peg picked up her sister Gwyn from the bus at Noojee. Gwyn joked that 'she was putting her life on the line' with Peg at the helm. They arrived safely back at the farm. The car and her new licence gave Peg more freedom, opened up further possibilities, and enabled her to engage more easily with the outside world.

Peg's first car, the Hillman van. She acquired her licence driving this car. L-R: Tim, Gerardine, Peg and Jack, 1968.

Gerardine remembers one of the first serious tests of Peg's driving ability, the two-and-a-half-hour drive to Sale when she commenced boarding school at the Convent of Our Lady of Sion at the beginning of 1967:

> I had just completed year nine and was about to commence my three years at Sion College in Sale. I will always remember that Christmas holiday as it was a lovely warm summer and we all seemed to be home. I recall doing house chores together where we cleaned and painted walls. Tim caught rabbits and we cooked them and we all worked on bringing in the hay.

This time the cleaning and house sprucing was for our plea-sure and not because Auntie Carmel was about to visit. We were really happy in each other's company and Mum thrived on having her teenage children around. We talked about all the important things in life and shared our thoughts on family, relationships, ambitions, values, behaviour and most prob-ably religion. Our connection to each other during this time deepened and was enriched by our shared time. This lovely point in time ended as I headed off with great trepidation to boarding school. After sorting out the books and uniform, my case was packed and Mum drove me to Sale in the little Rankin van. She walked me into the convent, an enormous cold building where we were met by one of the nuns. After settling me in it was time to say farewell. My heart broke as she drove away not daring to look back, as she too shared my grief but knowing that any display of emotion would only make things tougher.

Electricity came to the Icy Creek district in November 1967. It was probably about five years from the time it was mooted to its actual installation. Brothers Jack and Pat Spears, both farmers in Vesper, were the main protagonists who lobbied the local Council for the installation of electricity. There was a commu-nity meeting organised at some stage at the Icy Creek Hall to gauge the level of local support, and each household had to commit to about two hundred dollars for the installation of elec-tric power (SEC). That was a lot of money at the time but locals could clearly see the benefits. Nearly every family rallied around to support this planned infrastructure development for the local district, and they were committed to the payment of the upfront fee. People could see the potential for a marked improvement in the quality of their lives and the possibility for more modern farming techniques with the introduction of electricity.

Working bees were organised to clear the proposed line, helped by George Findlay, a local contractor and resident who owned a bulldozer. The community really got in behind the scheme. Jack Rankin was one of the few folk who was not so enthusiastic about this development. Unlike the others, he couldn't foresee the benefits to come through with this progress. Peg remembers:

> *Jack could not share the excitement. I was frustrated that Dad didn't get in behind this exciting development in the district. He was not that one bit interested in getting the power on. I remember two or three days of not speaking to him, giving him the silent treatment because of his lack of enthusiasm for this significant improvement in our daily lives. For children, it was an exciting time coming home and turning lights on at night. One day Paul, who was only five at the time, ran over to the cowshed and asked, 'Can we put the SEC on?' He simply meant a light switch but for weeks and possibly months he had heard about the SEC power coming to the house and it was approaching dark so this was his way of asking if he could turn on a light switch.*

SEC Power comes to Icy Creek, Vesper, Fumina

Icy Creek's oldest resident, Mr L. Green, had the honor of cutting the ribbon that switched on the electric power for the Icy Creek, Fumina and Vesper areas on Saturday night.

The ceremony took place in the Icy Creek hall, which was filled to overflowing, and among the distinguished guests present were the Minister for Fuel and Power, Mr J. C. M. Balfour, MLA, the Hon. H. A. Hewson, MLC, Mr I. McGowan, electrical sales engineer, and Mr E. W. Freeman, officer-in-charge of the State Electricity Commission's Warragul area, and Cr H. F. McCay of the Shire of Buln Buln, who made brief speeches in honor of the auspicious occasion.

Rejoicing

Mr Green's cutting of the ribbon also automatically and immediately lit up the Icy Creek Hall and also immediately furnished the much needed power to the many properties in the whole of Icy Creek area, to the great rejoicing of all those present and of all ratepayers and residents of the area.

Chairman of the meeting was Mr George Findlay, president of the district extension committee group, who expressed his and all other area residents' gratitude to the SEC for the realisation and solution of the power problem.

The ceremony concluded, all those present were guests

thorities'

Drouin Guardian, November 21, 1967.

Saturday, 19 November 1967 was a special night for the local community. It was colloquially dubbed 'The Switch-On'. That night celebrated the installation of electricity with a festive gathering in the Icy Creek hall. Peter was nine years old and remembers it:

The first thing that struck you was all the coloured lights, blue, red, yellow, orange and green, lining the gravel path between the hall and the school and the concrete path over to the amenities block. There were coloured lights everywhere.

I had never seen anything like it. And when you walked into the hall itself, it was a sea of fluorescent light. I was so used to seeing it so dark and dingy. It was a balmy November evening and spirits were high. The mood was so festive and celebratory. Community elder Mr Les Green, whose father was one of the early pioneers who had come to Vesper in 1894, was invited to cut the ribbon, a symbolic gesture of electricity coming into the district.

As the years rolled by, more and more electrical appliances and creature comforts were seen in the Rankin house. Very soon after the power was installed, a good-sized second-hand black and white TV was donated by relatives. This opened up a new world of entertainment. *Hunter, Homicide* and later *Division Four* became compulsory viewing, along with news and current affairs programs. Children were not allowed to watch *Coronation Street* and *Peyton Place*.

Herb was working with the PMG (now Telstra), and very generously brought home a new washing machine, an electric iron and an electric frying pan. Later Peg and Jack purchased a large freezer. Tim, who began his teaching career in 1970, paid for a large 10,000-gallon concrete water tank, and water was pumped to it from a nearby spring. Barry became a fully qualified carpenter and revamped the kitchen with a combustion stove and a sink with hot and cold water, and built a proper bathroom with shower, bath and a flush toilet. Things were really looking up in the Rankin homestead with these new amenities.

Most of the Rankin children who went to Icy Creek Primary School had an opportunity to go to a school camp toward the end of Grade Six. The two main places for the camps were the Lord Mayor's Camp in Portsea and the Lord Mayor's Camp in Somers on Westernport Bay. Peter recalls:

In 1969 I was in my last year at Icy Creek Primary school. As was the practice for a few years, the kids in Grade 6 often went on a camp towards the end of the year. Along with David Brock, Ron McDougall, Ernest Danks and Brenda Fleming we all spent nearly two weeks at Lord Mayor's Camp at Portsea. It was a great two weeks. There were new friends to make, new games to learn, there was a cruise out to Bass Strait, and generally a lot of fun, but also a bit of homesickness too. At the same time in Icy Creek there was some quite serious vandalism had taken place the weeks before the camp. A beautiful early twentieth-century piano had been lent by the Green family to the Icy Creek school hall to be used at dances, local functions and piano tuition. The piano was seriously vandalised. It had 'frilly bits' above the keyboard and near the pedals. In a few moments of thoughtlessness but no maliciousness, myself and a couple of others punched and kicked all the frilly bits in. It was done really without thinking, but certainly a careless action. Through other eyewitnesses, my name had been bandied around as one of the culprits. After Mum and Dad had been informed of my misdemeanour, and not being at home to face up to the music, I received a letter from my good mother. In the letter she mentions some local news, some family information and hoping I was having a really good time. Quite deliberately on her part no mention was made of the vandalised piano in her letter. To me this was prudent parenting. Why spoil a good holiday for a thoughtless son? Why have her son fretting about the consequences of a bad choice whilst he is away enjoying a rare opportunity? Why not wait and deal with the matter when he returns? If I remember rightly, I had to write a letter of apology to the Green family when I returned from Portsea. Personally, I think Mum read the situation well and her reaction was the right one. To me this was an example of good parenting.

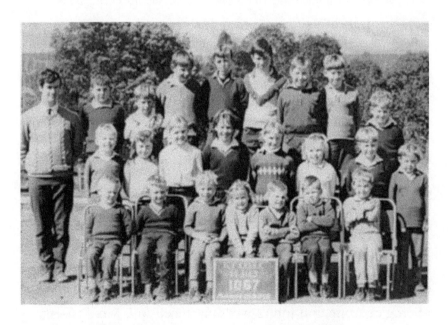

Mr Eric Barton and Icy Creek Primary School students, 1967.

In the early 1970s Mary became really close friends with Anne-Maree Gleeson. They later went to boarding school together. Anne-Maree would occasionally babysit children from the Pruser family and one time, Mary accompanied her. The Pruser children accused Mary of stealing a watch. Jack approached Mary, not in an accusative fashion, with the question: 'Did you take the watch, little Therese?' (Jack often called Mary Little Therese, Therese being her second name). Peg remembered the question and Mary's response:

> Mary responded, almost spitting the words out of her mouth: 'Thanks, Jack, for having that much confidence in me.' It was an unpleasant time. The mother would have frightened the children and ranted and raved as to the whereabouts of the watch. In the end they blamed this little girl from the bush. Mary was churned up about it. Afterwards the watch was found whilst they were stripping the bed. Mr Pruser rang me and told me they found the watch.

There is an interesting sequel to this. The mother of the children who made the initial complaint was an accomplished singer. Not that long after this incident, on 30 June 1973, Anne married John Schmid at St Ignatius Church, Neerim South. At the reception afterwards Mrs Pruser and her band provided the entertainment. When Peg had rung Mrs Pruser and invited her to sing at Anne and John's wedding reception, Mrs Pruser was flabbergasted that Peg would even approach her after accusing

Mary of stealing a watch whilst she was in their home. I think this shows a lot about Peg and her capacity for forgiveness and moving on. Not everybody can do that.

Not only were Mary and Anne-Maree Gleeson close friends, their two mothers shared a special friendship in the 1970s. Joan Gleeson reflected on her friendship with Peg:

> *Although I had known Peg for some time, we really didn't form a friendship until our daughters, Annie and Mary, started in Year 7 at the Neerim South High School. As the girls became very good friends, so the friendship between Peg and I developed. As mothers of large families we had much in common to feed our relationship.*
>
> *Peg was a bit older than me so I looked up to her as a source of wisdom and commonsense, as well as her down-to-earth attitude to life, which suited my outlook on life as well. Peg was always a cheerful soul, although it could not have been an easy life farming at Fumina and often isolated from reliable transport.*
>
> *When our girls got older, the High School was unable to provide the education at the senior levels, and so Peg and I decided to send them to the Lilydale Convent of Mercy to board from Monday to Friday, coming home each weekend. We shared the task of taking them to and from Lilydale on Friday afternoons and Monday mornings, meeting down on the Noojee Road to pick up or drop off the girls, always depending on whose car was available at any given time.*

For a few years in the early 1970s we ran the milk bar at Neerim South. Days off were rare as we opened every day of the year except Christmas Day, half of Boxing Day and Good Friday. Sometimes we would take the opportunity of a day off to drive up the mountain to visit the Rankins. It was always a great day as our mob was made very welcome and joined in the madcap antics of the Rankin mob.

Both the Rankin family and the Gleeson family can be jokingly scathing about the capacity Peg and I have to talk nonstop for a couple of hours when we get together. We are usually on the same wavelength regarding current affairs, have ever-growing and extending families, and are both very keen AFL Bombers supporters, so we always have plenty of ammunition to keep us going for hours. We are both, after all, champion talkers! I have always considered Peg not only a friend, but also a mentor. Her family is a credit to both her and her late husband Jack.

I don't see much of her since she has moved to the suburbs, but we can still talk up a storm whenever we are lucky enough to have the opportunity.

In the 1940s and 1950s there was a lot of community harmony in the hamlet of Fumina, with very little tension or discord amongst the families. The 1960s was a different kettle of fish, as different types of folk settled into the neighbourhood. Peg was accused by a neighbour of having an affair, and was labelled a 'f---ing mole'. In her innocence she had to inquire as to what a mole was. She was also accused of burning a neighbour's house down. There were psychologically unstable neighbours who threatened to kill Peg and Jack, entrenched alcoholics, a suicide, child molestation, and crops of marijuana were being grown. It is amazing that a place the size of Fumina could have had so much scandal and intrigue. In their later years there, Peg and Jack lived right in the midst of it all. This is not fiction. Everything mentioned here was part of Fumina's more sordid recent past.

There is a more positive note about people moving into the neighbourhood. Jack's niece, Kath Kilner, and her husband Ted and family decided it was time for a tree change and moved to Fumina in 1973. Kath reflects:

> *I went to New Zealand for two years and met Ted on board the ship coming home. Ted was serving in the Army and thus began a life of being constantly on the move. So it was only when Ted retired from the Army life twenty years later and wanted to try his hand at farming that quite by chance we ended up back at Fumina and the old farm was for sale.*

Kath had spent her childhood on the farm they now purchased thirty years on. Kath's mother Millie was Jack's younger sister and she and her husband Pat Gilsenan lived in Fumina from the late 1930s until the mid to late 1940s. Kath had met Peg as a thirteen-year-old when Peg came to Fumina during her engagement and stayed with her family.

Kath Kilner remembers:

When we came back to Fumina Ted knew very little about farm life and it was a long time since I had done anything like that, so it was great to have Peg and Jack close by for help and advice. Peg and I shared a lot in those couple of years. Shopping trips to Warragul, driving our children to boarding school, and things like blackberry picking and jam making. Peg was always there at the end of the phone if I needed advice about anything to do with the cows or other aspects of farm activities. She was a great comfort to me and was always ready to drop whatever she was doing if I needed help.

Kath's daughter Kerry spent some time at the Rankins' so she could begin school at the beginning of a new term at Icy Creek Primary School prior to her family moving to Fumina. Kerry writes:

My strongest memory of Aunty Peg is from the few weeks I stayed at her place when I was about twelve, just before Mum and Dad moved to the farm. Alongside memories of so much freedom and fun, I remember lining up with a bunch of other hungry kids, both older and younger than I was, as Aunty Peg sliced bread in a totally unique way! The block of white bread, recently delivered to the mailbox wrapped in tissue paper, was turned on its end, the crust sliced off and the top end spread with rich yellow butter and jam. Then she would horizontally slice off an inch thick piece of bread, butter, and jam ready to eat, proceeding to demolish the rest of the loaf in the same way, slapping on the butter and jam, slicing the bread and handing out sustenance to what seemed like a multitude of kids lined up and waiting for their piece in that warm and homely farm kitchen. There were so many of you!

Aunty Peg was wonderfully accepting of me during those halcyon days. She seemed to radiate warmth and love to all of us. Those years in Fumina were the best of my childhood and inspired me to live in the country as an adult. I often think fondly of Aunty Peg. She was such a pragmatic, sensible woman who just got on with all the work required of running a dairy farm and managing her many, many children. Her humour was always at the surface along with a quick smile and her large laugh. She obviously had the forbearance of the saints, pictures of which adorned the walls of the house. I remember her strong, worker's hands that showed all of the effort she had put into the farm, and all of the kids in her life.

Life hits you for six sometimes. You can't plan some things. Peg and Jack's fifth eldest child, Barry, was killed in a work accident in 1973. As to be expected, this hit the family hard. In 1973, Barry, was a fully qualified carpenter and working on the Upper Thompson Conversion Project, diverting water from the Thompson River to the Yarra River to be dammed further downstream. This project was designed to shore up water supplies for the growing city of Melbourne. Barry's job was to assist in the formwork, lining the tunnel with concrete, etc, to prepare for the water diversion between the two rivers. Inside the tunnel was a locomotive and mini railway track to assist with the transportation of workers, machinery and tools within the tunnel. Barry was working nightshift. His usual boss was not there at the time. It seems he was crushed by the locomotive, and died instantly. The Coroner's Inquest into his death delivered an open finding, indicating there simply was not enough evidence to determine exactly what happened on that fateful night of 11 September 1973.

The news of the accident hit hard. Police came up to the farm and were having some difficulty in finding the place. Luckily a night owl farmer was planting potatoes and directed police to the Rankin farmhouse. It was nearly one in the morning when the knock on the door came, informing Peg and Jack of their son's death. Peg's memory was sharp:

> There was a beautiful moonlight and I could clearly see the police car and the two policemen at the door. I instinctively knew I had lost one of my sons.

Life doesn't stop for anybody. Not even Peg. She didn't go back to bed that night. Cows were milked at the usual time of 6.00 am. Peg maintains:

> Dennis, Jack and I milked the cows as per normal. I don't think we said a word the whole time. Our hearts were filled with sadness. Words weren't much comfort.

Bernard recollects:

When Barry was killed, Peg, as his mother was heartbroken, probably more so than the rest of us. I was working at Ansett Airlines when Anne came in and delivered the news to me. Anne and John Schmid had not long been married. I left work and got into the car with them. Like all of us, I was gutted. I remember we drove to Lilydale and picked Mary up from school who was of course distraught. All the way to Fumina I was dreading to think the state Mum would be in. I knew she was tough, but losing one of her children may have been a bit too much. When we arrived at the farm, Mum was calmly sitting in the dining room talking to the funeral director, making preparation for Barry's funeral. The rest of us were crying. Each time someone turned up, whether it be family, friend or neighbour, the emotional roller coaster would restart. It was a dreadful day; I think all of us would agree it was the saddest day of our lives. Barry was a great fellow and he was really good to Mum. Just before he died, he had built the bathroom, laundry and toilet, to give Mum and the family at home some comforts we had never had previously. All that terrible day Peg was so composed, a small time spent weeping. She was so strong. Only a few years ago I talked to her about it. She said with little kids still at home she had to hold herself together; it was her responsibility to the youngsters in the family. Peg probably never really had a chance to mourn Barry properly. It was never about her; it was always what was best for everyone else.

Gerardine similarly recalls:

We all arrived home at various intervals throughout the day and each time Mum was there to greet us and assess how we were coping. The outpouring of grief was palpable. The enormous sense of loss felt by us all had ripped through our hearts and left us vulnerable with the world as we knew it changed forever. Mum had a special relationship with Barry. They both lived and worked in the local community and Barry had done a great deal to support her by renovating her home and keeping her up-to-date with the local chatter. This loss felt by Mum at the death of Barry was deep, but not always on display – she clearly saw her role as one of support for the rest of the family. However, several months later I witnessed her pain and sadness. We were out visiting and our friends commented on my mother's lovely car. At this point she broke down and informed us all that her darling son Barry had given the car to her.

POPULAR YOUNG MAN KILLED

Whilst working on the afternoon shift on the Upper Thomson tunnel project at 8.45 p.m. last Tuesday, well known Fumina resident Barry James Rankin was fatally injured.

The deceased who was the son of Mr Jack and Mrs Margaret Rankin, was born at Rongoa Private Hospital in Warragul and was educated at the Fumina State School and later at the Neerim South High School.

He subsequently became an apprentice carpenter to Mr Gus Marshall, and on completion of his indentures early this year took up a position with the Upper Thomson tunnel project, working for Atkinson Holland Constructions.

He was an exceedingly popular young man with very high ideals, and for these he was a prime favourite allround. His sad and tragic demise came as a great shock to many.

The genuine high regard in which he was held was shown by the attendance at the funeral on Friday. The Neerim South Catholic Church was packed with friends.

The parish priest, Rev. Fthr. J. Readman officiated at the service and he was assisted by the Rev. Fthr. Walsh, a personal friend of the deceased, who travelled from Cowarr to attend.

In his eulogy to the congregation, Rev. Fthr. Walsh outlined the excellent traits of character which the deceased possessed, stating that in all the years he had known him he had never heard him pass an uncharitable word. He was a boy of great potential for he showed many Christian virtues.

When the sad cortege reached the Warragul Cemetery, it passed through two guards of honour, one of workmates from Atkinson Holland totalling 60 in all who had travelled by bus from Warburton, and the other of sisters and students from the Lilydale Convent girls' school where the deceased's sister Mary is a scholar.

The coffin-bearers were four of the late young man's brothers—Tim, Kevin, Terry and Bernard.

The deepest sympathy of a large circle of friends is extended to the bereaved parents and their family of seven boys and four girls on their sudden and irreparable loss.

Rev. Fthr. Readman read the last sad rites at the graveside, and the mortuary arrangements were in the hands of Messrs Nielsen and Handley of Warragul.

Warragul Gazette, 22 September 1973.

General Montgomery defined leadership as 'the capacity and the will to rally men and women to a common person and the character which inspires confidence'. This was Peg. She was able to size up a situation and respond accordingly. With Barry's death she had to draw on inner reserves of strength and be there for others. She could also lean on people when necessary. She was good at getting her children to buy into a project or task. Whether it was fixing a neighbour's car, all hands on deck for hay carting, a working bee painting the house or sprucing it up, she had the ability to gather the troops.

Tim writes:

> *One thing I would like to say about our dear mother is her ability to get any and all of us to help her when she needed assistance of any kind. This happened in Fumina and later. If she needed us to help her on the farm in any way, she was able to cajole us to comply with her wishes. She went about it in such a way that you could not refuse and actually felt good doing whatever it was she wanted. She was generous in her praise and made us all feel important and very good about ourselves.*

Peg's parenting style was firm and consistent, giving space for growth. She didn't readily tolerate unnecessary weakness, and she loathed her children being 'sooks'. If a child was crying for what she thought was insufficient reason she would say, 'Oh, dry up.' Often enough when it came to children asking for permission for something, she would tell them to 'ask your father' and

Mary, Peter, Kathleen and Paul were dubbed 'the four littlies' by older siblings. There is a two-and-a-half-year gap between Dennis and Mary, so in age there was bit of separation. Peg had a special bonding with the four younger children, and described her four youngest in the following way:

> *Mary is extroverted, she would never walk past anyone who needed her, she was always cheerful. As a child we crossed swords a few times. Sometimes you might rouse Kathleen or Peter and it was like water off a duck's back. Mary was a different kettle of fish. However, she was bright and on the go. Peter was timid, needed assurance. Kathleen was an easy child to manage, she didn't easily get into a tiss. She could hit the nail on the head. When she was about twelve she said to me, 'You're mostly a happy mum, but when you get tired, you can get a bit cranky.' Not a truer word spoken. Paul was a bit of a misery guts. He cried a lot. He followed me around a lot as a kid. He developed self-confidence over time.*

By the end of 1975 there was light at the end of the tunnel for Peg and Jack. Their days of formal parenting were slowly drawing to a close. Peg's brother-in-law Jack McHugh had perceptively described their parenting style as 'giving their children enough rope, but not enough to hang themselves'. Their tenth child, Peter, had just finished HSC at boarding school in Sunbury. Kathleen and Paul were the only two children left on their hands. They had just finished four and two years respectively at Neerim

South High School. For Peg and Jack's youngest they were happy years, both educationally and socially.

But change was afoot. The curtain was being drawn on Fumina. Peg and Jack decided to sell the farm and move into the town of Warragul. A new chapter in their lives was about to take place. And these were to be good years for both of them.

CHAPTER 6

Keeping the Flame
of Faith Alive

PEG AND JACK both had strong Catholic faith. It was ingrained into the fibre of their beings, but they came to faith from different angles.

Jack had the exemplary witness of both his parents. He was also instructed in the faith by his religious education teacher, Larry Power. His mother was a cradle Catholic and inherited a lively faith from her own parents, who came from Ireland. One of the reasons Kate wanted to leave Fumina was so that she could attend Mass more frequently. In Fumina, it was celebrated once a year at most. Jack's father was steeped in Christianity. Herb loved the scriptures. He also loved Kate and converted from Anglicanism to marry her in the Catholic Church. These two were a formidable pair in passing on the faith to their children. All of their offspring treasured their Catholic heritage.

Peg, too, had the example of her own mother. She also attributed a lot to the nuns who taught her at St Patrick's in Lilydale in 1936-1937. The current ritual for infant baptism includes the practice where one of the godparents lights the Baptismal candle from the Easter candle, and the following words are addressed to the parents and godparents:

> *This light is entrusted to you to be kept burning brightly. These children of yours have been enlightened by Christ. They are to walk always as children of the light. May they keep the flame of faith alive in their hearts.*[20]

Peg and Jack together made every endeavour 'to keep the flame of faith alive' for their children by word and example. Peg usually had each child baptised as soon as possible after their birth, and before she returned to Fumina.

In that era, it was normal practice for a child to be baptised fairly soon after their birth. It is written in John's Gospel Ch 3 v 5 that 'unless one is born through water and the Spirit he/she cannot enter the kingdom of God'. This text mesmerised Christians for centuries. It seems to suggest that if a child/adult was not baptised and died, there is no possibility for that particular child to enter the kingdom of heaven.

In the fourth century, St Augustine grappled with this text. In fidelity to the scriptural text, he concluded that if the child

---

20　*The Rite of Baptism for Children*, p.29.

was unbaptised and died, he/she would not be admitted into the kingdom of God. However, for him, the child couldn't be consigned to hell as they had committed no personal sin, and so he devised a theology of limbo. Put succinctly, limbo was considered to be an in-between state for infants dying without the sacrament of Baptism who suffer the pain of loss, but not the pain of sense. It was understood that the child might not see God face to face, but would nevertheless be in a state of natural happiness.

To ensure their children had the gates of heaven opened to them, until quite recently parents rushed to have their babies baptised so they could be admitted into the fullness of the kingdom, if by any chance they died prematurely or in infancy. Peg had all her children baptised as soon as it was possible.

Passing on the faith was no simple matter. Initially at least, there was no opportunity to attend Mass. The local church was more than twenty miles away and there was no possibility of a Catholic education as they lived too far from a Catholic school. The Church, however, has always considered that parents are the primary educators of their children in the ways of faith, and Catholic schools, clergy, religious or lay teachers play a secondary role to parents.

Peg and Jack witnessed strong Christian convictions to all their children. The existence of God and the love of God was as real to them as the winter cold and the cows in the paddocks. Their combined faith was solid as a rock. Peg and Jack taught their children prayers, and they spoke about religion in their home. There was always a Bible nearby. They exercised Christian charity and they put into practice what they believed.

In the early 1950s, Fr O'Hea from Warragul thought Peg and Jack's eldest two children would benefit from the teaching of the Sisters in Warragul for one week, in preparation for their First Holy Communion. For this faith formation experience, it was arranged that they would live with Phyllis and Joe Malady in the town, and attend classes at St Joseph's school. The two youngsters had come out of the less formal, much smaller one-teacher Fumina state school.

Here are Anne's reflections on the experience:

> *We went into a combined 2/3 class and Sister had about eighty in her class, three to a desk. She marched up and down the aisles of the classroom with a feather duster in her hand and all that sort of stuff. I sat next to a girl who had come from the State school and the kids teased her and they were still teasing her at St Joseph's. The plan was for the nuns to take Terry and I to Noojee on Saturday for further instruction and preparation for our First Communion. The poor nuns were overworked yet had these extra two children foisted upon them. We were just an additional burden to an overcrowded classroom.*

Terry's memory is less subtle:

> *I reckon it was one of the worst weeks in my life. I thought it was horrible. There was no time for any social acceptance. I was an outcast. I wasn't sure if I was entitled to a bottle*

of milk. All the other kids had a bottle of milk. Maybe they paid for them. Nobody told me anything. I had to sort it out myself. It was absolutely bloody awful.

The story finishes more positively with Anne's recollection:

The nuns then escorted us to Noojee for further instruction to be joined by other children from the district in preparation for First Holy Communion. This was a much more positive experience. The nuns gave us lollies; it was more personal, they asked how you were, how your mother was, and what we did at home and the like. This was an opportunity for the Sisters to get to know these little tackers from the bush. It was very difficult for the nuns to engage us in learning with eighty others in the classroom in Warragul. They would have just seen us as an additional burden. In Noojee they were lovely to us.

The reception of the Sacraments of First Communion and Confirmation was always a big deal. Our Lady of Sion Sisters would come out from Warragul on a Saturday morning to this little timber town of Noojee, to prepare the children of the district. There would have been follow-up in the home. Peg ensured her children dressed nicely for the occasion. Neighbours would assist with transporting children to and from Noojee for their preparation classes. The day of the reception of the Sacraments was a highlight on the religious and social calendar.

Back L-R: Mary Horan, Terry Rankin, Anne Rankin and
Barry Horan. Front L-R: Herb Rankin and Tim Rankin.

One of Anne's childhood memories is of a particular Sunday
morning. Peg was often overheard to say, 'I wish we could go to
Mass.' She might be cooking a Sunday roast and feel the day was
not quite complete, but it just wasn't possible to go to Mass. The
local church was a long way away and the Rankins didn't have a
car. Priests from Warragul were known to take the trek out to
Fumina and celebrate Mass on occasional Saturdays, and this
brought some comfort.

Mass is the central weekly event in the life of a Catholic.
The word itself is derived from the Latin *missa*, which means to
be sent. At the end of Mass everyone is sent to go and live the
gospel. Mass is when the community gathers to hear the Word
of God, to listen to a sermon expounding Christian truths found
in the Word of God for that day, to witness the consecration of
bread and wine, and to receive Communion, to be nourished

and strengthened for service. Peg longed to attend Mass more frequently.

In the ideal world Peg and Jack would have sent their children to Catholic schools to complement the values being taught in the home. That was just not possible, but ten out of the twelve children finished their secondary education in the Catholic school system. The only two children who did not have the benefit of Catholic education were Terry and Barry, and this was for sound reasons – the Marist Brothers school in Warragul finished at Intermediate. When Terry was ready for the Leaving Certificate year he boarded with his relatives the Kealys, and attended Drouin High School. That was a reasonable option for him. By staying with his cousins and attending Drouin High, he learnt more than English, Maths and French – he discovered a great love for the Essendon Football Club, how to put on a bet, and probably an early liking for the amber fluid. At Neerim South High School, Barry had a really good woodwork teacher in Peter De Vries. He excelled in working with wood and went straight from Neerim South High School into a carpentry apprenticeship with local builder Gus Marshall. All the other Rankin children finished off their schooling in Catholic schools.

It should be noted that all of Peg and Jack's offspring who attended Neerim South High school left with positive memories, although some, like Gerardine, would have preferred to continue their education at Neerim South rather than leave home and attend boarding school. An indicator of fond memories was that when the Neerim South High School celebrated its 50th anniversary in 2013, five Rankin children attended the celebrations.

Jack would gather the Catholic youngsters of the area and teach them the Catechism. Sometimes this was on a Friday night, and at other times it was Saturday morning. He let it be known to the local curate (assistant priest of the parish), Fr Hynes, that the children found it difficult to concentrate. Fr Hynes enquired as to how long he talked to the kids. Fr Hynes surmised that in these classes there may not have been much dialogue, but more monologue. Jack responded that he more or less taught the children for about an hour and a half. Fr Hynes is reported to have said, 'Hell, Jack, not even at University do lectures go for that long without a break.' Dan Holland was a student at that time along with Anne and Terry, Barry and Mary Horan, and possibly one or two others. Mary recollects:

> Mr Rankin would teach us catechism around the fireplace. I could not wait for the lesson to end so we could have supper. Mrs Rankin would have the nicest supper for us, sponges, cream cakes, etc. He was a wonderful teacher, but we would get lots of homework. He would check the homework when we came back the next week. Dad would bring us over. Supper was a highlight.

One particular day Lindsay Rankin got a tough lesson on religion in Fumina, when the idea that all the children were the same and held the same values was thrown out the window.

I learnt a tough lesson one day. A Catholic priest turned up unannounced. Great excitement abounded amongst the Kealys, Rankins and indeed myself. I muscled in and took my place with the children of these families to be taught some religious instruction by the visiting priest. All good. It was only then that Pat Kealy sidled up to me and told me to 'nick off, you are not one of us, you are a Protestant'.

This was my own first clash with sectarianism and it left me hurt and bewildered. I thought we were all the same. I reported the events of the day to my parents. They decided we needed a bit of good old-fashioned religion, so they sent myself and my siblings over to the Sturtevants' for Sunday school. It was led by Mrs Sturtevant. We heard Bible stories, which was all new to me. Doug Connolly (a teacher) would play the violin, we would sing. This was my real introduction into the Christian faith. In hindsight, I wish I had kept my mouth shut because in effect Sunday was the only day I had off and now we were putting on our Sunday best and spending Sunday afternoons at the Sturtevants'. Half a day of a precious weekend time was spent there because I had asked a question!

In 1960, Neerim South High Elementary was putting on a special evening on sex education for the students. The plan was for Anne, Terry and Herb to attend school as normal, attend the session 'on the birds and the bees' in the evening and then stay with Eric and Linda Rankin, who had not that long before moved to a house in Neerim. Herb picks up the story from here:

Mother saw the value in her children attending such an evening for their overall education. We were just about to board the bus that morning and Dad got wind of what his children were about to be part of and intervened forcefully. He forbade his three oldest children from attending this program. He told us it was the parish priest who is the one who is specially trained in these delicate matters. He has special knowledge in this all-important area and he is the one and only one that his children should speak to about such matters.

When Jack felt strongly about something Peg didn't interfere, and she supported him. She would not have been entirely happy with this intervention but she would have gone along with it. When push comes to shove, they were a united front. As a postscript to the incident, Herb says:

It would have been much better if we attended the night firsthand. The playground talk and the commentary with other children who attended the evening the next day wasn't helpful The sniggers and the children's take on it all was not very enlightening.

In 1957 or 1958, when Peg went to Warragul and stayed with Phyllis Malady whilst preparing to have one of her babies, she attended a Parish Mission at St Joseph's Church. The mission preacher really encouraged families to recite the Rosary, with the injunction that 'the family that prays together stays together'.

In one form or another, the Rosary has been an important devotional prayer recited by Catholics since the sixteenth century. The word 'rosary' comes from the Latin *rosarium*, a rose garden. The term was applied to medieval love lyrics, so by extension the Rosary became a love lyric to Mary. Monks in the monasteries of Europe would recite the one hundred and fifty psalms over a week. However, most of the people living around the monasteries couldn't read or write, and were encouraged to pray the Hail Mary 150 times over in a similar time frame. People began to use a rather primitive form of beads attached to a piece of string to keep count of the number of times they had recited the Hail Mary. The short prayer recalls the words of the Angel Gabriel to Mary, as found in the gospel of Luke: *Hail Mary full of grace, the Lord is with you, blessed are you among women and blessed is the fruit of your womb.*

St Dominic Guzman, who preached widely in Southern France, Italy and Spain, was having little success in his mission to bring back into the Christian fold those who strayed. In a vision, he was exhorted to pray the Hail Mary multiple times a day to invoke Mary's help to assist him in his pastoral endeavours, which he duly did. His Marian devotion and the frequent recitation of the Hail Mary ensured hardened souls were being won over to God and returning to the life of the Church. In the middle of the sixteenth century, Pope Pius V is attributed to having composed the second part of the Hail Mary which contains the words: *Holy Mary Mother of God, pray for us sinners now and at the hour of our death. Amen.*

Over time the Rosary prayer was further refined and amplified. Catholics were encouraged to contemplate the joyful, sorrowful and glorious mysteries, each mystery beginning with the Lord's Prayer and followed by ten Hail Marys, which was duly called a decade of the Rosary. Pope Pius IX had a very strong devotion to Mary and when he was on his deathbed, one of the prelates attending him asked what was on his mind in these moments. He answered:

> *Actually I am contemplating the fifteen mysteries of the Rosary depicted on the walls of this room. If you only knew how encouraging they are to me! Considering them is most comforting. Meditating on the joyful mysteries, I forget about my pain. Considering the different phases of the Passion I am greatly heartened, since I tread the path of suffering in the company of Christ who went before me. When I bring the glorious mysteries to mind, I am filled with joy. It is very clear to me that all my pain is being converted into glory. What great solace the Rosary has been on my deathbed!*

In the early years of white settlement in Australia, there were few priests to celebrate Mass and administer the Sacraments, and the recitation of the Rosary was the main devotional practice that kept the flame of faith alive. On Sundays, clusters of families might gather in the one house and possibly hear a passage of scripture, but they would definitely recite the Rosary. Even if you couldn't read much, you could learn the basic prayers of the Rosary off by heart and feel part of the prayer gathering.

Fr Patrick Hartigan (pen name John O'Brien) was a priest who ministered widely in southern New South Wales at the turn of the twentieth century. He wrote some beautiful poetry accurately capturing Catholic life and customs in rural Australia in that period of our history. In a poem entitled *The Trimmings on the Rosary*, he depicts what was happening in many homes at the time:

> *I can see that little mother still and hear her as she pleads,*
> *'Now it is getting onto bed-time; all you childer get your beads.'*
> *There were no steel-bound conventions in that old slab-dwelling free;*
> *Only this – each night she lined us up to say the Rosary;*
> *E'en the stranger there, who stayed the night upon his journey, knew*
> *He must join the little circle, ay, and take his decade too.*
> *I believe she darkly plotted, when a sinner hove in sight*
> *Who was known to say no prayer at all, to make him stay the night.*
> *Then we'd softly gather round her, and we'd speak in accents low,*
> *And pray like Sainted Dominic so many years ago...*

So when Peg returned from having baby number nine or ten, before the children went to bed, she would gather her brood and instruct them to kneel down and say the Rosary. Initially she would have followed a leaflet, then after a while she would have learnt the entire prayer off by heart. It has been said that for a new behaviour to settle, you need three weeks of daily practice for it to be a successful and ingrained habit.

This new prayer wasn't to become a passing fad, but became an entrenched ritual in the Rankin family. Peg always instigated it and Jack always led. After he introduced each decade of the Rosary and the prayer intention, a different child was assigned to lead that particular decade of the Rosary. Peter recalls:

> I envied my youngest brother Paul. He would be often allocated the first decade and then he could skip off to bed. The older siblings had to endure the whole lot and with the trimmings it would take about twenty minutes. My older sibling Dennis would rush through his Hail Marys and occasionally would be told to slow down. My sister Gerardine was miffed that she was always allocated the intention of praying for purity!

The family that prays together, stays together was the mantra at the time. Peg and Jack obviously couldn't attend Mass on a Sunday, so on most nights Peg gathered her brood to recite the Rosary. Remember, her day started at 5.30 am, so she would have been going all day. Springtime was extra busy on the farm. The cows were at their peak of milk supply, there were calves to feed, weeds had to be controlled during the spring growth, there was extra care of the cattle to prevent bloating. After another full day, Peg was obviously tired. She picks up the story:

> I was wavering in my commitment to pray the Rosary one night. Maybe this was 1970. Bernard and Dennis were in boarding school. It was springtime. I was awfully tired but somehow mustered up the energy to pray the Rosary. I somehow found the strength to get on my knees with Jack and

the children at home. I rationalised to myself that if I wanted Our Lady's protection for my family, I needed to honour her and invoke her maternal blessing. That very night Herbie and six of his drinking mates, all of whom worked in the same Bank in Morwell, were celebrating the birthday of one of them. They all piled into an FC Holden car and drove from Morwell to Walhalla. On the return journey the car careered out of control. No-one would have been wearing seat belts. The car got into a spin and rolled several times. A 17-year-old Dutch boy died in Herbie's arms. The driver also died.

One or two others had serious injuries. Herb escaped with a broken arm and a cut on his head. After this horrific accident, it would have been a skeleton staff in the bank the following morning. Herb was with the PMG (later called Telecom) and the only one of those inside the car who didn't work in the bank. This all happened the same night that Peg was wrestling with whether or not to pray the family Rosary, and she attributed Herb's safety to Our Lady's special intervention and protection.

This incident demonstrates the power of prayer. Prayer has been called turning the mind and heart towards God. Thérèse of Lisieux, the young Carmelite nun who died in 1897, described prayer as follows:

> *... a surge of the heart, it is a simple look towards heaven, it is a cry of recognition and of love, embracing both trial and joy.*

Dietrich Bonhoeffer, a Lutheran pastor who was incinerated at Auschwitz, talked about prayer in these words:

> *It matters little what form of prayer we adopt or how many words we use. What matters is the faith which lays hold on God, knowing that He knows our needs before we even ask Him. That is what gives Christian prayer its boundless confidence and its joyous certainty.*

Peg's prayer life was well grounded. She didn't ask the impossible or expect extraordinary miracles, but she had a belief that if she did the right thing by God, God would do the right thing by her and her family. Anne put it this way:

> *In my mother I witnessed a woman of sound and sensible faith. She did not take the path of sentimental piety but her praying was constant and she lived with a confidence in the goodness of Almighty God.*

Peg would have begun each day with the Morning Offering and throughout the day her heart would have turned often to God. Her last act would have been to kneel down by her bed and say her night prayers.

Fr Cusack, parish priest of Neerim South in the early 1960s, was a zealous and energetic pastor. He organised a three-day parish mission in Fumina in 1961. A parish mission of that time consisted of sermons, Mass, the opportunity for confession, adoration, Benediction, silence, review of one's life and resolutions. The facilitator was Fr McMaster, a Redemptorist priest. He stayed with Frank and Phyl Horan for the duration of the event. Mary Horan recalls:

We had the Blessed Sacrament in the house. The Horan children had never been so well behaved.

In Catholic devotional life, the Blessed Sacrament is the consecrated host(s) reserved in the Church for quiet prayer and adoration. In earlier times, excess hosts were consecrated at Mass and taken to family members who could not attend Mass. If you walk into any Catholic Church and see a red lamp at the front, this indicates the presence of the Blessed Sacrament reserved in the tabernacle of the Church.

Since the venue for the parish mission was a community hall which was used as the local primary school during the day, it was deemed best to reserve the Blessed Sacrament in the home where the priest was residing for the duration of the Mission. There were quite a few Catholic families in the district of Fumina, Icy Creek and Vesper in 1961. There were Rankins, Horans, Van den Brocks, Findlays and van Boxtels, and a photograph taken at the time shows almost forty participants in the parish mission at Fumina.

The Mission in Fumina in 1961.

Fr Phelan succeeded Fr Cusack as parish priest in Neerim South in the mid-1960s. He was Irish, dedicated to his flock, and valued the importance of catechising schoolchildren. Each week he visited Neerim South High School and taught the rudiments of the faith to the Catholic secondary school age students who attended the school. However, he did not always build rapport with the pupils in front of him. Sometimes he would direct questions to individuals and they were found wanting. Not infrequently there were red faces. Peg remembers Barry coming home from school as a fourteen-year-old and blurting out, 'Fr Phelan hates me!' Other times, Fr Phelan might quiz the students as to who attended Mass the previous Sunday. In one sense it was an unfair question as it wasn't a level playing field and the Rankin children would look down at their shoelaces. Up until the time Peg got her licence, it was not possible for them to attend Sunday Mass on a regular basis, and to be ticked off for something outside their control was unfair.

After Peg gained her licence in 1966, the Rankin family attended Mass either in Noojee or Neerim South. From that time on they were very much a part of the life of the Church. This included attending Benediction, Stations of the Cross, and any special events in the Church. Sometimes there would be as many as seven or eight children crammed in the back of the van. There weren't any seats in the back, simply an iron floor. On one particular Sunday in the winter of 1967, there was quite a severe snowstorm in Fumina, but that wasn't to be used as an excuse not to attend Sunday Mass. Peg and Jack gathered their brood. A foot of snow did not prevent the Hillman van from winding its way down to Noojee in time for 10.30 am Mass. Noojee itself is in a valley and wouldn't get much snow, but the surrounding district was blanketed in snow. The parish priest, Fr John Phelan, would have driven through snow himself in Neerim North on his way to Noojee. When he saw the Rankin children file out of the back of the van one after another, he said, 'This is taking religion a little too far.'

For decades Mass was held in the Noojee Hall each Sunday.

Sometimes there would be two or three cars heading off to Mass at Noojee. Ian Rankin would often be staying with the family over the weekend and he helped with transport. Herb and Terry had cars at this stage and if and they were home their cars weren't written off, they would help with transport to and from Mass. There was always the Hillman with 'Rankin's Radio' plastered on both sides of the van, winding its way down to Noojee with Peg at the helm.

It was a pretty loose arrangement as to who got into which car. The same loose procedure followed in the return journey. Drivers merely looked around to see if there were any stragglers, and it was simply a matter of piling in and returning to the farm. However, there was that Sunday when, about half an hour after everyone had supposedly returned home, Peg for some reason had a quick count and couldn't find her baby, Paul, and it dawned on her and others that he had been left behind at Noojee. So back to Noojee it was and five-year-old Paul was found unfazed, a few kilometres into walking back to the farm.

Peg took seriously her role as a parent, and the primary educator of the faith for her children. For a while after she had acquired her licence, once a week she would drive across to Icy Creek Primary School to teach catechetics to the Catholic children. Phyllis Horan would teach the younger children and Peg would take the older children. When her children were attending high school, she ordered catechetical material to be sent to her by the nuns in Sydney. This was like religious instruction by correspondence. Her children didn't look forward to the occasional Sundays when they were to sit down and work through the material. Peg would work through the questions and answers with them, and the children remember that the questions were quite difficult. Herb insists the emphasis was on 'law and doctrine and not so much on love and compassion'. Peter remembers the material as dry and unengaging. Occasionally Peg would be quite frustrated on the limited Christian knowledge of her offspring.

When quizzed about the depth of her faith and her understanding of God at the time of Barry's death, Peg shared:

> When Barry died, neither Jack or I went down the path of
> being angry with God. That is such a fruitless exercise. Faith
> gives us consolation. I rang Barry's friend Fr Pat Walsh, who
> reassured me that Barry would be saved, that God would
> permit him into the kingdom. A few years after he died I
> crossed paths with a neighbour who had lost a son in a tractor

accident and she was so sad, it partially destroyed her. She was forever sad, there was such a sad look on her face. The mother was a good person but had no faith in an after-life or God helping her in that situation. God is not callous. God does not think 'I will take that Barry Rankin today'. I didn't dwell on it or get angry with God. We have a life to live, we are here, we just have to get on with it. How we accept or reject what life dishes out to us is critical to happiness. You have to make your own life.

By the end of her time in Fumina, Peg was well renowned as a really good cook. At dances, her cream puffs and sponges were legendary. If visitors popped unannounced into the farm any morning or afternoon, freshly made hot scones or a cream sponge would be prepared in no time. All the time Peg would be chatting away. She always had the ability to juggle a few balls in the air – she could multi-task before the term came into vogue. That little stove and oven in Fumina were overworked preparing meals and delicacies for whoever might pop in.

In 1973-1976, the parish priest of Neerim South, Fr John Readman, had two caps. He was the pastor of the local community, and he co-ordinated the Catholic Education Office for the Diocese of Sale. This meant he would organise in-service days for teachers in the diocese, which was sometimes a live-in experience, and Neerim South would be the venue to host these occasions. Three times Peg was asked to cater for these occasions. Three times she said yes. It meant preparing meals for about thirty people pretty much all by herself – all in a day's work for her. Food and Peg went hand in hand.

Fr Readman was a zealous pastor and had quite a bit on his plate. In his time there he negotiated with the Anglican Church for the use of St Andrews Church in Noojee so that Mass could be celebrated in a designated place of worship rather than a community hall. Occasionally a dance or similar function was held on the Saturday night in the hall, and when Mass was celebrated the following morning the stench of beer and tobacco was overwhelming. The new venue was more compact, more prayerful, more aesthetically pleasing. In the negotiations with the Anglican Church, it was agreed the Catholic Church would pay for the new carpet and the provision of individual chairs rather than pews. In the end it was a vast improvement for worship. Peg told one funny little story from this time:

> *During Fr Readman's time he scolded the latecomers to Mass. He said, 'There are twice as many people in the Church now than when Mass started.' The very next week he was late himself. When he finally arrived for Mass, I think it was Tim who tapped his finger on his watch letting Father know he was late. The good priest took it on the chin and knew he was in for a bit of good-natured ribbing.*

One of the features of Church life in Neerim South/Noojee was the cordial relationship between the different denominations. On the occasion to mark the 100th anniversary of

St Ignatius Church in Neerim South on 6 November 2005, Peter Rankin was invited to preach the homily, which included the following words:

> It is right and fitting that we should acknowledge the presence of members of other Churches today. I believe St John's Cooperating Church (combination of Anglican-Uniting Church has cancelled their service today to be here with us. What a marvellous ecumenical gesture. We rejoice in you being here with us to celebrate this occasion. There is definitely more that unites us than divides us.
>
> Churches working together in this community go back a long way. In 1904 there was a big fund-raising effort to build the original Church. A four day bazaar was organised at the Mechanics Institute Hall. The Anglican, Presbyterian and Methodist Churches assisted the Catholic Church in a tremendous way in this fund-raising effort. The bazaar was written up in the Neerim Star and concluded with these words: 'I was pleased to see the Rev. Newton Wood (Church of England) in the hall for some time, which served to show that he was a gentleman capable of seeing worth in other denominations as well as that of his own. Would that there be many like him.'

Fr Joe Flynn wrote in the foreword to the initial history of St Ignatius, and he made mention of this event:

> *We tend to think of ecumenism as a fresh movement. How delightful it is to read that our forerunners did the deed half a century before the Churches would sanction a name for it.*

It was 1973 when Fr Readman was instrumental in negotiating with the Anglican Church to utilise St Andrew's Church in Noojee for Mass each Sunday.

After a fire in April 1981 destroyed the original St Ignatius, the Uniting Church under the leadership of Rev Leonard Jones came forward to offer the use of their little Church for Mass on Sunday. This continued for almost two years until the new Church was built. I think the Uniting Church even slightly changed the time of their morning service to accommodate the needs of the St Ignatius folk.

The first donation to come in after the fire was from the Anglican Church in Drouin. At the opening of the new Church in December 1982, the ladies from both the Uniting Church and the Anglican Church served the afternoon tea at the local hotel. This community is to be congratulated for the way the different Churches work and pray together. May it be a feature of Church life over the next hundred years.

St Ignatius Church Neerim South was an important part of the faith life of the Rankin family. Most received their First Communion in that Church and all twelve children received the sacrament of Confirmation. Up until quite recently it was nearly always the Bishop who presided over the sacrament of Confirmation. The Bishop of Sale would come to Neerim South every second year and Confirm the children of the district, who were usually in senior primary school at this stage. As its name suggests, Confirmation confirms one's Baptism. It is one of the three sacraments of initiation; Baptism and Eucharist are the others. In the post-war period, preaching at Confirmation usually stressed the challenge of being a soldier of Christ, of standing firm in faith and witnessing to the gospel. More recent preaching might focus on Confirmation as full membership in the Church.

St Ignatius Church Neerim South, 1970s.

246

In the mid-1970s, St Ignatius Church was the venue for a number of significant family occasions. Anne, the first of the Rankin children to tie the knot, married John Schmid at St Ignatius on 30 June 1973. Barry was buried from there on 14 September 1973, and Gerardine married Paul Christou on 7 December 1974. Just several weeks later Herb married local girl Jackie Spears on 25 January 1975. There was a popular English film made in 1994 called *Four Weddings and a Funeral*. The Rankin family celebrated three weddings in a little over eighteen months and mourned the loss of a son and brother during that time. For them, it was three weddings and a funeral.

Gerardine and Paul Christou's wedding taken
outside St Ignatius Church at Neerim South.

Fr Readman was present at all of them, assisting the family through happy moments and sadder occasions, and has shared the following reflection:

I first met Peg Rankin when I was Parish Priest of Neerim South (1973-1976). She must be among the finest, if not the finest, Catholic lay-person I have met. A woman of great faith and generosity and someone who reached out to others, no matter what the call might be. Even though the family lived in a remote area of the parish I was absolutely amazed to see them at Mass, Benedictions and all other parish and community activities. Her energy was hard to match, seemingly tireless and then her good humour was ever present. Surely, a woman of great faith and endless good works. She is one of a kind.

Fr Readman, Parish Priest at Neerim South from 1973-1976, was instrumental in negotiating with the Anglican Church to allow Mass to be celebrated in St Andrew's Anglican Church Noojee each week, rather than in the community hall.

When a person decides to enter training for the priesthood, that enormous sacrifice and commitment normally requires the witness of faith of either or both parents. Peg and Jack's son Peter began training for the priesthood in late 1977 and was ordained a priest in December 1989. He attributes the decision to a call from God, and also to the witness of the faith of both his parents for him to undertake that journey. At the celebration to mark the twenty-fifth anniversary of his priestly ordination in December 2014, Peter spoke in the homily with these words:

> *It is wonderful that my Mum can be here to celebrate this occasion. Her faith and love has always been an inspiration to me. I was brought up by two people who demonstrated different aspects of the gift of faith. Mum's faith was strong, practical, active and adaptable. She made sure we attended Mass when we could. She ensured we were prepared well for the Sacraments. She decided when we would kneel down and pray the Rosary. She made sure we attended catechetical instruction on Saturday mornings. She saw to it that nearly all of us finished off with some Catholic education after having attended local state schools. She ensured we loved our neighbour. St Augustine, whose life straddled the fourth and fifth centuries and whose mother prayed for his conversion for many years, said of his own mother, 'Never can I describe what her love was for me. By her glance as well as her words, she raised our hearts to God. If I am God's child, it is because*

though didst give me such a mother.[21] *On the twenty-fifth*
anniversary of my ordination I would like to acknowledge the
faith and witness of my good mother. Dad's faith was cere-
bral thoughtful, traditional, old-school. He hankered for the
older pre-Vatican II Liturgy. He liked to read the scriptures
and ponder the great texts. He was fascinated by the notion of
the end time and thought it was fast approaching. One faith
with two different expressions was evident in my upbringing.

Christian faith is a gift. It is not earned or deserved. It is not
magic. It gives one meaning and direction in life. Faith enables us
to believe in things we can't see. Faith is not so much a body of
doctrine or ancient creeds to assent to, but is essentially trust in a
higher being than ourselves, and in the Christian understanding
this means faith in God. Faith is a way forward. Pope Francis in
his first encyclical wrote that 'faith is not a light which scatters
all our darkness, but a lamp which guides our steps in the night
and suffices for the journey'. Peg has been blessed with abun-
dant faith, not blind faith but well-grounded faith. God, to her, is
real, tangible and to be served with active faith. In the Letter of
St James we read:

> *Take the case, my brothers and sisters, of someone who*
> *has never done a single good act but claims to have faith. Will*
> *that faith save him? If one of the brothers or sisters is in need*

---

21   *The Confessions of St Augustine.*

of clothes and has not enough food to live on, and one of you say to them, 'I wish you well; keep yourselves warm and eat plenty,' without giving them the bare necessities of life, then what good is that? Faith is like that: if good works do not go with it, it is quite dead.[22]

One of the ways Peg put this into practice was to invite people of all ages into the home. Her nephew, Michael McFadden, spent months at a time living in Fumina and attending school there. Peter and Patrick Mitchell, relatives on Jack's side, were very small, undernourished children when they came to spend a couple of months on the farm in Fumina. Local bachelors living on their own were invited to the family meal table. This ritual of hospitality lasted for the entire time she lived in Fumina. Nearly every week for over thirty years the door was open to lonely, broken and occasionally alcoholic men. If there were any people on their own on Christmas Day, Peg would make sure they were invited to lunch. Faith without good works is dead.

---

22   Letter to James 2:14-17.

Jack, Peg (holding her granddaughter Katie) and Peter
on the day of Katie's baptism. At this stage, Peter was a
Deacon and administered the Sacrament of Baptism of
his niece at St Joseph's Church in Warragul, 1989.

The flame of faith is to be kept alive. Peg kept the flame alive
through personal prayer, a rich sacramental life, and a faith which
worked through love. She ensured all her children were taught
their prayers, were prepared for the sacraments, and were raised
in an environment where faith could be openly talked about.
She took her children to Mass when she could, she instigated
the family Rosary, and she immersed herself and her family into
the life of the local Church. In the current Rite of Baptism for

Children, the Church challenges parents by making them aware of their Christian responsibility as they present their children for baptism. We find these words addressed to parents at the beginning of the ritual:

> *You have asked to have your children baptised. In doing so you are accepting the responsibility of training them in the practice of the faith. It will be your duty to bring them up to keep God's commandments as Christ taught us by loving God and our neighbour. Do you clearly understand what you are undertaking?*[23]

Peg and Jack took this undertaking very seriously. They did all in their power to ensure they passed on the faith to their children.

---

23   Rite of Infant Baptism.

CHAPTER 7

Eking Out a Livelihood in Fumina

Yet in spite of all this toil, perhaps in a sense, because of it, work is a good thing for men and women. It is not only good in the sense it is useful or something to enjoy; it is also good as being something worthy, that is to say something that corresponds to human dignity, that expresses this dignity and increases it. If one wishes to define more clearly the ethical meaning of work it is this truth that one must particularly keep in mind. Work is a good thing for men and women, a good thing for his or her humanity, because through work men and women not only transform nature, adapting it to his or her own needs but individuals also achieve fulfilment as a human being, and indeed, in a sense become more a human being.

– POPE JOHN PAUL II

A photograph of Fumina taken in the 1940s. Although the land was cleared, the menace of the bracken fern can clearly be seen. Also evident are the remnants of the 1939 bushfires in the background on Mt McDonald, as many trees can be seen with no foliage.

Thomas Edison once said that there was 'no substitute for hard work'. Hard work had never frightened Peg. She had already proved herself as a reliable, competent and conscientious worker for four years in her father's grocery store in Mount Evelyn. Now she was to learn a new craft, the art of farming in the hostile physical environment of Fumina. When she arrived, at least most of the farm had been properly cleared of trees. Though there was always the problem of rocks and weeds and market forces, at least Jack and Peg were making a life together after the hard toil of the previous fifty years had cleared the land for agriculture.

Peg and Jack's early farming experience was with potatoes. Both during and immediately after the Second World War, there was considerable demand for potatoes. Until the post-war immigration impacted on the average family's eating habits, potatoes were daily fare for most Australian families. The soil in Fumina was good for potatoes and they grew like wildfire. The Romanins and Murphys planted potatoes around logs and other patchy areas, and they still flourished. Fires would rip through, there would be lots of logs lying around but potatoes would grow abundantly around them. They thrived in the virgin soil.

In those days, potatoes were harvested by hand. Prices fluctuated and it was hard to predict them. Dennis, who spent five years working on the family farm from 1971 to 1975, heard stories from earlier times. He remembers:

> The first five years or so of Mum and Dad's marriage, Dad grew potatoes. Potatoes were always hit and miss, some years good and some years bad and there was no irrigation or anything.

In the 1940s, at its peak a bag of potatoes was worth up to ten pounds. That was a lot of money. Other times it was worth much less. Apparently at the time of the Melbourne Olympics in 1956, potatoes were a scarcity and prices went through the roof.

Joy Rankin was a young child in Fumina when most of the cleared land was turned over to planting potatoes. She recalls:

> Most of the farms in those days grew and sold spuds. The spuds were sold by allocation and each supplier had their own number and could only send a certain number of bags when their number came up. My Mum and Dad had a wireless so they would listen for the numbers. When the numbers came

up a carrier by the name of Hedley Keane came in his truck and collected the bags of spuds. He took them to the train at Noojee. The spuds were inspected at Neerim station and if the inspector found a rotten spud or some small ones the whole lot was condemned and no money paid to the farmer. I don't know how often that happened but I know that the spuds were pretty much freshly dug.

Joy's memory is a vivid reminder of the fickle nature of the potato industry, when a small potato or a rotten one in a bag may have incurred forfeiting any payment. Sometimes when potatoes were bagged and ready for sale, there was a problem with the availability of couriers. This was people's livelihood on the line. Some local farmers were more pro-active in ensuring there were no problems in the distribution side. A bottle of whisky or the gift of a good pen or a wad of money was known to change hands with both railway employees and inspectors, to ensure the smooth transfer of potatoes to their destination. Jack was not known to engage in these sorts of underhand transactions, and he sometimes paid the price when his potatoes were left on his property.

Above: Ploughing potatoes in Fumina in the 1940s.

Left: Picking potatoes in Fumina in the 1940s.

Peg and Jack had a regular source of income to supplement the fickle nature of the potato industry. As soon as settled into their house in Fumina, they assumed responsibility for the Fumina Post and Telegraph Office from Bert and Katie. The Post Office part was more lucrative, whilst the telephone aspect was more time-demanding with little remuneration.

The mailman would deliver not only the mail and newspapers, but also groceries, meat, and even occasional supplies from the chemist. Technically, residents should have come to the Post Office to collect their mail but it was a commonsense practice for the mailman to deliver the mail with his other deliveries.

The mail arrived with a Government seal on the mailbag which had the King or Queen's head on it. Peg had to ensure the mail was sealed when it arrived. If the mail was sealed improperly or if it seemed to be tampered with, it was her responsibility to report it to higher authorities in the PMG Department. She had to cut open the seal and sort out the mail there and then, and the mailman then delivered it to residents in Fumina.

For outgoing mail, letters had to be stamped and placed in a special PMG cotton mail bag, which was sealed with a heated red wax seal with the imprint 'PMG' on it and tied with a string. Later on Peg had a little crimping machine which entailed threading the bits of string through a crimp and squeezing it with a pair of pliers. Mail would be transferred to Moe, where it was re-sorted. In the 1950s, as well as delivering mail, newspapers, groceries etc, the mailman picked up the cream from local farmers and despatched it to the Moe Butter Factory.

It was the responsibility of a Post Office agent to keep a float with cash in it, and to always have sufficient stamps, telegram paper and an updated logbook for records, etc. Herb tells the story about this:

> One day a PMG official turned up in Fumina to check the books and the till and realised quickly enough it was insufficiently stocked. This official asked Mum to sign a document indicating there was a deficiency in the cash float, stamps, record keeping etc. Mum, thinking as quick as a flash, said she couldn't possibly sign on behalf of the Postmaster. (Technically Jack

Rankin was the Postmaster). When he enquired of the where-
abouts of the Postmaster, Mum simply said, 'I have no idea, Sir.'
Funny thing is it would have been more embarrassing if Dad
had been there because he wouldn't have known where anything
was and more or less been forced to sign the document. Mum
certainly showed a bit of spirit, and was able to diffuse a poten-
tially embarrassing situation. There was no follow-up from the
PMG visit and everything just resumed as normal.

Telegrams were an important part of communication in earlier Australia. Everywhere, the local Post Office was the home of the telegraph apparatus. In fact, for decades they were known as Post and Telegraph Offices. When a telegraphic message reached its destination, it was written or typed out on an official sheet of paper in the Post and Telegraph Office, and then the paper – the telegram – was placed in an envelope and delivered to the intended recipient:

> *From the 1890s the bicycle was used to deliver the telegram*
> *on the short, final leg of the journey to the front door of a shop,*
> *factory or house. The price of sending a telegram would become*
> *cheaper but the arrival of a telegram was still an uncommon*
> *event in most Australian houses as late as 1900. A typical house*
> *probably did not receive more than one telegram a year. Often*
> *the telegram carried the news of a death.*[24]

---

24   Blainey, Geoffrey, *Black Kettle and Full Moon – Daily Life in a Vanished Australia*, 2004, p.97.

A couple of generations later people even sent money through telegrams. Countless telegrams would have been sent during wartime, as relatives of servicemen and women who died or were seriously injured were informed through telegrams. Post Office agents had the task of personally delivering telegrams.

Telegrams were meant to be delivered as soon as they were received. As the agent in Fumina, Peg would have to record the message on a special piece of yellow carbon paper, place it in an envelope, and personally deliver it. The message would have to have been accurately dictated onto the carbon paper to give the precise message. The official telegram would arrive some days later through the post. This procedure was designed as a way for Post Offices to be accountable and transparent.

Occasionally in Fumina a telegram would come through late at night, and that meant Peg would have to walk in the dark to a neighbour's place and deliver the telegram, which was sometimes good news but often bad. Terry remembers, as a child, delivering a telegram to Dom and Mary McHugh informing them that their son Jack had contracted pleurisy. Occasionally the telegram message would be phoned through if the neighbour had a telephone. This was left to the discretion of the agent. The information was usually quite personal: babies being born, people gravely ill, possibly the news of the death of a relative being conveyed to a family.

In the 1950s and 1960s it was still common practice in Australia to send congratulatory telegrams to be read out at wedding ceremonies and wedding receptions. When Margaret Potter and

Keith Ferguson married in Fumina in September 1956, Peg had the task of reading out the many telegrams on their special day. Joy Rankin remembers:

> *Sometimes the mailman would deliver the telegram for Peg. Often enough people would know the mailmen delivered mail and groceries etc on Monday, Wednesday and Friday and quite deliberately they would phone in a telegram to be delivered to coincide with the mailman's run.*

Right: Margaret Potter and Ken Ferguson's wedding in Fumina, September 1956. Peg read out the telegrams at their wedding.

When Peg and Jack first settled in Fumina they had the telephone exchange in their home. Anybody in Fumina who wanted to receive a call or make a call had to come to their house. Anne recalls:

There was a so-called public phone in the corner of the kitchen for general use.

> It wasn't until about 1948 that telegraph wires went to individual homes so they could receive and make calls from home, although obviously they first went through the Fumina exchange.
>
> When little Janet Rankin was have only been three or four and she was in the city shopping with her mum, somehow she wandered off. When someone noticed this distraught little girl and enquired about a name, address and contact number, she was able to say it was Fumina 4. That was brilliant for a three- or four-year-old, because contact could be made with the family and they could take it from there. Fumina 4 was the right number. Each household in Fumina which was connected by phone had a number, and Eric and Linda's number was 4.

Joy Rankin recalls with fondness:

> I remember the wires going in for the telephones to the various homes. This would have been in about 1948. This made life so much better. One of my memories of the new phone lines was that one day I was bringing in the cows for milking and the copper telegraph wires were glistening in the

sun. Mum and Peg would have been on the phone most days when the lines were put in catching up with the local gossip.

Dennis remembers:

All of my childhood we had the telephone exchange in the corner of our living room. All calls in and out of Fumina had to come through the exchange, manned mostly by Mum and also us kids. It was a weird system of buzzers and Morse codes and plugs going in and out. The exchange was not manned all the time. It didn't really open till 9.00 am when we began dairy farming and the morning milking had been completed, and the exchange was closed again from 4.00 pm till 6.00 pm for the evening milking. If any of the older kids were home they operated it if Mum wasn't there.

Occasionally if an important phone call was expected and Peg was busy, one child would not go to school so they could look after the exchange. Bernard remembers staying home from school to man the phones on a couple of occasions. Dennis also. Their teacher Mr White was not happy that children were missing school to man the phones for the Fumina exchange. Lindsay Rankin maintains that:

Every kid in Fumina knew how to work that switch. Peg would instruct the kids to plug in the switch if she was busy outside. We would simply plug it through and connect the folk ringing in or wanting to ring out.

The telephone component to the Post and Telegraph Office did not pay well. In addition it was demanding time-wise, unlike the postal service which involved more intense work for only a few minutes – opening mail, sorting out mail, readying outgoing mail, and ensuring mail bags were sealed properly. This part of the business paid more handsomely.

Around the hamlet there was sometimes the occasional whinge, with neighbours complaining there was no-one manning the phone when they wanted to make an outside call. The PMG put pressure on Peg to ensure the phones were being manned throughout the day. At this stage Peg had a tractor and was hell-bent on making a fist of controlling weeds and improving farm productivity. She was out and about on the tractor and often enough the telephone exchange commitment was ignored. The upshot of all this was a meeting with the PMG at Fumina, and it was decided to transfer the exchange from Fumina to Icy Creek so that there was a central exchange connecting the entire district of Fumina, Icy Creek and Vesper. For some time after that the switchboard apparatus was idle and taking up space in the home. In a moment of exasperation one day, Peg rang the PMG department and told them to come and collect all their phone apparatus, or it would be thrown out on the road. She was known to be quite fiery from time to time.

It seems that fairly quickly there was a shift in agricultural practice in the West Gippsland area. Farmers were moving in droves away from cropping and into dairying. Peg was in the loop, talking to people around Trafalgar who were in the vanguard of this move. Jack and Peg joined the throng of farmers making the switch. Dennis remembers that:

267

By the early 1950s Mum and Dad used to milk about twenty cows by hand and then they would wind up the separator to take the cream off the top. The cream was then taken to Trafalgar by the mailman and sold.

The skim milk was fed to the few pigs at that stage. Peg certainly helped with the milking. Already she had had a number of children but that never stopped her helping Jack milk the cows. Sometimes this meant restraining her youngest children in the process. Others were left to fend for themselves. It is amazing that there weren't any serious accidents in the house whilst the milking was taking place. There was always a stove burning and plenty of places where a young child might be hurt, but there were no major mishaps.

Peg had good business sense and could see that there was a future in dairying but to make the whole enterprise more viable, they needed to build up the size of their herd and invest in labour-saving modern machinery. Jack was conservative by nature and needed to be convinced about such a significant change of operations. Anne was eight at the time and remembers her mother wooing her father into taking the risk of investing in machinery. She recalls:

Mum and Dad discussing the matter after tea. Mum would say, 'Jack, to make a future of this, we need to invest, we need this new way of milking cows so we can increase the size of our herd, increase production and make it more profitable.'

And that would have been the conversation for goodness knows how long, and as an eight-year-old I remember Mum gradually cajoling and coaxing Dad into accepting the idea of the machines. Dad wouldn't have been champing at the bit, jumping up and down with excitement and when it eventually happened and he agreed. I was so thrilled for Mum. who had to work on Dad and convince him of the merits of investing in these new farm techniques. I remember Mr Brewster putting in the modern machinery. I was so enthusiastic about milking the cows, learning how to tie up the cows, put on the leg-rope, ensuring feed was in the trough, washing the teats and then placing the cups on the teats of the cows. I was so pleased for Mum. I remember having a good time mucking about. Mum decided I should be at home doing the babysitting. so that was the end of my farming career; brought to an abrupt halt at the age of eight and a half. I was demoted/promoted, which-ever way you look at it, so Mary Kealy and I would look after the babies. Mary Kealy soon found it boring so she went home and I was left on my own to do the babysitting.

Jack and Peg were the first couple in Fumina to acquire the motorised milking machines. Eric and Linda Rankin, the Potters, the McHughs, Jack Beale and the Sulcases pretty much followed their lead. Peg and Jack had a choice between the more expensive, stronger British-made Bamford engine or the locally made, smaller and less costly Donaldson and Tippet engine. They chose the former. The Bamford motor never missed a beat and served the farm well for twenty-three years. Sometimes with machinery it is the luck of the draw; the Horans in Icy Creek bought the same motor and had nothing but trouble with theirs.

Dennis remembers that starting the motor required a bit of skill:

> You had three functions, to crank the handle with one hand, hold the choke chamber in place with the other and release the handle at the pivotal moment when the engine fired up.

The machinery meant the size of the dairy herd could be increased significantly from twenty to thirty, as the milking time was halved.

Peg recalls the dairy farming years fondly:

> In the nice weather, milking the cows was great. The noise of the machines whirring away, I quite liked it. I found it quite meditative. Luckily enough, we had no trouble with the Bamford motor. It worked like a dream, unlike our poor neighbour Frank Horan. Even the engineers couldn't fix his motor properly. Only a handful of times in that twenty-three year period did we have to milk the cows by hand. Our milking machine proved incredibly reliable.

Unfortunately, a constant problem was the bracken fern. The younger cattle particularly liked to eat the juices of the young plants. It was important to keep the calves and yearlings away from the bracken fern if possible, because if they ate enough of it, they could be poisoned.

This particular plant thrived in Fumina and it was always hard to contain. Another early piece of farm machinery was purchased to combat the weeds. The Allen's slasher was a power-driven two-wheeled machine with a see-sawing blade at the front. The knife went forwards and backwards, and a series of metal fingers protruded at the front for the protection of the cutting apparatus. It was ideally suited for the slashing of weeds, particularly the bracken. However, although it was power-driven, the machine was hard to handle. It required a bit of strength. Herb notes:

> It really put pressure on your legs. It wasn't easy to manoeuvre. It was cumbersome. It was okay on the flat but our farm was full of hills, rocks, rabbit burrows and difficult terrain. If you accidentally hit a wombat hole or a ditch, the machine would jerk, the wheels would keep spinning and it was painful on your arms and legs. Mum just took it all in her stride. She would have used this machine for more than fifteen years. There wouldn't have been too many women able to do that.

Allen's Slasher. Peg used a similar one for 15 years in
an effort to contain bracken and other weeds.

In the 1950s and early 1960s, one of the really positive aspects
of farming in Fumina was the community participation at the
time of harvesting. Neighbours helped neighbours.

Harvesting hay in the summer for winter feed for the cows and
calves was essential. There was very little grass around in the winter
as it was too cold for any to grow. When the grass was cut and dried,
it needed to be stored in haystacks and sheds before there was any
rain. Timing was everything. Farmers needed to keep an eye on
the weather forecasts as it was necessary to cut the grass, rake it
and have it stored before it rained. This necessitated all hands on
deck, and the whole community supporting one another. Whoever
was on hand in the hamlet, children included, would go from
farm to farm bringing in the hay. Earlier on, the pitchfork was the
essential tool; later, tractor and trailer picked up the hay bales and
transferred them into the shed in an orderly fashion. Hay carting
together really cemented community spirit and cooperation.

Community involvement including children in hay carting.

Peg relished working on the farm. It wasn't drudgery to her and she was always pushing herself to ensure optimum achievement with the resources at hand. The family was growing, and to ensure they were all fed, clothed and educated, calculated risk and sound decision making was required every day on top of hard work.

In 1964, after Jack's stomach operation brought the change in his personality and deteriorating energy levels, Peg definitely became more proactive in leadership and drive on the farm. The days of horses and sledges and antiquated practices were over. Jack's precarious health, his stepping back, and Peg's leadership on the farm ushered in the use of more modern farming accessories and techniques.

The first purchase was a little grey Ferguson tractor. This was a very popular tractor at that time – reliable, inexpensive and very functional for small-time farmers. They were great work-horses for farmers in Gippsland and beyond. Peg attended a clearing sale in Neerim South in late 1964 and instructed farming colleague Jack Spears to do the bidding for a Ferguson tractor. He was instructed to bid up to three hundred pounds. Herb was at the sale and he tells the story:

> *Jack Spears did the bidding. Mum had decided to with-draw from bidding after three hundred pounds. I am not sure how it happened but we put in a final bid of three hundred and three pound and it came in. The tractor was ours. Jack Spears had the job of driving it home from Neerim South. Tim and I taught Mum how to drive it. Peg had to take out a loan to purchase the tractor – it was a calculated risk. She decided to rear more calves and sell them at the market to pay off the debt. When she lost calves to bracken-fern poisoning etc. it was always touch and go whether she could keep up the loan repayments.*

Apart from one hiccup, the tractor was a godsend. Within a few months of its purchase, the engine needed an overhaul. Local mechanic Paddy Kane from Warragul came to the rescue and the tractor was soon back in farm use. The tractor made a difference immediately. Weeds and certain grasses were such a menace on the farm and hard to contain. Prior to the purchase of the tractor, the Lands Department were hired occasionally to spray weeds, particularly the blackberry weed. This was obviously expensive. The acquisition of the tractor meant Peg could do that work herself.

Jack never learnt to drive the tractor. After one or two lessons with Tim, he gave up and left all work with the tractor to Peg. Jack and machinery didn't really go well together. He even loathed having to crank the milking machines motor and when he could, he delegated that task to someone else.

Dennis recalls :

> *With the investment of a boomspray which consisted of a forty-four gallon drum of pesticide on the trailer, a pump on the tractor and a spray bolted onto the bonnet of the tractor, we could at least partially control thistles, wild radish, and the aftermath of the burr medic clover which caused the cows to suffer from bloating.*

In the first summer after acquiring the tractor, Dennis was driving the tractor and trailer as bales of hay were hoisted up onto the trailer. This was before his tenth birthday:

> *I could hardly reach the pedals.*

In the summer of 1967/68, Victoria was drought-stricken. The main water tank near the house was completely empty. Every other day the little 'grey fergie' would be driven over to a spring at the western end of the farm and drums of water would be transported back to the house.

The burr medic clover grew profusely in the springtime. It was full of water. Although it made a fantastic pasture and was ideal for hay, the high water content would bloat the cows. In one springtime Peg and Jack lost several cows due to bloating. The burr medic grass would also clog the mower when it was cut for hay. As Dennis points out:

> Another downside to the grass was that when it dried, it would frizzle up to nothing. Because it needed plenty of water, as soon as summer came, it would dry out, crack the ground and make perfect conditions for thistles, wild radish, and cape weed to grow. With no tractor, weeds were a nightmare to control. With the acquisition of the tractor, controlling weeds became manageable if not highly successful.

In the springtime bloating was a real challenge for farmers. The white clover grew in the springtime. This was a lush grass for the animals. If the cows ate too much of a certain clover they could bloat, and they bloated terribly on this burr medic clover. To contain the amount of grass on which cattle were masticating, farmers used the electric fence to restrict feeding.

Peg reflects on the issue:

Our farming days were almost over when we got on top of this bloating curse. Different clovers would take over the dreaded burr medic clover. It was difficult to find a grass that would override the burr medic clover, but we eventually got on top of this and sowed a different clover which was not as damaging to the cows and prevented the burr medic from gaining ascendancy. In one day, we might have lost three cows, nearly ten per cent of our herd. Dad found out that certain clovers were better than others and these other types meant the cows didn't bloat.

A separate problem was the blackberry weed. Without vigilance, it could take over whole portions of a property in Fumina. Again the tractor came into play, together with a specially designed two-hundred-and-fifty-gallon trailer/tank which was hired from the Lands Department. This was used to spray a pesticide which curtailed the spread of blackberries. In the summertime it was common practice to pick the blackberries, preserve them for jams, and then spray the weeds. During the autumn the remnants of the blackberry bush would be burned and space for grasses and crops reclaimed.

In the incredibly hot summer of 1967-1968, in which a drought persisted, Peg was out as usual spraying the blackberry weed one Saturday. When she came back to the house and put the radio on, she heard that the Mercury level had reached 110 degrees in Melbourne. When it came to work on the farm, Peg simply did what was required at the time. She didn't flinch. She was made of tough stuff.

The Grey Ferguson tractor and hired trailer
for spraying blackberries, 1971.

Another source of income was rearing calves for market. Peg
used to go to the cattle markets in Warragul to buy and sell the
calves. At her peak, Peg reared up to one hundred calves at a time,
which she bought in the spring and sold at the end of autumn.
They were fed with the skim milk after the cream was separated
for sale. While getting them ready for market, she had to ensure
they didn't kill themselves on the juicy young bracken fern. This
seemed to be more a problem for the calves than it was for the
fully grown dairy cattle.

Peg feeding calves during the late 1950s. Note
the primitive cowshed in background.

Ken Rankin (neighbour) to the right in the photo.

Bernie Rabl was an auctioneer at Warragul and he has fond memories of Peg:

> *She was the standout among the few women who bought and sold calves. She had a good eye for calves, didn't mind getting her hands dirty. Peg was most respected by the auctioneers.*

Kevin Quirk, another auctioneer from those days, also remembers Peg:

> *She would buy the second tier quality Friesian calves only a few days old. She would keep them for eight or nine months.*

We had what was known in the trade as late October sales. This was the most popular time for Peg to buy. The calves were well and truly weaned when she sold them at the end of autumn.

With the advent of electricity in 1967, other farmers in Icy Creek and Vesper invested in switching from selling cream to full cream milk. Again, this was a sizeable investment, and for Peg and Jack it meant basically rebuilding the cowsheds. Milk trucks needed direct access to the shed itself to transfer the milk from a vat into the truck, and it was impossible for milk trucks to access the cowshed on its current site.

They pondered this option and selected a piece of land close to the road on the eastern side of their property, where they might rebuild a cowshed and make provision for access by a milk truck. However, it really meant starting from scratch. So the idea was considered but in the end it didn't get much traction. The sums didn't add up because the farm wasn't quite big enough. To make it a viable concern, you needed to be milking one hundred cows and not thirty. The cost of a new cowshed as well as purchasing or leasing further land and tripling the size of the herd was simply too much. And would a truck come all the way to Fumina for just one client? After weighing up their options, Peg and Jack stayed with selling cream and rearing calves to the end.

Ken Rankin observing Peg feeding her calves during the 1950s.

Dennis spent five years on the farm after he left school, up to the time the farm was sold. He reflects on the rabbits:

There was little money in farming, but my parents raised twelve kids, gave us all the education we required from the earnings from a thirty-cow dairy farm. Most of us went to boarding school. We were a bunch of very happy, healthy kids. But as kids we were a fairly skinny bunch; we never stopped. We didn't have much but we had three meals on the table every day and a braised rabbit stew was often on the menu. My father often told the story of how it was time to stop the rabbit plague so he laid some 1080 carrot bait on his farm and the farm next door. After curtailing the rabbit population, neighbours complained they were going hungry.

Dennis slashing weeds with the Mobilco during 1971.

Although they were a plentiful source of cheap food, rabbits were a nuisance. When they swelled in numbers, as they did in the 1960s to plague-like proportions, they ate up all the best grass. Farmers periodically had to cull the them, and the most effective way to do that was to poison them. Poison was placed on carrots or apples and placed in furrows throughout the farm. It had the desired effect and reduced the rabbit population very quickly. It also returned the grass to those for whom it was intended, the cattle.

Crown Land allotments at the beginning of the twentieth century were usually in the vicinity of eighty acres. The Rankin farm was not a large property. Peg and Jack leased farmland from their neighbour Ken Rankin, so they could milk more cows and rear more calves. One funny little story in the mid-1960s was about a farm next door that was not being farmed. The owners had left the district. They had not sold the property and they had no cattle on it, so this productive land was not being utilised. Peg and Jack decided to put their cattle on the property to chew some of the grass which otherwise would have gone to waste. That very day, the owner brought up a truckload of cattle to graze on the property! Peg and Jack's cattle made a stealthy and hasty exit from their neighbour's farmland. Jack and Peg eventually purchased this farm and it gave them extra grazing land for their cattle and calves. It was bought in 1971 for $8000 and sold in 1975 for $30,000 – not a bad mark-up.

It is quite mind-boggling to look back at that time and reflect on how Peg and Jack managed to feed, clothe and educate twelve children on a small rocky farm in the middle of nowhere. But they did it. Maybe they had to slog away during their farming years, but the sale price of their property ensured no more sleepless nights and, for the first time in their married lives, financial security.

The thirty-two years of raising a family and farming in Fumina came to a halt at the end of 1975. In one sense it wasn't a planned decision, but more opportunistic. What sparked the decision to sell the farm was the inflated price of land in Fumina. The Kilners next door sold their property in May 1975 and were recompensed handsomely. From when they purchased the property in 1973 to the time of the sale just two years later, there was a considerable mark-up. There was no doubt they'd purchased at a good time and sold at a good time.

The Kilners' sale set Jack and Peg thinking. Beef prices had plummeted during the time of the Whitlam Government. Cream prices bottomed out. It was a lot of toil for little reward. It was hard to make a living, yet there were others champing at the bit to try this farming caper. Hobby farms were the rage, and professional people were seeking weekend properties not too far from their workplaces. Fumina was only two hours from Melbourne and it was certainly picturesque. It was affordable and there were ready buyers out there.

Jack was flabbergasted at the price the Kilners had received in the sale of their property. He was sixty-three, facing another long winter with little reward for effort, and now he could see a way out. I sense that Peg and Jack came to the decision, without much argument, to sell up and move to the largest town nearby, and that was Warragul. Jack was ready to slow down, move out of Fumina, have more time to smell the roses and write poetry. Peg was only fifty and still full of energy. With her small but able body and sharp mind, she still had plenty of good working years in her. She was more than ready for a new challenge, and Warragul was to give her that opportunity.

CHAPTER 8

The Warragul Years

FOR MANY REASONS, the move into Warragul was a sensible decision. It was a larger service town with a higher prospect for employment for Peg. Their son Barry was buried in Warragul. There was an active parish community in which to be involved. It was on the train line, and it was only an hour and half from Melbourne for their family to visit. It all made good sense to settle there.

Peg very quickly landed on her feet in Warragul. Whereas Jack was ready to slow down, she was too young to receive the pension. She had just turned fifty and she was fit and healthy, still in her productive years and champing at the bit to join the workforce. The Warragul years were very happy years for Peg. She spent the next thirty-seven years of her life there.

Corner Victoria and Queen Streets, Warragul.

Peg had let it be known to Barbara Malady, who was the secretary to the Matron of West Gippsland Hospital, that she would be happy to put her hat in the ring for any employment opportunity that might arise, even if it was washing dishes or something quite menial. Peg and Barbara were well known to each other. Peg was very good friends with Barbara's mother, Phyllis Malady, and she had stayed with Phyllis and her family before giving birth to eight of her twelve children. Barbara, who was a teenager and young adult at the time, remembered Peg coming to their house to prepare for the birth of her children. By the time Peg and Jack moved to Warragul, Barbara had been working at the hospital for more than a decade and was well known and highly respected. She also had clout and influence.

West Gippsland Hospital, where Peg was able to gain
employment when she and Jack moved to Warragul.

Barbara's antenna tuned in when she overheard a colleague
and team leader in the diet kitchen. Thelma Gould expressed
concern that three of her staff would be taking long service leave
in the next year or so, and she needed someone to fill in during
this time. Barbara instinctively knew that Peg could more than
adequately fill that vacancy; she had fed a large brood for many
years, and was conscientious and reliable. Barbara had no hesitation in recommending Peg to fill the breach, and she informed
Thelma that she had a person in mind.

Very soon afterwards an interview at the hospital was arranged
for Peg:

It was arranged that I meet Thelma at about 10.00 am. She put me at ease. She explained that cooking would be straight-forward, pretty much home cooking except with reduced salt and sugar. Cooking for a large family, Barbara's recommendation and my performance at the interview all contributed to being offered the job.

She began cooking at the hospital on Jack's sixty-fourth birthday, 2 February 1976, and she continued working there until her retirement at the end of 1990 when she turned sixty-five. Paul, the youngest child, remembers Peg coming home from work at the hospital with her first payslip:

She proudly displayed it to all and sundry saying it was a much easier way to make a few bucks than farming.

Peg reminisces about those early days in the diet kitchen and her work:

Over time a permanent vacancy in the diet kitchen became available and I was told by the Diet Kitchen manager that I would have to speak up for myself if I was to secure that position rather than merely continue as a relief cook. An older cook who had been on the staff for many years was retiring. The diet kitchen management was delighted to have me continue in the role as relief cook. Without big noting myself I was reliable, competent, independent and team orientated. They thought I would be difficult to replace in the role and for them to find someone who would tick all those boxes wasn't going to be easy. Sometime later the head of the Kitchen Department came up to me and said, 'I was being a bit selfish. I wanted to keep you on as the relief cook as the "go to person." Let's face it, you are not getting any younger so to secure your future, we intend offering you a permanent position on the diet kitchen staff rather than continuing merely as a relief cook.'

So Peg transitioned from being a mere relief cook covering staff who were on holidays and long service leave to an employee with a full-time permanent position in the diet kitchen, and she never looked back.

Diet kitchens are an important part of the functioning of a hospital kitchen. At the West Gippsland Hospital there were two people assigned to the diet kitchen. The cook preparing the lunches commenced work at 7.00 in the morning and the one preparing the evening meal started at 9.00 am. The earlier cook prepared the salads for lunch and the later cook prepared the vegetables for tea. Peg maintains:

One had to be aware that vegetables varied so much in their calorie intake. Cabbage, cauliflower, beans etc were high in calories and were to be avoided in some diets. When patients returned from surgery they were often on special diets. It meant that there always had to be a good batch of

chicken broth on standby to help patients get their stom-
achs re-oriented to functioning normally. Healthy chicken
soup was always a good start, with onion and carrot added
to flavour the soup and ensure any chicken fat was skimmed
off. Jelly was an important component of the diet kitchen food
preparation as this was so easily digestible for people immedi-
ately after surgery. Steamed chicken too was always available
for patients with a light diet. Diet fruit was always on hand if
needed. It was made clear what size portions to give patients.

It seems that Peg was well on top of her game, with no food preparation causing concern for her. Sometimes patients with private health insurance had particular needs, but there was never a problem meeting those needs. Peg could cope readily with any change of game plan in the kitchen. She was not ruffled easily.

Barbara Malady saw Peg's work at first hand over a long time and says:

The first time she had a sick day was in her final year.
She enjoyed the work. She would go anywhere, she would do
anything. She would peel the potatoes, do all the vegetables,
she gladly worked weekends, she had to learn the intricacies
of diet cooking, she learnt how to use unfamiliar ingredients.
She was a quick learner, she was a marvel, she really was.

The Food Services staff in 1978. Peg is in
the front row, sixth from the left.

As part of a significant refurbishment of West Gippsland
Hospital in the mid-1980s, an entirely new kitchen was
constructed, and the diet kitchen was amalgamated into the
main kitchen rather than left as a separate entity. The diet cook
for each shift had his/her name on the whiteboard indicating
they were responsible for the diet patients. On the board, it was
earmarked what was to be cooked for that day as well as a weekly
menu to guide staff.

In this major overhaul of the working of the kitchen, no-one
was actually put off but some were re-trained to work in the
main kitchen. With the refurbished kitchen, cooking preparation changed. A conveyor belt was now in operation and meals
were plated in the main kitchen and not in the wards. Kitchen
staff worked together to ensure food was dished out closer to the
time patients were eating.

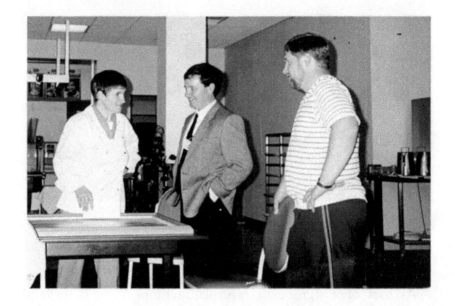

Peg in the kitchen at the West Gippsland Hospital.

Peg even enjoyed working on Christmas Day:

> *Because of my preparedness to work on Christmas Day and
> other holidays, one of my main tasks was to make sure Christmas
> lunch was prepared on time. I had to oversee and be responsible
> for the main meal at lunchtime. I relished the opportunity.*

Reflecting on the fifteen years cooking at the hospital, Peg said:

> *It was just fantastic and of course it just so happened that
> I was one of the lucky ones to turn up at the right time and
> be offered a position that would see out my working years.
> Work was never a drudgery; there was usually good company*

and something meaningful to do. I never felt it was back to the salt mine. The Hospital Union was quite a militant one and they put a case forward that the technically unqualified cooks (myself included) who didn't receive the same remuneration as the trained staff, yet they were doing exactly the same work (and a good number had been working for a long time), should be remunerated equally. The Union organised a practical accreditation assessment for individual staff who were technically unqualified as cooks. An Assessor from the Apprenticeship Board evaluated me. The assessment was both verbal and practical, though not in written form. As well as answer a few basic questions, I was asked to demonstrate how I would pass a knife to a colleague in the kitchen. The main point being that the person receiving the knife should receive it by the handle and under no circumstances should the blade be pointing toward anybody. My mother taught me in childhood to be careful with knives and always to pass the handle first. I passed the test and received a little leather book with my official accreditation. Not bad for an uneducated woman from the bush to be granted such recognition.

Peg could have retired at sixty but chose to continue to work. To give him his due, Jack never resented her working. According to Peg:

Some husbands couldn't bear to see their wives working but Jack was always supportive of me. He knew I was happy at work, enjoyed what I was doing, and he encouraged me to continue. I took two sick days in my fifteen years of work at the hospital. Those two days occurred in my final year of working, probably in the May or June of 1990. I was never late for work once in fifteen years. That in itself was a major feat when you think I started at 7.00 am for nearly all of my time there.

Reflecting on the Warragul years, she said:

It was good to be alive and having the capacity to get out and about. There was a lot of happiness, weddings, engagements, 21st birthdays. Oh yes, they were very happy times. There were family members coming home, some studying at university, children preparing for exams, others fronting up to boarding school. There were beginnings of relationships and bringing boyfriends and girlfriends home to meet Dad and I. They were blessed times indeed.

'The Girls'
Back Row L-R: Jackie Rankin, Gerardine, Christou, Marg Rankin,
Mary Rankin, Deb Rankin. Front Row L-R: Anne Schmid,
Kathleen Cantwell, Brigette Rankin, Peg Rankin and Jo Rankin.

Peg has always had an amazing work ethic. After a long shift at work it was not uncommon for her to come home from the hospital and then oversee a meal for her family. Maybe there were up to fifteen, twenty, or even twenty-five visitors at different times, and Peg would see it as her duty to provide the evening meal for whoever happened to be in Warragul. She took it all in her stride – there was no doubt as to who was in charge in the kitchen at 1 Edinburgh Street, Warragul. Daughters, daughters-in-law and others might have helped, but it was Peg who was calling the shots and directing proceedings all the time.

In the late 1970s and early 1980s, Mary was nursing at Royal Melbourne Hospital and she often brought colleagues and friends home to Warragul. She travelled quite a bit at that time, too, and brought international visitors home. Mary tells the story:

> *I had friends from England come to stay at Warragul with Mum and Dad. They first met Mum after she arrived home from work, having cooked for eight hours. They watched in amazement as she chatted, never sat down, donned her runners, ran back and forth around the kitchen and produced a superb meal. There was no stopping this woman. Steve, one of the Pommies, was particularly in awe of Mum because she had given birth to twelve children over eighteen years. He enquired, 'How did you do it, Peg?' As quick as a flash Peg retorted, 'With a strong back and weak head,' laughing merrily.*

Paul was the only child who lived in the house in Edinburgh Street and attended a local school, Marist Sion College, for one year in 1976. He writes:

> *When we first moved to Warragul, I was pretty much the only child living at home. Kathleen was at boarding school, Peter at University, and Dennis remained in Fumina/Icy Creek during the week and worked for the new owners on the farm we had sold. As a kid, the good part about Warragul was that there were always visitors. Being closer to Melbourne and such*

an easy trip up the Princes Highway, there was great opportunity for family members to visit. I know I enjoyed seeing a lot more of the family, which also made Mum and Dad happy. Because Mum nearly always worked on Christmas Day, family would appear in droves late afternoon, for the family Christmas get-together in the evening. On Christmas Day 1977, Mum had prepared an easy lunch of curried sausages which simply had to be reheated for the few who were home at lunch. I distinctly remember that Christmas. Dad, Dennis, Kathleen and I were the only ones home for Christmas lunch. Bernard rang to wish everyone a happy Christmas and I answered the phone. Enquiring how was Christmas lunch, I blurted down the phone that: 'It was the worst Christmas ever. There were no visitors as yet, everyone at home was asleep, and all we had for Christmas lunch was curried sausages.' Mum had a bit of a laugh when the story was relayed later that day and it became a joke for many years afterwards.

When Peg and Jack first moved into Warragul, one of the first relationships to really blossom was the romance between Tim and Marg Maloney, and they married on 14 May 1977. Tim spent the summer of 1976-77 at Warragul working in the Drouin Butter factory during university holidays. Marg, a nurse working at St Vincent's Hospital in the city, was a regular visitor to Warragul that summer, and of course many times after they married. She remembers:

I had heard so much about Jack and Peg before I met them and I expected a large, loud and hearty man backed up by a quiet and constantly busy cook. My expectations were upended and I very quickly realised Peg was central to each and all of us. Peg is a magnificent cook! For all of her married life she prepared Jack's meals according to the way his mother cooked them and then produced miracles for the rest of us. I always think of her in that tiny kitchen in Warragul (before renovations) with a bowl under her arm and a wooden spoon, beating away while she talked. She was an amazing hostess, feeding us loaves and fishes and similarly producing beds as needed. In the early days in Warragul it was about the boys' room and the girls' room. Later it was by couples and eventually by families, but there was always room.

She so loved Jack and anticipated his every need, but especially for her company. They shared everything, but did not tie each other to the same point of view. They enjoyed travelling around the outback and we often saw them on their bus tours during which they camped each night in a tent. They shared a very strong faith and commitment to their parish. They shared the great joy of supporting Peter in the priesthood, and one of the most marvellous family occasions was the weekend of Peter's priestly ordination. While I missed the opportunity to know Barry, his place in the family was treasured and always recognised by his loving parents.

Another relationship to flourish in the reasonably early years at Warragul was that between Dennis and Joanne (Jo) Blizzard, who met through the church activities provided for young adults. The Assistant Priest stationed in Warragul, Fr Denis O'Bryan, was a mutual friend of theirs. Dennis and Fr Denis were at boarding school together at Rupertswood in Sunbury in 1969-1970. Understandably, Fr Denis O'Bryan was the priest who officiated at their wedding on 30 October 1982.

Fr O'Bryan celebrates the wedding of Dennis
and Joanne Blizzard in 1982.

Fr Denis O'Bryan shared this reflection:

> *When I was first ordained a Priest I was appointed to the*
> *Warragul Parish, and formed a close association there with*
> *the Rankin family. Jack and Peg were parents of a large family*
> *and I enjoyed many occasions of hospitality in their home.*
>
> *Peg was always welcoming, cheerful, seemingly unflap-*
> *pable, blessed with energy, prayerful and amazingly capable.*
> *She gave herself unsparingly to Jack and her family and her*
> *home was a place of fun, hospitality, good humour and faith.*
> *It was a busy home with family and friends coming and*
> *going. While I was in Warragul it was a home which gave*

great support to young people involved in Youth Ministry in the parish. Peg was a good listener and wise in her advice. She was not one to seek attention for herself, but took interest and delight in the wellbeing of all.

Peg was always grounded in her faith, prayerful and one of the people who made St Joseph's Parish a terrific parish. Her faithfulness and dedication to parish ministry amongst her many other responsibilities inspired me and was a wonderful witness for her family and fellow parishioners. She had a particular gift for encouraging people, recognising their goodness, being a loyal friend to them. She had great inner strength born of her prayerfulness, a great sense of God's goodness and love and the closeness of her family, parish and community life.

Jo remembers the first time she was introduced to her future parents-in-law:

I first met Peg in 1981 when Dennis walked me into the kitchen on his way to his bedroom and just said, 'This is Peg and Jack,' and left me to it! I have always felt at home with Peg and have always felt very blessed to have a mother-in-law that I not only admire but truly feel as if she is the mother I have not had for a very long time. I remember not long after meeting Peg that she asked Dennis where I came from as she knew my surname, that being Blizzard. Dennis tried to tell her that was impossible as I was from Traralgon, but Peg being

Peg wouldn't have that; she was certain she knew the name from somewhere. I suppose it was a couple of weeks later that Peg quizzed me as to what my father did. I thought it was odd as my father had died in 1975. Peg disappeared for a little while and then came back with an envelope with a letter inside. When she opened it, she handed it to me and to my utter surprise, the page was written in my father's handwriting! It was signed 'Max Blizzard' and as I read it, I realised it was a letter from him on behalf of the Australian Workers Union in regard to the death of Barry. It was quite surreal standing there looking at this letter from Dad, but that's why Peg knew my name; she had this letter from my father which she had kept all that time.

Over the years, Peg and I grew closer and closer. In fact, we used to joke that if Dennis and I ever split up, I would go and live with Peg, not Dennis! Having Peg so close to us in Warragul was great, the kids really loved having Nan around the corner, especially because they didn't have any grandparents on my side of the family. Even when she was working up the hospital, it was still a benefit for me. I remember when I was in hospital trying to give birth to Sarah, I was on a diet of clear broth and jelly for a week which was not the greatest menu. Being a specialised diet, Peg was in control of it, so she would come up and ask me which broth I preferred and which colour jelly would I like; little things, I know, but it was knowing she cared enough to ask was the greatest. The day I went to surgery for delivery, Dennis went down to the kitchen

to get his mother to sit with him to quell the nerves! Not every
impending father could have the benefit of his mum waiting
with him! I miss Peg not being in Warragul. It was like having
my best friend move away when she went to Greensborough,
but I am very comforted by the fact that she is comfortable
coming to stay with us here in Warragul for visits and feels
very happy to be here.

Another great event for the Rankin family that decade was
the ordination to the priesthood of Peter at St Jude's Scoresby
on 9 December 1989. Since a lot of people from Melbourne were
attending, it made sense for the ordination ceremony to be held
there. The first Mass of the newly ordained priest took place
in Peter's home parish of Warragul the following day. Peg had
the task of liaising with the local clergy and local community to
ensure everything was ready for the First Mass and the sump-
tuous afternoon tea held in the Warragul Arts Centre. Peg, and
to a lesser extent Jack, were involved in the life of the Church,
and many of their friends from the parish were able to attend the
First Mass. It was such a great day for the family. It was one of the
highlights of all of the Warragul years.

Photo taken on the day of Peter's ordination to the
priesthood, 9 December 1989. This was a grand day
for the Rankin family. The faces tell the story.

The family celebrations kept rolling along. Kathleen might
have been starting to think that love had passed her by, but she
married Peter Cantwell at St Joseph's Church on 12 October
1991. Peter, the priest in the family, presided over the ceremony.
It was a magic spring day and a beautiful celebration, a day for
the family to savour. The bridal party dressed in Peg and Jack's
house, and Jack was able to walk Kathleen down the aisle. It was
especially significant because the following year Peter Cantwell's
mother died very suddenly just before the birth of the couple's
first child.

Kathleen and Peg on the day of Kathleen's wedding, 12 October 1991.

Kath and Peter's wedding

Photo of family taken outside St Joseph's Church in Warragul.

When Peg and Jack moved to Warragul, from the outset they immersed themselves into the life of St Joseph's Catholic Church community. One group they both joined together and greatly contributed to was the Legion of Mary. Although they joined the group, their pathways were different as Peg was working and Jack had time during the day to visit families and so on. In effect, they joined different groups under the one umbrella, the Legion of Mary. Peg recalls:

> *The Assistant Priest of the time possibly put out expres-*
> *sions of interest to anyone who might want to be part of the*
> *Legion of Mary. The group had been operating for many*
> *decades in the parish, but the priest wanted to ramp it up a*
> *bit and strengthen its numbers and outreach.*

Peg and Jack responded to the call, attended a meeting and became part of the Legion, for the next twenty years or more in the case of Peg. They joined this group within a year or two of their arrival in Warragul.

Their involvement in the Legion meant a commitment to a weekly meeting and some door-to-door visits to Catholic families in the parish, with the aim of connecting them to the life of the parish. Visitation always took place in pairs and it was decided beforehand which streets to concentrate on. Peg remembers that reception varied:

> *Older people seemed to appreciate our visits more. Since we visited during the day, often there was no-one home as occupants would have been at work. But if we visited in the evening, who would want to answer the door after a busy day to a Bible basher? This was valuable family time. Overall, we were insulted only a couple of times.*

Fr Herman Hengel, Parish priest of Warragul from 2003, valued Peg's common-sense approach to sharing her faith:

> *Some members of the Legion were too right wing. This is one of the great things about Peg. She was such a mature, well balanced, sensible, practical woman, including in her faith. Some people became fanatics about the Rosary and Apparitions of Our Lady, and explicitly converting people. Peg had an extraordinary touch of being so balanced in her faith, sharing it beautifully, never pushing it down people's throat, she was terrific.*

For a long time, the Legion in Australia had been front-line foot soldiers connecting people with their local parish. In the earlier post-war period, the Legion of Mary had done a power of good visiting newly arrived migrant families. Peg remembered that on some visits, people would say, 'The Legion visited us when we first came to Australia.'

Meeting times changed over the years. Peg remembered that there were morning meetings and afternoon meetings as well as a 'workers' group' who would meet in the evening. In the late 1970s there would have been up to 25 people involved. Because Peg had such a strong commitment to the Legion, she became in a sense the linchpin to its success, and meetings were scheduled to suit her, so they coincided with her days off work. For a good deal of her time as a member of the Legion of Mary in Warragul, Peg was President of the local branch:

> *For years and years I had the same two days off work mid-week and so our meeting times were scheduled around that. This extra voluntary commitment on my days off was never an issue as hard work never worried me. I kept on finding something to do.*

Peg and Jack celebrated their golden wedding anniversary on 12 February 1994. Jack was already dealing with bone cancer but he was well enough to really enjoy the day. The mood was both celebratory and subdued. Everyone present at the gathering would have been aware that Jack was coming to the end of his time on this earth. There was also the awareness that after all, he had just turned eighty-two and he had been a heavy smoker until he was seventy-eight – not a bad innings when you consider that scenario.

The mood at the celebration was marked by gratitude for fifty good years of marriage. Peg and Jack had learnt the art of marriage long before. The key to their successful marriage was acceptance, trust, and space to move. Neither tried to change the other and they instinctively trusted each other. Sufi prophet Kahlil Gibran said that for a healthy marriage 'there must be spaces in your togetherness', and this was evident in spades in Peg and Jack's marriage. They each gave the other room to breathe.

Jack wanted to die at home. His wish was granted. He died peacefully on 1 July the same year.

WARRAGUL/DROUIN GAZETTE, February 15, 1994.

Celebrating 50 years

Jack and Peg Rankin celebrated their Golden wedding anniversary with a party at their Warragul home on Saturday.

The celebrations began with a special mass said by their son the Rev Fr Peter Rankin at St Joseph's Catholic Church, Warragul.

Mr and Mrs Rankin were married at Mt Evelyn in 1944. They farmed at Icy Creek before moving to Warragul in 1977.

They have eight sons, Terry, Kevin, Tim, Barry (dec), Bernard, Dennis, Peter and Paul and four daughters, Anne, Geradine, Mary and Kathleen.

They also have 17 grandchildren.

A special guest at the party was Mrs Rankin's sister and brother-in-law Carmel and John Fahey of New Zealand.

● *Peg and Jack Rankin in the garden of their Warragul home.*

Peg and Jack's grandchildren. Photo taken on the day of
their golden wedding anniversary celebration in 1994.

When Jack died, and after a period of adjustment Peg immersed
herself in the life of her family and resumed her involvement in
the life of her parish community. She was a reader/lector in her
parish church, and after Mass one Sunday she was approached
by a teacher at St Joseph's Primary School and asked to consider
volunteering her time to help children with their reading. She
duly obliged, and this ministry too became part of her weekly
ritual. She built up a relationship with her students and they
looked forward to her visits.

Children had been part of Peg's entire life. She had younger
siblings, she had twelve children of her own, and she had twenty
one grand-children. At one time she worked with a very difficult

child, and brought him a gift of some pencils. She was a little miffed when the teacher thought that the gift was inappropriate and may have shown signs of favouritism, and the gift never reached the child.

We are all a product of our times. The influences of childhood are paramount. Psychologists tell us that the first few years are pivotal to our later psychological make-up and emotional health. In our faith journey, too, the early years are important. Early religious experience can be quite telling, and the way we remember being taught about First Communion often stays with us. One of the strong devotions in the early part of the twentieth century was devotion to the Sacred Heart of Jesus. The heart is a symbol of love, a symbol of compassion. Most Catholic families had a picture of the Sacred Heart of Jesus prominent in their houses. There was certainly a picture of the Sacred Heart in the Rankin house in Fumina, but in the move to Warragul somehow the picture was lost or accidentally discarded.

This image was in Peg's house in Warragul and later sat in pride of place on her wall in Leith Park, Greensborough North.

In the eighteenth and nineteenth centuries the spiritual life of Catholics was influenced by Jansenism. In short, this movement stressed our unworthiness in the sight of God, our sinfulness, our wounded human nature. There were vestiges of this movement in the early part of the twentieth century. Devotion to the Sacred Heart was designed to counteract this spirituality. It rekindled belief in a loving God, a merciful God, a God who had a heart for humanity, and counteracted the pessimistic Jansenist influence with the reminder that ultimately God is Love.

Like many others of her vintage, Peg was brought up on a religious diet of Eucharistic adoration, the cult of Mary and devotion to the Sacred Heart. The picture told the story. Jesus was depicted with a gentle face, looking slightly heavenward with an emblazoned red heart visible on the image, and the forefinger of the left hand pointing towards the heart. Peg made it very clear that she wanted a picture of the Sacred Heart in her house in Warragul. Her eldest son, Terry, and his wife Deb were on a mission to track down the image.

These pictures were not easy to find in the first decade of the twenty-first century. As devotion to the Sacred Heart had waned over the years, so too had the availability of the image. But they were eventually successful and tracked down a picture. It was not quite the traditional image but it met with Peg's approval and liking, and was given pride of place in her house at Warragul in the last few years of her time there.

Parish Pastoral Councils are relatively new in the Catholic Church. Up until the 1970s the parish clergy were the sole decision makers in the parish. They decided what, where and when things would happen. They prepared couples for marriage, prepared families for the baptism of their children, they initiated the direction of pastoral outreach, they were the sole financial administrators, they were the Liturgy Committee and decided which events would occur. The role of the laity generally was caricatured as 'to pray, pay and obey'.

After the Second Vatican Council (1962-1965), there was a considered move towards decentralisation of decision making and more lay collaboration in the process. We find in one of the documents of the Council these refreshing and revealing words:

> *Pastors indeed, know well how much the laity contribute to the welfare of the whole Church. For they know that they themselves were not established by Christ to undertake alone the whole salvific mission of the Church to the world, but that it is their exalted office so as to be shepherds of the faithful and also recognise the latter's contribution and charisms that everyone in his or her own way will, with one mind, cooperate in the common task.[25]*

Elsewhere in the same document we read that:

> *Pastors should recognise and promote the dignity and responsibility of the laity in the Church. They should willingly use their prudent advice and confidently assign duties to them in the service of the Church, leaving them freedom and scope for acting. Indeed, they should give them courage to undertake works on their own initiative. They should ... consider initial moves, suggestions and desires proposed by the laity.[26]*

This is definitely new thinking in the Catholic Church, since for centuries priests were considered an 'elite caste' superior to the laity.

One of the offshoots of the Vatican Council and the revision of Canon Law following the decrees of the Council (1983) was

---

25 *Dogmatic Constitution on the Church No.30.*
26 *Dogmatic Constitution No.37.*

the formation of Parish Pastoral Councils to assist in the decision-making process of the local church. The opinion of the laity was meant to be heard, they were to be given freedom and scope for acting, and their initiatives were to be respected and encouraged. For many priests this change of mentality was not always easy to accept. Some priests who were trained in the old way were now challenged to serve in a new way, and it wasn't easy for them to adjust. Peg reflects:

> *I was on the Parish Pastoral Council for a while. It was frustrating for members. If anyone had an idea, no matter how good it sounded, Fr McCartan's (the parish priest at the time) initial response was always negative. It didn't matter what you brought to the table, he would never say 'that is worth a thought'. He would always howl you down but later on, he may come around. You just had to be prepared for his instinctive negative reaction.*

The Rite of Christian Initiation of Adults (RCIA) is a revamped method of welcoming adults into the life of the Catholic Church. It is technically the process whereby adults seeking initiation in the Catholic Church are accompanied along the journey by committed Christians towards reception of Baptism, Confirmation and Eucharist, which would normally take place at the Easter Vigil Mass. In the good old days a person who expressed interest in becoming a Catholic would have classes in the evening with the parish priest or his assistant. The model was the familiar inquiry class and the primary goal was instruction in Catholic teaching.

The RCIA is about conversion, about the spiritual journey of the whole person – heart, mind and soul – towards God. This process involves a lot more than knowing what the Church teaches. It is initiation into a community of believers, not simply an introduction to the parish priest or his associate pastor. From the early 1980s, in parishes around Australia it became the practice to form a team of committed Catholics in assisting enquirers, catechumens and candidates for full reception into the Church. *Enquirers* are those who dip their toe in the water, but are yet to make the decision to become Catholic. A *catechumen* is the technical term for an adult who is yet to be baptised and opts for Christian initiation. *Candidates* are those who are baptised into another Christian tradition, ie Anglican Church, Uniting Church, Pentecostal Church etc, but have stepped forward in faith and are on the journey to be received into the Catholic Church.

At St Joseph's Parish, Warragul, Peg had retired from work before the RCIA process was in full swing. This meant she could give it her heart and soul, and she worked for many years as part of the RCIA team. It was a significant involvement for Peg and one which she enjoyed immensely. It often meant a change of routine and worship time. She reflected that:

> *You might attend Mass on Sunday that wasn't your usual Mass with catechumens and candidates.*

During Peg's involvement with the RCIA, the Co-ordinator for a good while was Joan Robertson. Joan valued Peg very highly and remembers:

Every Wednesday night at ten past seven the little red Ford Laser pulled up in front of my house and we went to the gatherings together. Peg was a great supporter of the RCIA. She was such a help to people enquiring about the faith because she was such a faith-filled person herself. She always had great stories to tell, especially when it came to unpacking the scripture stories. She was able to relate them to everyday life. She was able to bring the Word of God to life for participants and give them a better understanding of the message of the gospels. It was Karl Bath, the great Protestant theologian, who said we must have the gospel in one hand and the newspaper in the other. She was always very good at drawing out the text and applying it to everyday life. Peg had a great knowledge of her faith and the scriptures.

Joan Robertson, RCIA Team Leader and close friend of Peg during her final years at Warragul.

At some point Peg wondered if at her age she could continue to make a worthwhile contribution to the RCIA team, and she expressed these concerns to Joan, who recalls:

> *Peg approached me on the quiet and suggested maybe her best years were behind her and it might be time to step back from the team. I reassured Peg that her wisdom, mature faith and scriptural insights were still valued and appreciated, and encouraged her to stay on the team. We also loved her cream sponges at the end of the meetings! She was certainly treasured both within the RCIA team and by individuals working towards full membership of the Catholic faith.*

For more than fifteen years Peg was the sacristan at St Joseph's Church. This entailed setting up for Mass and other liturgical celebrations such as Benediction and funerals. When the parish priests were away, Peg took it upon herself to open and close the church, which was left open all day to allow anybody to pop in for a private prayer. Occasionally, late at night Peg might have remembered she hadn't locked the church and off she would go in the little red Laser to do her duty and secure the building. She would go out of her way to assist any visiting priest, making sure everything was ready for Mass and enlightening him as to any local customs, and ensuring he was comfortable. Sometimes she would have also provided meals for the visiting priest.

Fr Herman Hengel, parish priest of Warragul from 2003, reflected:

Peg was well and truly ensconced as sacristan when I hit the scene. She was responsible and reliable, she was great to work with. She was organised. She loved the job, she wanted to do it. It gave her a mission in life. When it came to the big celebrations, Peg knew what to do, how to set the Church up for certain celebrations and events. Just one time, however, we arrived at the point of baptism in the Easter Vigil Liturgy. I lifted the lid off the font to administer the adult baptisms and there was no water and in a friendly manner I turned to Peg and said, 'Oh, we might need some water, Peg.' Peg immediately scurried off to the sacristy and returned with a bucket of water, poured it into the baptismal font with smiles all round. It wasn't a problem.

Joan Robertson remembered the occasion well:

One funny little story is the Easter Vigil, the highlight of the liturgical year when the Church welcomes new adult members. Everything was ready, lectors, music, sponsors, all was thought to be in readiness for a wonderful uplifting liturgy with several baptisms and receptions. At the critical point Father Hengel lifted the lid off the font and there was no water. Every year since that we always remember that little episode. Peg enjoyed being sacristan. She was good at it too. I remember Bishop Christopher Prowse, Bishop of Sale (2008-2014) commenting on the quality of the linen on the altar and how lovely it was, and once publicly thanked Peg for she

always had the altar linen beautifully starched. Truly, she did
so much. It was a bit of a joke around the parish that when
Peg finished up as sacristan in 2012, it took three people to fill
her shoes.

Bishop at Warragul

BISHOP Prowse meets sacristan Peg Rankin at the Warragul Mass.

By Anne Keating

WARRAGUL - Parishioners were pleased to welcome Bishop Christopher Prowse to Warragul and Drouin for weekend Masses on August 22-23.

He commended those who had contributed so well to the celebration of the Eucharist. He reminded us that many parishioners attend Mass with joy rather than through a sense of obligation and in so doing give good example to others, particularly members of their own family who perhaps have not attended Mass on a regular basis for some time. After the 7pm Mass in Warragul on Saturday evening Bishop Prowse blessed and declared open the new Marian Room and met many parishioners.

In speaking to the people his sense of humor and relaxed friendly manner delighted those who shared supper with him. The lovely supper was provided by parishioners and the Catholic Women's League.

Bishop Prowse also celebrated the 9am Mass in Warragul and the 10.30am Mass in Drouin on Sunday morning. A warm welcome was extended to him by parishioners of St Joseph's and St Ita's who look forward to further visits in the future.

Peg knew the people in the parish well. She was a mine of information for the local clergy. Fr Herman Hengel noted:

Peg knew everybody in the place, who's who in the town, she knew about them, their family situation, and she was always positive about people. She knew them all. She was a most extraordinary person to have around when a new priest who knows few people is trying to find his way in a new parish. Peg knew strengths and weaknesses. Obviously her contacts with the hospital was a way in, but her knowledge transcended the hospital scene. It was possible to know a lot about the Catholic community and little outside that, but Peg had a strong foothold into the wider community.

Joan Robertson similarly remembers calling on Peg and her good friend Marie Beasley to write up a list of older people whom they could invite for a special Mass and lunch. Joan tells the story:

Peg and Marie hand wrote a list of all those we might invite to a Mass of Anointing and Luncheon. These names were handwritten and between them they knew so many older people in the parish. I remember Peg and Marie coming to the office next door and getting their heads together to work on the list. All these years later, we still refer back to the list, and we have added to it along the way. Peg would know about anniversaries. If I wasn't sure when somebody had died, Peg would know. If I wasn't sure about something, I'd ring Peg. She was always ready to help.

Peg and Fr Herman Hengel, Parish Priest, at the occasion of Peg's farewell from Warragul. 2012.

Peg was always prepared to go the extra yard in service of others. Barbara Malady remembered Peg for the extra care she gave her mother Phyllis in the nursing home:

> *Peg was wonderful to Mum after she had a stroke. She used to make her pea and ham soup. She personally took the soup over to Phyllis for her to eat; there was nothing that was too much trouble for her.*

Similarly, Prue Walkinshaw, parish secretary, remembers:

> *Peg was absolutely marvellous to my mother-in law. She visited her many times.*

Tim and Marg remember the time Peg gave them when they had a milk bar in Balaclava in the mid 1980s. She would work five days a week in the hospital and then spend her two days off helping them in the shop! Tim reflected:

Mum seemed to love working with us on her days off. She was excellent with the customers and they all loved to have a chat with her and she knew a lot of them by name. Working with us may have taken her back to her youth because she took to it like a duck to water. She was a tremendous support to us during this time and made life so much easier for us. She was there when Nicola was born and for all the birthdays, which was a wonderful gift to all of us. I hope the rest of my siblings did not feel left out during these few years but we certainly appreciated her help. I think she has demonstrated her ability to be wherever she thought she was needed most at the time and I am sure we have all benefited from her generosity in this way.

Gerardine pondered:

I was 42 when my first and only son Jackson was born. I had been a teacher and had then held a number of management roles where my commitment to work was high and I was a bit of an achiever. I also lived in Ballarat, about 200km from Warragul. Once Jackson was born I felt totally out of my depth. The Dr Spock book certainly didn't have the answers. I rang my mother for help and her response was brilliant:

'My professional daughter finally needs my help. I will be on the next train to Ballarat.' And true to her word, she arrived in Ballarat later that day and stayed with us until things settled.

Paul had similar memories:

Mum was so generous with her time. She never hesitated to come to Melbourne and babysit our girls for an evening or two, often at short notice. Our kids loved it, as she would always bring some sort of cooked treat with her, yo-yos, lemon meringue pie, chocolate cake or another favourite 'Granny soup'. Peg has proved time and time again her ability to be there for family and friends in need. Nothing ever seemed too much trouble for her, and she never went about telling anyone how good she was.

Little things matter. Deliberate and random acts of kindness count. Martin Luther King once said that 'the way you begin to change the world is through service'. St Francis de Sales similarly wrote that 'there is nothing small in the service of God'.

Peg's life has been renowned for continual acts of kindness. After Jack died in 1994, she immersed herself in the life of her family and community. She drove herself down to Greensborough and helped Kathleen and Peter with their children. When one of her adult children was sick or run down, she would be right by their side in no time. When Peter, her son the priest, took his religious community away from Don Bosco in Brunswick on a couple of occasions, she cooked for them. She would babysit grandchildren at short notice. When St Joseph's primary school was relocated, she was be busy sticking address labels onto envelopes for those who were to be invited to the new school opening. She helped with providing supper for parish functions; she would drop what she was doing and visit some member of the community who was sick. Peg's life was filled with deliberate and random acts of kindness.

Current Bishop of Bathurst, the Most Reverend Michael McKenna, spent the early part of his priesthood in the parish of Warragul. He remembered Peg well:

> I met Peg thirty one years ago as an assistant priest. It was my first appointment and Peg was welcoming and supportive from the start. She was a real Christian; full of love, mercy, joy and a lively sense of humour. We shared wonderful talks about faith like a brother and sister in the Lord. Of course, she was an older sister who helped me a lot with her greater wisdom and understanding of people. I got to know and love her boisterous family too, and could see the love of life she'd passed onto them. My words are inadequate, but when I remember Peg, it makes me happy. I think of what St John wrote to a fledgling Christian community: 'How can we say we love God who we can't see unless we love the brother and sister we can see?'[27] Peg made God's love real for me and for so many others.

---

27 1 John 4:20.

'Pretty soon after I retired from work I got involved in taking Communion to the sick,' said Peg. Again, this is a modern ministry within the Church now opened to lay people. For centuries it was the sole prerogative of the priest and deacon to bring communion to the sick and lay people were not allowed to touch the consecrated host. It was part of the clericalisation of the Church in the Middle Ages whereby certain ministries were closed to laymen and laywomen and reserved for ordained ministers, bishops, priests and deacons. However, in the early Church, laymen and laywomen would take communion to their sick relatives who were not well enough to attend Mass.

After the Second Vatican Council, some ministries were given back to the laity, including taking communion to the sick. As Peg said:

> *I couldn't do this particular ministry whilst I was still working as this normally took place on Sundays and I worked most Sundays. It usually meant taking Communion to three or four elderly or sick people.*

People looked forward to Peg's visits, and being nourished by word and sacrament. Peg recalled that:

> *A nun came to our parish from Sale and instructed us in preparation for this ministry. She insisted that ministers always have a little chit-chat before administering Communion to the person.*

Peg would have easily and readily adhered to this format. She has always had the gift of putting people at ease in her presence by initiating and being part of a conversation. Again, Joan Robertson explained that when she was visiting the sick and elderly, sometimes in the presence of their family:

> *Peg would move into the moment and lead families in prayer with grace and poise. Peg would have known the prayers and what to say and put the family at ease and feel really comfortable in that setting. Peg would instinctively know what to say and know what not to say to the children about their mother or father.*

In addition to her ministry on Sunday, Peg took Communion to the sick at Cooinda Nursing Home every Friday:

> *One woman in Cooinda had a mild case of dementia and on a particular day she was following me around and heard me read a passage of scripture and she blurted out, 'Don't talk that s--t.'*

All in a day's ministry for Peg!

Peg had the advantage of being well known and her commitment to the Church was obvious. Families crossed her path in her ministry to the sick and elderly. For some time (possibly years) she had been administering Communion to a retired farmer at Cooinda by the name of Jim. Over time, Pag had built up quite a relationship with Jim and his family. At some point his health began to deteriorate quite rapidly, and one day his family directed staff on duty at the Nursing Home to call Peg to see if she could come down and administer the last rites to their dying husband and father. Peg was mortified at the request, since in effect the family was asking for the Sacrament of Anointing of the Sick. This particular pastoral ministry has always been the reserve of priests, and not even deacons can administer this sacrament. We find in the letter of St James the text:

> Are there people sick among you? Let them send for the priests of the Church and let the priests pray over them anointing them with oil in the name of the Lord. The prayer of faith will save the sick persons, and the Lord will raise them up. If they have committed any sins, their sins will be forgiven them.[28]

Here was Peg being requested to administer the sacrament to the dying. In her own words:

> I panicked a bit, I didn't want it getting around the town big noting myself that I was a quasi-priest. I reassured the family that I would do all in my power to find a priest. Father McCartan was away at the time and we had to call on Fr Pat Walsh to come over from Korumburra to administer the

---

28 Letter to James 5:14-15.

sacrament. I didn't want to go to the Nursing Home and give the wrong idea that somehow I had the authority to administer the priestly anointing. In hindsight, I should have gone down there and presided over prayers with the family for Jim, but I panicked. I knew my place. Later on, my priest son Peter would often joke with me that we had two priests in the family, Peter and Peg!

Papal medal to Warragul woman

PEG Rankin proudly wears the Benemerenti Medal alongside parish priest Fr Herman Hengel who displays the framed citation.

WARRAGUL - Peg Rankin, a parishioner of St Joseph's Parish, Warragul has received a Papal Award of the Benemerenti Medal for her services to the Church.

It only the second awarded in this diocese.

She has received a medal and a citation recognising her contribution to promoting Christian living.

Mrs Rankin is the greatly loved matriarch of her large and extended family. She has also contributed enormously to the Catholic Parishes in which she has lived.

For many years she has visited people in their homes, nursing homes and hospital on behalf of St Joseph's Parish, organised and brought Communion to those not able to come to the Church.

She has been a member of the parish council, helped prepare adults for baptism and reception into the Catholic Church, listened to children reading at the parish school and is the sacristan at St Joseph's Church.

Peg was aware that she served her church community well, but not so much the wider community. One day whilst she was doing her shopping, she came across a community leader who was looking for volunteers to assist by ringing up older people who were confined to their homes, to give them a bit of companionship and support. Peg responded, and each Friday from 10.00 am to 12.00 midday she would turn up at the Warragul Police Station and report for duty. She had a list of older people to contact and she would proceed to ring them up. Peg was a natural on the telephone and was well able to initiate a conversation, put people at ease and have something interesting to say. If the person was not at home when Peg called, she would report it in the book where notes were recorded. Peg performed this weekly task pretty much until the time she left Warragul. On the eve of her departure, at least two families wrote her thank-you notes for the comfort she had given to their parents, and said how much they looked forward to her weekly phone call.

During 2011, Peg was beginning to think of her future. There would come a time when she couldn't drive, and her house was more than two kilometres from the church and shopping centre. It was going to be too costly to move closer to the town as property prices were significantly more expensive nearer to the town centre. Jo and Dennis lived in Warragul, but nearly all her children lived in Melbourne. Could she leave her beloved Warragul, a place which meant so much to her, a place where she had invested so much energy over the last thirty-six years, and which in return had given so much to her? Options were discussed with her children. In the end it was decided that Peg would 'pull up stumps' in Warragul and move closer to the city, nearer to her children, where she could receive the care she would need in her final years. She was eighty-six.

Once the decision was made, Peg never really looked back. She had spent her whole life adapting to new situations. She went to Fumina as a young bride and mastered the skill of parenting. She played a strong hand in raising twelve children. In 1964 she stepped up to the plate when her husband had a serious operation, and basically took over the running of the farm.

The years in Warragul were great for Peg and Jack. A whole new world had opened up to them when they moved there. And now a move to Melbourne beckoned for Peg to be closer to most of her family.

St Joseph's parish gave Peg a farewell afternoon in June 2012. It was very well attended. It was a truly fitting way to thank Peg for her outstanding contribution to the life of the parish for almost forty years. Her CV was impressive. She had been:

- an active member of the Legion of Mary including in the role of President
- a well-prepared lector
- a trusted Eucharistic minister
- a well-received reader at St Joseph's School
- a valued RCIA team member
- a skilled minister to the sick and elderly
- a valued Parish Pastoral Council member, and
- dedicated sacristan.

The parish gave Peg a beautiful chair for her new unit at Leith Park in Greensborough North. It was now time for her to put her feet up after her many years of labour in the Lord's vineyard.

CHAPTER 9

Time to Ease Off

NOW IT WAS time for Peg to ease off a little and settle into a quieter life. From August 2012, Peg resided at Leith Park in Greensborough North, a retirement village on the outskirts of Melbourne. Leith Park was established in 1963 and is located within a leafy setting typifying the natural beauty of the Diamond Valley. It had one hundred and eighteen self-contained independent living units in which residents can maintain their privacy and independence with reassurance that help and support is readily available upon request.

Peg's younger sister Gwyn had moved into Leith Park a year or so earlier and that helped make Peg's transition a little bit easier. Peg lived comfortably in her own unit close to family and amenities. And since part of her childhood was spent in Eltham, she was only a few kilometres from a place which held memories for her.

Leith Park, where Peg lived from 2012.

Kathleen reflects on Peg's transfer from Warragul to Leith Park in these words:

> *The main factor in Mum's decision to leave Warragul was that she realised that she shouldn't be driving. Her reflexes and spatial awareness were not what they had been, and without her licence her life in Warragul would change dramatically. As most of her children live in various parts of Melbourne she decided to move to Melbourne rather than stay in Warragul. It was a courageous decision to say goodbye to her friends and the parish in which she had spent almost four decades. She put her name down at Leith Park and waited for a unit to become available. Her home at 1 Edinbugh Street, Warragul, for thirty-six years was spruced up a bit and put on the market. It took a while to sell but once it was sold the time came to sort out all of Mum's possessions and memories. I really admired Mum's positive attitude at this juncture. Unlike lots of people at this stage of life, Mum didn't want to be burdened with too much clutter and hang on to possessions she no longer needed. She was fully aware she was moving into a very small unit and wanted to live simply and only take what she needed.*
>
> *After many small farewells and goodbyes and a moving celebration from the St Joseph's community, moving day arrived. It was a very stressful time for Mum and a bit overwhelming, but she was ready for the move. Mum's unit at Leith Park is one of the older ones. It is small but cosy and surrounded by lovely trees and gardens. It is a safe, peaceful*

place and she has settled in well to her new life. Leith Park is close to St Helena Shopping Centre and this has most of the facilities she needs. One of the best things about Leith Park is that her sister Gwyn also lives there. It is wonderful that they are able to support each other and keep each other company in their last few years. We all go grocery shopping together on Tuesday and have coffee and a chat. Mum is also able to catch the Leith Park bus to St Helena, so she does that regularly and meets friends for coffee.

Mum has made a real effort to become involved in the social activities provided. She attends movie outings, sausage sizzles, and plays cards regularly on Saturday mornings. On Thursdays she enjoys lunch at the Greensborough RSL with Gwyn and other friends including Godfrey and Doreen, Joan and Marj.

We go to Mass together on Sunday morning to Francis Xavier in Montmorency. Mum now recognises some familiar faces who greet her warmly. It has been a difficult transition to move from a parish in which she had been such a part of for so long, to a parish where she is still a stranger. We have coffee after Mass at our favourite coffee shop in Montmorency.

Mum comes regularly to our house for dinner and is a welcome visitor at all of our family celebrations. It has been fantastic for her and for us to have this special time with her. She also really enjoys having Mary close by, and they see each other regularly. Mary and I both feel blessed to live so close to Mum, and treasure the time we are spending with her.

Sisters Peg and Gwyn, who both resided in
Leith Park, Greensborough North.

CHAPTER 10

A Life Lived to the Full

The good life is one inspired by love and guided by knowledge.
Life isn't about finding yourself. Life is about creating yourself.

GEORGE BERNARD SHAW

CONFUCIUS SAID THAT life is really simple but we insist on making it complicated. Peg chose not to live this way. She led an uncomplicated life. She lived a rich life. She seized the day. She lived life to the full. In one sense it was quite an ordinary life, but in another sense quite extraordinary. Peg maximised the potential of each moment. She read her situation well and made the most of it.

From a very young age Peg lived the maxim:

There is more joy in giving than in receiving.

It was her ritual as a child to bring each family member tea and toast in bed. She gave her all to help her father in the family business. She gave every fibre of her being into her relationship with Jack. Often there was not much in return. She taught all her children the value of faith, integrity, hard work and tough love. She served her family, her church and her community well.

And Peg was tough. There would not be too many eighty four-year-olds who could manage the camping caper, sleeping on a lilo like she did in Ocean Grove in 2009. Hers was indeed a journey of faith and resilience.

A beautiful reading in the Book of Proverbs captures a rich life, one filled with wisdom, dignity, hard work, practical skill and outreach. There is hardly a phrase or sentence in this passage that does not in some way apply to Peg:

> *A woman of character, where is she to be found? She is more precious than jewels.*
> *She brings only good, not evil all the days of her life.*
> *She is always busy with wool and needles, she does her work with eager hands.*
> *She is like a merchant vessel, bringing her food from far away.*
> *She gets up while it is still dark and feeds her household.*
> *She sets her mind on a field, then she buys it.*
> *With what her hands have earned she reaps a rich harvest.*
> *She puts her back into her work and shows how strong her arms can be.*

*She finds her work well worthwhile; her lamp does not go out at
night.*
*She puts her hand on the sewing machine and her fingers work the
spindle.*
She holds out her hand to the poor, she opens her arms to the needy.
Snow may come, she has no fears for her household,
With all her children warmly clothed.
*She is clothed in strength and dignity, she can laugh at the days to
come.*
*When she opens her mouth, she does so wisely and her words are
kind.*
She keeps an eye on her household and is never idle.
Her children speak up and call her blessed.
Many women have done admirable things but you surpass them all.
*Charm is deceitful and beauty empty, the woman who is wise is the
one to praise.*
*Give her a share in what her hands have worked for and let her
works tell her praises in the hamlet, the town and city.*[29]

All these qualities were amply evident in Peg's long life.

Congratulations, Peg. You lived life to the full. You were graced. You gave it your best shot. All that awaits is for you to enter the Kingdom of our Lord.

---

29 Adapted from the Book of Proverbs 31:10-31.

Peg passed away peacefully surrounded by her children and many grandchildren on 9 May 2018. She left behind a legacy of love, resilience, and unwavering faith in the face of life's challenges.

Treasured Memories

The following are tributes written for the occasion of Peg's 90th birthday on 19 November 2015.

SONS-IN-LAW AND DAUGHTERS-IN-LAW

Peg always maintained a warm relationship with sons-in-law and daughters-in-law. In their own way, all the in-laws felt loved and valued.

JOHN SCHMID **Married Anne in 1973**

In earlier days Peg had boundless energy and stamina. She could fix any problem, had loads of common sense. She 'wore the pants', looked after John Simon Rankin. She tended to get fired up or worked up on a subject of interest or a cause she supported. She knew all the goings on. Peg was a very good cook. Best scones I have eaten, plum puddings 'yum yum'!

MARG MALONEY **Married Tim in 1977**

The beginning and end of the story are the same: I love my darling mother-in-law Peg with all my heart and I am absolutely uplifted by her love for me. She is inspirational to me as a wife, a mother, a grandmother, sister, mother-in-law, woman of faith and woman. She is a marvellous confidante and colleague. She has incredible empathy with people in any and all stages of life, and endless energy to care for all.

Each of her twelve children is loved for themselves. Each was allowed to go and each one loved to come home (still do). No matter how many miles away we were, Tim and Peg always discussed the weather in the style of true farmers. When we moved back to Melbourne from West Wyalong in 1983, when we took on the shop in Balaclava in 1985, when Tim began to build his masterpiece, a mudbrick home, in 1999 Peg was right into it and full of practical support... It is the same for everyone's dreams.

One of my favourite reflections is on Peg as grandmother. I could hardly wait to take Louisa to see Peg and Jack in Warragul, but I wondered how helpless I would look as a new mother in the eyes of a mother of twelve! Peg greeted me with 'what a lovely job you are doing with her' and I immediately relaxed and enjoyed talking over every detail of Louie's progress, then Mick's and finally Nicola's. The night that Nicola was born we were in the Milk Bar and waited until Granny arrived to go to hospital. We all loved Granny's amazing support at the shop, especially

Tim. Of course, we are only one of the families of grandkids who have spent school holidays, beach holidays, birthdays, Christmas, Easter and many happy times with Peg.

It is a privilege to be a woman alongside Peg. It is to share the very best of those roles: partner, wife, mother, nurturer, encourager, listener, peer, friend – and it is to share the striving towards them. It is to watch someone grow, welcome each new arrival, see someone off, be both independent and dependent, to build community. It is to bring your faith to life in every relationship, joy and hardship. It is never to be alone.

PETER CANTWELL **Married Kathleen in 1991**

Peg filled a big hole for me as not long after meeting Kathleen and just before the birth of our first born, Lachlan, I lost my own mother at the extremely young age of sixty-nine.

Peg filled the void of being both first and second grandmother to Lachlan and our next three children. Peg has given an amazing amount of her time in ringing the children around special events – birthdays and attending various school activities.

I was working crazy hours in Lachlan, Felicity and Marcus's early years. (Thomas had not yet arrived at that point.) Peg would jump in her car from Warragul early in the morning and arrive at our place in Greensborough before 9.00 am to help Kathleen with managing the housework and entertaining and looking after the children. On a number of occasions if Peg had been at our house for five to ten minutes and had still not picked up the iron, Lachlan would question Peg on *WHY* she had not as yet commenced ironing as he assumed that was the natural part of her visit.

Peg, as part of being my surrogate mother, selflessly chose to accompany me to Minyip in the Wimmera to attend the funeral of my Uncle Frank in the mid '90s. Kathleen was unable to attend with juggling young children at the time. Peg drove to Greensborough the morning of the funeral and later that morning she and I headed up the highway to Minyip. Without Peg's company for an eight-hour round road trip, it would have made such a journey very tedious. Having someone to talk to whilst completing such a journey and attending the funeral was much appreciated, and a very selfless act on Peg's behalf.

Christmas time at Peg's was always a time the children and *BIG* children enjoyed and remember. It was always amazing that food would just appear – much like the loaves and the fishes. Regular trips to Warragul with the children during the year were always greeted with a fresh batch of scones, lamingtons and jelly cakes. We were always welcomed and fed up to our 'pussy boots'.

BRIGETTE **Married Paul in 1983**

M	*Mother, Matriarch, Mother-in-law*
A	*Active, Amazing*
R	*Resourceful, Reliable, Responsible*
G	*Generous, Groovy Granny*
A	*Admirable, Awesome*

R	Respected, Religious
E	Entertaining the masses
T	Time honoured, Talented
P	Persistent, positive,
E	Energetic, engaging, encouraging
G	Graced, grateful, gregarious

DAVID Dahlenburg **Married Gerardine in 1999**

For someone who has read that right wing rag the *Herald Sun* all her life, Peg has a great capacity to be open-minded about modern-day issues and politics. Well done! But maybe it was the crosswords she loved, as her ability to knock over a crossword with or without Herbie's help is a symbol of the agility of her mind.

I thank her for welcoming me into the family in spite of the rushed and very non-Catholic approach to the conception of our child Jackson. Although I planted the parsley to assist with the potting procedure, Peg simply laughed and said, 'Oh no need for parsley, Jack only had to look at me!'

Now, about that waddle. The Rankin waddle perfected by Peg lives on in each of her daughters, especially Gerardine. Hopefully Peg will see a few more Geelong premierships in her time.

CAROLINE **Married Bernard in 2000**

I first went to Ocean Grove in January 2007 while Bernie was away and working in the Solomon Islands. I went for a few days and Lara came too. Tim and Marg offered me a spot in their tent and I shared the front room with Peg, who, like me, slept on her inflatable mattress with a sleeping bag. It was quite fun chatting at night in our beds and I occasionally accompanied Peg on a dawn trek to 'the ladies'. We were very comfy.

I think it was the following year that I went again, and again shared the tent with Tim, Marg and Peg. Peg was still recovering from her hip operation so getting up and down off the ground was difficult. When nature called, I woke in the early hours of the morning and helped Peg up off her camping mattress and helped get her back down. She never complained but I knew it was proving to be hard work. The next day I decided Peg needed a camp stretcher to get her off the ground, allowing easier access to and from the bed. Off to Rays Outdoors we went and picked out a suitable stretcher. She slept on that for a number of years and it was just amazing to have a lady of her age, camping with the family. It was evident she enjoyed her time there and she was always available for a glass of wine and quiet chat when needed. Her resilience is remarkable.

On a more personal note, Peg has always made me feel important and an integral member of the family. She has a very inclusive nature, welcoming all those she meets, and I thank her for her support of me, Bernie and our children as a blended family.

GRANDCHILDREN AND STEP-GRANDCHILDREN

At the time of her passing, Peg had twenty-one grandchildren and six step-grandchildren, sixteen great-grandchildren. She was variously called Granny, Grandma or Nan.

ISAAC SCHMID

Yo-yo biscuits, plum pudding icy-poles! There was always plenty of yummy food at Grandma's house. As a kid, I loved visiting her house in Warragul. Grandma always made us feel welcome. But it wasn't just because of her great cooking. She took a great interest in all her grandchildren (and still does). Grandma enjoyed talking to us and sharing a joke.

Over the years nothing much has changed. There are now more grandchildren and also a few great-grandchildren! I'm so glad my own kids have had the chance to meet their great-grandmother. Turning 90 is a fantastic achievement.

OLIVE SCHMID

I was born in January 1976, in the week that Grandma and Granddad moved to Warragul, and my story starts at 1 Edinburgh Street. Grandma and I were friends from the beginning. Long before I mastered the art of conversation with anyone else, Grandma and Granddad were regaled with my incessant chatter for the whole week that I stayed with them as a 4-year-old.

Grandma taught me how to make her famous yo-yo biscuits and I still remember being told very firmly that I was too big to be caught licking the bowl. Grandma was my favourite MasterChef decades before the TV show hit our screens and these days, Grandma's shortbread, sponge cake and banana cake recipes are still my go-to references next to the Margaret Fulton and Karen Martini cookbooks on my bookshelf.

The grandkids would often run amok at the Warragul North Primary School oval, and the chance to hang out with our cousins was definitely the priority at Rankin family gatherings and school holiday visits to Warragul. Despite our lack of social engagement with the grown-ups, when we finally trudged home Grandma would always spoil us with lamingtons, jelly cakes and yo-yo biscuits. We would be offered a treat from the giant deep freezer in the laundry that was permanently stocked with our favourite ice creams. With an ever expanding troop of grand-kids to cater for, Grandma's ability to keep track of our likes and dislikes never faltered.

Peg with Olive and Isaac Schmid, 1979.

Grandma is one of the kindest, most compassionate people I have ever had the privilege to know. I discovered the limits to her patience on the day that a vicious, swooping magpie pecked me between the eyes when I was playing hide and seek with my brothers at a Warragul Park. I would have been about ten. After whisking me off to the GP for a tetanus shot and then enduring my hysterical wailing for the next 2 hours, Grandma had finally had enough. She demanded that I stop crying because she couldn't stand listening to it for a moment longer. In hindsight, I think this was a fair call, but my fear of magpies persists and I still flinch at the slightest flapping of a wing.

Come Christmas time, our always-groovy Grandma would find each grandkid an outfit that fitted them perfectly and matched their personal style. I remember Grandma cheering from the sidelines at my junior netball grand finals and coming on beach holidays to Dromana with a whole tribe of grandkids. Grandma is just as involved in our lives today. On visits to Leith Park, it's obvious that befriending my cousins, aunties and uncles on Facebook just can't compete with all the family news to which Grandma is privy.

I moved to Hobart in 2012 and Grandma, Great Aunty Gwyn and Aunty Kate were my first visitors from across Bass Strait. They were at the mercy of my boot camp holiday itinerary. When I suggested an early morning hotel pick-up for 8.00 am Mass before hitting the road for a full day of sightseeing, Aunty Kate thought my octogenarian rellies might prefer a more relaxed pace for their holiday. But my 87-year-old grandma was an enthusiastic tourist as we explored Salamanca Market, Mt Wellington's summit, the Tasman Peninsula and a winery in between. I remember Grandma even set the pace with her mental arithmetic to split the bill at dinner. My housemate was from Nepal and had no contact with elderly relatives of her own but declared her fear of ageing well and truly assuaged after meeting my sprightly Grandma and Great Aunty that weekend.

L to R: Anne, Peg, Adrian and Ollie, 1993.

Grandma is the matriarch of four generations of Essendon supporters and we watched a lot of footy together in 1993 as Kevin Sheedy coached the Bombers to their fifteenth flag. I reckon Grandma despises Carlton more than any other Essendon supporter I know, so victory against our archrivals that year was particularly sweet. But twenty years later, when the 'peptide scandal' threatened to bring the Essendon footy club to its knees, Grandma was my only ally in believing that James Hird, as senior coach, should be held accountable for what transpired. We were outnumbered by Rankins and Essendon supporters across the country in our steadfast belief that Hird should resign or be sacked. In the interests of family harmony and on-field success we can only hope that in 2016 the club can make a fresh start with a new coach at the helm.

ALISON RANKIN

Grandma Peggy has always fascinated me. She gets three jobs done at a time. She can stick at things and she genuinely cares about people. She is very religious but not self-righteous at all and I admire that too.

To state the obvious, Peggy as far as I know has been accepting of the non-traditional couples among the Rankins. This would be against her natural inclination so it shows an inner generosity and an ability to accept people.

Peggy used to able to work really hard. She could cook for 40 people at once in between sorting out church duties and catching up with everyone. I've seen her do it!

When Jack was dying, his future inevitable, she kept at it and found help and made him as comfortable as possible. She sticks at it even when failure is inevitable. I admire this. She doesn't walk away, she confronts life and tries pretty hard to make things as good as possible and doesn't give up. In my mind this is an admirable trait.

She always takes time for everybody. She is interested in everyone and when things are bad she tries to help. I'm not really like this but Peggy showed me it is valuable.

Outside my immediate family Peggy has been the most positive role model I had growing up. Mostly I look at her as a person to be like.

DOMINIC SCHMID

As a young kid, I remember that Gran always seemed to be around helping Mum. Obviously at the time I didn't appreciate the effort involved in driving down from Warragul to Boronia until I was older. She always made time and continued to do so as the pool of grandkids continued to grow. Visits were usually accompanied with a box of yo-yo biscuits, and birthdays always involved a card and a fresh $20 note, which seemed like $2,000 to a kid back then. On a trip to the Melbourne Show I can only assume that Mum gave me one too many red cordials and I became quite restless (which I understand was rare!). Gran took over the reins, literally, and was tasked with holding onto my harness. I'm sure I was a little 'turd' that day but Gran kept her cool. I guess she had had a lot of practice by that stage in her life.

Gran always showed an interest in what I was up to, from a sports mad kid to my uni days, and since joining the Constabulary. She genuinely showed great understanding of life's pressures and always seemed to know the right things to say. I admire how Gran seemed to understand others' perspectives and how she would always make an effort to make sure everyone was all right regardless of the circumstances. Always caring, she recounted to me a number of times the tragic time when two young police officers made their way to Fumina to advise of Barry's passing. Despite her grief, Gran invited them in for a cuppa knowing they had come a long way.

JOHN (CRACKER) RANKIN

Grandma has always been very inclusive and welcoming , even when you had not seen her for quite some time. She would never hold a grudge; she is just happy to hear the update on your life and how it's progressing. I have found her to be immensely proud of everyone in the Rankin clan, even when people and things are not working out as she might have hoped. Grandma to me is a role model. When it came to bringing up kids and family, it is a very rare thing to have a family as big as hers that all get along relatively okay and have time for each other. In summing up, Grandma to me is a lovely and genuine person, with time for everyone. I have never felt that she has favourites, just loves us all equally. If that is true or not it doesn't really matter because that is how she makes us all feel.

LOUISA RANKIN

My strongest memories of Granny are all about her simply 'being there', offering love, care and support in the form of a choc-chip biscuit, a cup of tea, a hot meal, a place to stay – her presence in the most understated way, representing the value, the influence, the loyalty, the love of family. Granny's strong family values have been passed on to all her children and grandchildren, and she is a centre of gravity for a huge but nonetheless close-knit family. Being a member of the Rankin clan has shaped me in ways that are fundamental to who I am and this is something for which I will forever be thankful.

ADRIAN SCHMID

Granny was a big part of my childhood and has continued to be there for every significant moment of my life. I remember when I was little, Isaac, Ollie and Dom had all started school and were going to lots of places without me – so I decided I needed an adventure of my own and the first place I could come up with as a 4-year-old, was Granny's house. So Mum and I caught the train up to Warragul and I was spoilt for a few days eating yo-yos and ice cream. There were trips to the footy, Christmas and Boxing days in Warragul, and beach holidays. Every birthday I excitedly waited for the post and a birthday card from Granny with $20 stashed inside, and a Christmas gift always included a new T-shirt.

Her resilience, quiet, yet strong resolve, care for others and cooking skills are all traits Granny possesses – and I'd like to think they have at least partly been passed on.

Watching Isabelle grow up over the two years has certainly been rewarding – but also with its challenging and difficult moments. I couldn't imagine having 12 running around on an isolated farm without all of today's modern technology and conveniences. Being able to stay in control and achieve so much is certainly inspiring… although two kids, not 12, might be enough for us!

It's great that Isabelle has been lucky enough to have a great-grand-mother, and despite seemingly spending the last 70 years around new babies in the family, Granny has still made an effort to get to all of Isabelle's events and was genuinely excited and happy to see us during the times Isabelle and I have called in to visit her.

Adrian and Marina's Wedding, 2011: Peg, John Schmid, Marina Schmid Adrian Schmid, and Anne Schmid.

MICHAEL RANKIN

Most of my early memories of Granny centre around the tiny kitchen at Edinburgh Street. The TP Rankin's favourite were the choc-chip cookies, but the huge roasts with innumerable veggies (the roast potatoes remain the best ever and are still unbeaten), chocolate cakes and pavlova, yesterday's Christmas leg of ham on the bone covered in a tea towel in the centre of the table, Boxing Day cricket clicking softly in the background – all of these memories loom large in my mind. Family functions were always overflowing with people and as a kid, the fact that such a huge amount of food must've been required to feed such a massive family never really registered, but looking back now it's hard to believe so much was pumped out of such a small kitchen by just one Granny! It speaks of her nurturing and accommodating nature, her desire for everyone to be comfortable and happy. It is something I think she passed on to her children as they have to theirs.

NICOLA RANKIN

I'm always amazed at how Granny has managed to be a part of the significant occasions in my life, despite having so many other grandkids to concern herself with, and despite living 1.5hrs away for most of my life. I have no doubt that she manages the same for everyone else, and her ability to make you feel important in such a large family is remarkable. Mick and I had some great times when we spent some of our school holidays with Granny down in Warragul and she even let us bring a friend each, which was very generous. I feel very fortunate that Granny could be at my wedding last year and share in such a special day, and the way she has made Fontaine feel welcome in the family has meant a lot to me. I'm sure I've got the best Granny in the world.

SARAH MURTAGH

I was very lucky to grow up in Warragul, so Nan was local to us. She was always there supporting us at our important and not-so-important events, right from when we were very young.

Whenever Mum had to work, Nan would pick us up from school and stay with us until Mum got home. Most nights this would also mean that Nan would have dinner cooked before Mum walked through the door. In fact, I remember Nan coming over to cook us dinner long past the time when we needed a babysitter, but we enjoyed spending that time with her and her cooking was amazing!

Nan is and forever will be the best cook I have ever known. Every time Mum planned a roast for dinner we tried to organise Nan to come over, as her roast potatoes are the best and Mum could not compete. At Christmas time Nan would always invite Katie and I over to help her make the fruit mince pies. It was always a great fun day that ended with us taking home a pile of mince pies for our help.

Nan has always been very encouraging and proud of our

achievements. On the day I received my VCE results, I had slept in. By about 9.00 am, Mum woke me up and said, 'Can you PLEASE get up and find out your results? Nan has already called three times!'

When I first told Nan that I was pregnant with Adara, my eldest daughter, I was a little nervous, as Justin and I were not married at the time. I will always cherish how supportive she was of us. She did not judge, but rather congratulated us and asked how I had been feeling etc. When Adara was born I had trouble breastfeeding her. Nan encouraged me by telling me that she had trouble feeding Mary, even after all the babies she had had before that. Nan was none too pleased at that time when a nurse in the hospital asked her, 'Is this your first baby, dear?'

I feel blessed to have such a wonderful Grandmother and I am so glad that Adara and Matilda are lucky enough to know and love their great-grandmother.

Sarah's Debutante Ball..

LUKE RANKIN

Having Nan as the only grandmother I have been able to really know has been great. Her cooking, taking time out of her own life to pick us kids up from school, also running us to sporting events and training, all memories.

As well as being there at birthdays, Nan was one of my sponsors at Confirmation which was an honour.

I will always cherish these memories of Nan.

KATIE MACK

There is so much I could say about Nan, but I thought I should keep it as simple as possible and not take up the entire book, so I thought I would reminisce about the time I have spent with Nan over the years and share some of my favourite memories.

I think anyone who knows her, knows she is an incredible cook. I know most people try to argue that their own grandmother makes the best of something, but it is just not possible to find a better sponge cake or chocolate pudding than Nan's. Yet even though she can cook pretty much everything all of the time, Nan has always saved her best skills for December. It became a tradition that she would spend mornings leading up to Christmas at our house so Dad could re-tie the plum pudding. A more important tradition though, was that one day in December I would head to Nan's and spend the day assembling the fruit mince pies. A little mini production line which resulted in the best fruit mince pies the world had ever tasted (I might be biased but... I still think I'm right).

Growing up with Nan just up the road made it so easy to spend as much time with her as we could. There was rarely a day we didn't see her, and that was always one of my favourite things about living in Warragul. I can't wait to celebrate her 90th birthday with her.

Sarah and Justin's wedding.

LISA RANKIN

When I think of Peg, I remember family Christmas parties when I was a kid. Rather than joining the Kris Kringle, she would buy a thoughtful gift for each and every grandchild. I remember thinking that it must cost her a small fortune because there are so many of us. Whenever I see Peg, she always remembers what I've been doing at work/uni and I think it's amazing that she can keep track of all of us and what we get up to. She really is an amazing Nanna.

JARYD RANKIN

I will always remember as a child walking into Nanna's house and being greeted with the smell of her delicious cooking. A trip to Nanna's house always meant a good roast lunch and if we were lucky some of her famous lemon meringue tart.

LACHLAN CANTWELL

I am lucky enough (unlike my younger brothers) to have many memories of a younger Granny, who was always around at our house when I was growing up. Before my 7th birthday I welcomed another brother to go with the younger brother and sister I already had. With Dad working long hours and four kids under seven, it was enough to drive Mum mad. In came Granny to help Mum along and to provide unwavering support. It became such a regular occurrence to see Granny arrive at the door from Warragul with freshly baked scones and kids' trifle. Apparently I once queried her as to when she was going to start the ironing. It would have been within five minutes of her walking through the door!

I know Mum, as well as her brothers and sisters, will be forever grateful for Granny's support in their hour of need. As I've become older I have heard all of them talk of how at the drop of a hat, she would drop everything to come to their homes and help out wherever she could.

We could not have asked for a better Granny. She has touched my life and the lives of so many others through acts of kindness and care that will never be forgotten.

FELICITY CANTWELL

Christmas has always been my favourite time of year. Growing up we always spent Christmas in Warragul with Granny. I remember always being shocked that Santa was able to find us. Granny has always made Christmas so special for me. She never failed to deliver us an amazing roast for lunch and a delicious vegetable soup for dinner. Let us not forget Granny's classic kids' trifle! I have so many fun memories of us kids playing in Granny's playground and amusing ourselves for hours on the garage wall. The Christmas nights were always so much fun as there was always far more people than beds. I can remember the corridor being filled with people sleeping on the floor. Paul and Bridgette even parked their campervan in the back yard one year! Granny is such a special person in my life and has always been there for me. She inspires me so much and I am so grateful we are so close. Love always, Felicity.

MARKUS CANTWELL

Granny has always been a part of my life. When we were at Primary School and something good happened, or we won something or got an award, she was always the person we would ring and she was always proud of us. Granny spent a lot of time with us when we were young and I loved having her around. Granny camped with us at Ocean Grove for nearly ten years. So many campers would comment about how fantastic it was that Granny came with us in spite of her being in her eighties. Now that Granny lives near us, it is good that she can come and have dinner with us often and still celebrate our birthdays and other family events.

Right: Peg and Markus Cantwell, 1998.

THOMAS CANTWELL

Granny has always been someone I look up to and you do not have to look far to be inspired by her. It was only a couple of years ago when I perceived Granny as any other grandparent – a supplier of ice creams, scones and kids' trifle. I adored her for that. I also loved how I always felt loved and treasured when I was in her presence. I appreciated how she always made the effort to make time for me. Whether that be watching me get smashed in footy, having me and my relatives over for Christmas lunch, or simply... just being there to comfort me.

But as I became a little older and my ability to understand things grew, I started to comprehend how special my Grandma was. I overheard my aunty speaking about my Granny and her story and I realised that she wasn't your ordinary kind of lady. Deep inside her lay the ability to overcome more battles than I could even begin to imagine. I learnt of her aptitude not to be disheartened by the hurdles and obstacles the world put in front of her, difficulties that an average person would not be able to withstand, and all with such grace and humility.

There are so many words in the English language, but I don't think any single word can begin to explain the vastness and complexity of who my grandma is.

Love you always, Granny.

A child needs a grandparent, anybody's grandparent, to
grow a little more securely into an unfamiliar world
- CHARLES AND ANN MORSE

JACKSON DAHLENBURG

I have always called you Peg for as long as I remember. I'm not sure why I have, though you are also my Grandma and such a kind and caring one.

I believe you have played a huge part in influencing and shaping the lives of people of whom you've been a part. I think this is largely due to your generosity, positivity, nurturing and open-minded outlook on life, which others have found a comfort and inspiration.

You don't have to look far to see the influence you have made, as all your extended family have developed a kind and caring nature from you. I would like to thank you for this influence you have had on me.

What an eventful and special 90 years, and hopefully another 90 wonderful years to come.

Much love and care.

HAYLEY AND SAMANTHA RANKIN

Reflecting on our childhood with Granny brings to mind fond memories of Warragul, Christmas time, Easter and Ocean Grove. Family has always been such an important part of Granny's life, and it is from her influence that we have learnt to appreciate the love and close bonds the Rankin family share.

What stands out to us most when thinking of Granny is her generous nature. Granny would regularly buy us ice creams, make us delicious baked treats, or on our birthdays it was always exciting to receive her card in the mail because we knew a little something awaited us inside! She would also often make our favourite meal, 'Granny's Soup'. It would be the highlight of any family occasion at Warragul. Perhaps of more importance to us, Granny was generous with her time. The number of grandchildren did not detract from the quality time she spent with each of us growing up.

Granny would always make the trip down from Warragul to Melbourne to watch our dance concerts. It would give her such pride to be there to watch us, and in return it gave us a great amount of joy that she was able to see our five minutes of fame! Following the performance was perhaps the most exciting part of all, Granny's famous chocolate cake. It wouldn't have been a dance concert without the reward at the end, which we could also look forward to in school lunches the following week.

Granny also endured many 10-hour trips up to Sydney, crammed with us in the backseat. She was subjected to kicking, screaming and countless arguments between us both as she sat in the middle seat to act as a peacekeeping barrier. Granny would also talk and talk and talk the whole way! The only time there was ever silence was when she had nodded off to sleep momentarily. We appreciate now that Granny did all of this just to be able to spend quality time with our family and support Hayley's gymnastic competition.

We want to wish our Granny a Happy 90th Birthday. We both aspire to be as big-hearted, selfless, generous and kind as you are. We love you, Granny!

Jackson Dahlenburg, Hayley Rankin, Lachlan Cantwell, Samantha Rankin, Felicity Cantwell, Danielle Schmid, Markus Cantwell, Peg and Thomas Cantwell.

LARA WEST

Going to Peg's house in Warragul and playing with all the cousins at the local primary school (where the obsession with 'Kick The Can' came alive). I also remember, many times (before meeting Peg) Bernie raving about how delicious Peg's lemon meringue pie was going to be. When we arrived for lunch there was no pie to be eaten. However she had made scones and this is when I learnt to always mix my batter with a metal knife – my scones have been light and fluffy ever since. Thankfully, I have been blessed with an abundance of lemon meringue pie since!

SAM WEST

I remember chatting to Peg at the last Rankin Christmas party at our house in Booran Rd. She asked about my carpentry job even though she hadn't seen me in ages.

In loving memory of

Fr Peter Joseph Rankin
Salesian of Don Bosco

Fr Peter Joseph Rankin
Salesian of Don Bosco

Born in Warragul, Victoria, Australia
14 September 1958

Religious Profession at Lysterfield, Victoria
31 January 1979

Priestly Ordination at St Jude's
Scoresby, Victoria
9 December 1989

Entered Eternal life
at Greensborough, Victoria
14 January 2022

Pastoral Ministry
Vice Provincial, Formator,
Youth Worker, Educator, Pastor

Well done, good and faithful servant!

Come and share your master's
happiness!' [Mt 25:23]

Peter Rankin was born in Warragul in 1958, the tenth child among twelve born to Peg and Jack Rankin. Growing up in the close-knit community of Fumina, he attended schools in Icy Creek and Neerim South before completing his education at Salesian College in Sunbury, where he boarded.

In 1979, Peter entered his religious profession and was ordained as a Salesian Priest in 1989. Throughout his priesthood, he served in various parishes across New South Wales, Victoria, Tasmania, and South Australia, earning the love and respect of parishioners for his caring demeanour, humility, unwavering faith, and deep inner wisdom. Beyond his religious duties, Peter was an avid Essendon AFL supporter, enjoyed playing cards, and cherished engaging in heartfelt conversations.

Despite claiming he wasn't Peg's favourite child, Peter cherished a unique bond with his mother, attributing it to having her favourite job. He began writing Peg's book while serving in Engadine, New South Wales, in 2014.

Tragically, in 2021, Peter was diagnosed with cancer and passed away in 2022. He entrusted this book to his family as a token of his immense love for his mother, with the hope that it would be shared widely as a testament to Peg's extraordinary life.

———

I am pleased that Peter's request for his book to be published has been accomplished. I would like to thank my family and Green Hill Publishing for their support throughout this process. Thank you, dear Peter, for bringing our mother's story to life.
Gerardine

www.ingramcontent.com/pod-product-compliance
Lightning Source LLC
Chambersburg PA
CBHW031329031125
34900CB00011B/467